The Complete Nonprofit Corporation Kit

(+ CD-ROM)

Mark Warda

Attorney at Law

SPHINX® PUBLISHING
AN IMPRINT OF SOURCEBOOKS, INC.®
NAPERVILLE, ILLINOIS
www.SphinxLegal.com

First Edition: 2007

Published by: **Sphinx® Publishing, An Imprint of Sourcebooks, Inc.®**

<u>Naperville Office</u>
P.O. Box 4410
Naperville, Illinois 60567-4410
630-961-3900
Fax: 630-961-2168
www.sourcebooks.com
www.SphinxLegal.com

This publication is designed to provide accurate and authoritative information in regard to the subject matter covered. It is sold with the understanding that the publisher is not engaged in rendering legal, accounting, or other professional service. If legal advice or other expert assistance is required, the services of a competent professional person should be sought.
From a Declaration of Principles Jointly Adopted by a Committee of the American Bar Association and a Committee of Publishers and Associations

This product is not a substitute for legal advice.

Disclaimer required by Texas statutes.

3454 1754 1/07

Library of Congress Cataloging-in-Publication Data
Warda, Mark.
  The complete nonprofit corporation kit (+CD-ROM)/ by Mark Warda. -- 1st ed.
    p. cm.
  Includes index.
  ISBN-13: 978-1-57248-544-0 (pbk. : alk. paper)
  ISBN-10: 1-57248-544-2 (pbk. : alk. paper)
  1. Nonprofit organizations--Law and legislation--United States. 2.
Charitable uses, trusts, and foundations--United States. I. Title.

KF1388.W37 2006
346.73'064--dc22

                                                          2006022856

Printed and bound in the United States of America.
SB — 10 9 8 7 6 5 4 3 2 1

Contents

How To Use the CD-ROM

Thank you for purchasing *The Complete Nonprofit Corporation Kit*. In this book, we have worked hard to compile exactly what you need to form a nonprofit corporation, including how to get it started, file the proper incorporation and charitable recognition documents, and manage the day-to-day activities. To make this material even more useful, we have included every document in the book on the CD-ROM in the back of the book.

You can use these forms just as you would the forms in the book. Print them out, fill them in, and use them however you need. You can also fill in the forms directly on your computer. Just identify the form you need, open it, click on the space where the information should go, and input your information. Customize each form for your particular needs. Use them over and over again.

The CD-ROM is compatible with both PC and Mac operating systems. (While it should work with either operating system, we cannot guarantee that it will work with your particular system and we cannot provide technical assistance.) To use the forms on your computer, you will need to use Microsoft Word or another word processing program that can read Word files. The CD-ROM does not contain any such program.

Insert the CD-ROM into your computer. Double-click on the icon representing the disc on your desktop or go through your hard drive to identify the drive that contains the disc and click on it.

Once opened, you will see the files contained on the CD-ROM listed as "Form #: [Form Title]." Open the file you need. You may print the form to fill it out manually at this point, or you can click on the appropriate line to fill it in using your computer.

Any time you see bracketed information [ ] on the form, you can click on it and delete the bracketed information from your final form. This information is only a reference guide to assist you in filling in the forms and should be removed from your final version. Once all your information is filled in, you can print your filled-in form.

*   *   *   *   *

Using Self-Help Law Books

Before using a self-help law book, you should realize the advantages and disadvantages of doing your own legal work and understand the challenges and diligence that this requires.

The Growing Trend

Rest assured that you will not be the first or only person handling your own legal matter. For example, in some states, more than 75% of the people in divorces and other cases represent themselves. Because of the high cost of legal services, this is a major trend, and many courts are struggling to make it easier for people to represent themselves. However, some courts are not happy with people who do not use attorneys and refuse to help them in any way. For some, the attitude is, "Go to the law library and figure it out for yourself."

We write and publish self-help law books to give people an alternative to the often complicated and confusing legal books found in most law libraries. We have made the explanations of the law as simple and easy to understand as possible. Of course, unlike an attorney advising an individual client, we cannot cover every conceivable possibility.

Cost/Value Analysis

Whenever you shop for a product or service, you are faced with various levels of quality and price. In deciding what product or service to buy, you make a cost/value analysis on the basis of your willingness to pay and the quality you desire.

When buying a car, you decide whether you want transportation, comfort, status, or sex appeal. Accordingly, you decide among choices such as a Neon, a Lincoln, a Rolls Royce, or a Porsche. Before making a decision, you usually weigh the merits of each option against the cost.

When you get a headache, you can take a pain reliever (such as aspirin) or visit a medical specialist for a neurological examination. Given this choice, most people, of course, take a pain reliever, since it costs only pennies; whereas a medical examination costs hundreds of dollars and takes a lot of time. This is usually a logical choice because it is rare to need anything more than a pain reliever for a headache. But in some cases, a headache may indicate a brain tumor, and failing to see a specialist right away can result in complications. Should everyone with a headache go to a specialist? Of course not, but people treating their own illnesses must realize that they are betting, on the basis of their cost/value analysis of the situation, that they are taking the most logical option.

The same cost/value analysis must be made when deciding to do one's own legal work. Many legal situations are very straightforward, requiring a simple form and no complicated analysis. Anyone with a little intelligence and a book of instructions can handle the matter without outside help.

But there is always the chance that complications are involved that only an attorney would notice. To simplify the law into a book like this, several legal cases often must be condensed into a single sentence or paragraph. Otherwise, the book would be several hundred pages long and too complicated for most people. However, this simplification necessarily leaves out many details and nuances that would apply to special or unusual situations. Also, there are many ways to interpret most legal questions. Your case may come before a judge who disagrees with the analysis of our authors.

Therefore, in deciding to use a self-help law book and to do your own legal work, you must realize that you are making a cost/value analysis. You have decided that the money you will save in doing it yourself outweighs the chance that your case will not turn out to your satisfaction. Most people handling their own simple legal matters never have a problem, but occasionally people find that it ended up costing them more to have an attorney straighten out the situation than it would have if they had hired an attorney in the beginning. Keep this in mind while handling your case, and be sure to consult an attorney if you feel you might need further guidance.

Local Rules

The next thing to remember is that a book which covers the law for the entire nation, or even for an entire state, cannot possibly include every procedural difference of every jurisdiction. Whenever possible, we provide the exact form needed; however, in some areas, each county, or even each judge, may require unique forms and procedures. In our state books, our forms usually cover the majority of counties in the state or provide examples of the type of form that will be required. In our national books, our forms are sometimes even more general in nature but are designed to give a good idea of the type of form that will be needed in most locations. Nonetheless, keep in mind that your state, county, or judge may have a requirement, or use a form, that is not included in this book.

You should not necessarily expect to be able to get all of the information and resources you need solely from within the pages of this book. This book will serve as your guide, giving you specific information whenever possible and helping you to find out what else you will need to know. This is just like if you decided to build your own backyard deck. You might purchase a book on how to build decks. However, such a book would not include the building codes and permit requirements of every city, town, county, and township in the nation; nor would it include the lumber, nails, saws, hammers, and other materials and tools you would need to actually build the deck. You would use the book as your guide, and then do some work and research involving such matters as whether you need a permit of some kind, what type and grade of wood is available in your area, whether to use hand tools or power tools, and how to use those tools.

Before using the forms in a book like this, you should check with your court clerk to see if there are any local rules of which you should be aware or local forms you will need to use. Often, such forms will require the same information as the forms in the book but are merely laid out differently or use slightly different language. They will sometimes require additional information.

Changes in the Law

Besides being subject to local rules and practices, the law is subject to change at any time. The courts and the legislatures of all fifty states are constantly revising the laws. It is possible that while you are reading this book, some aspect of the law is being changed.

In most cases, the change will be of minimal significance. A form will be redesigned, additional information will be required, or a waiting period will be extended. As a result, you might need to revise a form, file an extra form, or wait out a longer time period. These types of changes will not usually affect the outcome of your case. On the other hand, sometimes a major part of the law is changed, the entire law in a particular area is rewritten, or a case that was the basis of a central legal point is overruled. In such instances, your entire ability to pursue your case may be impaired.

Introduction

The nonprofit organization is a particularly American institution. As early as the 1830s, political and social observationist Alexis de Tocqueville remarked that Americans were "constantly forming associations." Today, the United States has the most advanced system of nonprofit organizations in the world. Americans often rely on each other, and are eager to volunteer when needed to improve society and show the independent spirit that has always influenced this country.

Over a million nonprofit organizations exist in the country. Nonprofit organizations make up over 12% of the economy. They are estimated to control nearly two trillion dollars in assets. As society becomes wealthier, you can expect many more nonprofit organizations to form.

Whether you have enough money to fund a nonprofit organization yourself or plan to rely on the generosity of others, the nonprofit corporation is the best vehicle for aiding a cause you believe in. Whether you seek a cure for cancer or just closer ties among your ethnic group, the nonprofit corporation can help you claim all the benefits given to such organizations and establish something that can continue forever.

The benefits of nonprofit status are numerous. The best known benefit is the tax-free status. Nonprofits also enjoy lower postage rates, discounts from some businesses, lower governmental fees, the ability to qualify for private and government grants, and free air time or ads by some media outlets. Many nonprofits can attract funds from taxpayers because donations to the organizations are tax-deductible.

You can show that you have another American trait—the do-it-yourself entrepreneurial spirit— by using this book. Instead of hiring a lawyer, you can do a lot of the work yourself and save a lot of money to put toward your cause. However, you should realize that the law of nonprofit organizations is complicated. There are a lot of strict government rules that must be followed in order to qualify for all of the benefits. In some situations, you may need to pay for expert advice to be sure you have done everything right. The most complicated areas are noted in the text, and you are advised when legal guidance may be necessary.

Fortunately, many organizations exist whose purpose is to help other nonprofits. Also, a wealth of information about nonprofit organizations can be found on the Internet. (Perhaps too much—a recent search turned up over a million sites.) Some of the best sites are referred to throughout the text.

For more information regarding the required IRS forms and links for your state, please visit **www.sphinxlegal.com/extras/nonprofit**.

Good luck with your organization!

Chapter 1:
Definition of a Nonprofit Organization

If you are reading this book, then you have probably made a serious decision to start your own nonprofit organization. A nonprofit organization is one that does not pass its income to its members or shareholders, but instead uses the income to further a goal that benefits the community or some part of the community.

This does not mean that the operations of a nonprofit cannot be profitable. Many nonprofit organizations make large profits on their operations, but those profits cannot benefit private parties. They must be used to further the organization's stated goal. If a nonprofit disbands, no one except another qualified nonprofit organization (with goals as similar as possible) can take over its assets.

To ensure that your nonprofit will be successful and meet your goals, you need to treat it like a business by following the rules imposed on businesses and following good business practices. Some of what follows may seem obvious, but to someone wrapped up in getting started, this information is occasionally overlooked.

Know Your Strengths

You should consider all of the skills and knowledge that running a successful business requires, and decide whether you have what it takes. If you do not, it does not necessarily mean you are doomed to fail. You can be successful if you know where to get the skills you lack. Perhaps you just need a partner who has the skills you lack. Perhaps you can hire someone with the skills you need, or you can structure your organization to avoid areas where you are weak. If those tactics do not work, maybe you can learn the skills.

For example, if managing employees is not your strong suit, you can:

◆ have a partner or manager deal with employees;

◆ take seminars in employee management; or,

◆ structure your organization so that you do not need employees (use independent contractors or set yourself up as an independent contractor).

When planning your business, consider the following factors.

◆ *Are you willing to put in a lot of overtime to make your organization a success?* Like for-profit business owners who work long hours seven days a week, you have to enjoy running your organization and be willing to make some personal time sacrifices.

◆ *Are you willing to do the dirtiest or most unpleasant work of the organization?* Emergencies come up and employees are not always dependable. You might need to mop up a flooded room, spend a weekend stuffing ten thousand envelopes, or work Christmas if someone calls in sick.

◆ *Do you know enough about accounting and organizational management?* Do you have a good head for business? Some people naturally know how to save money and do things to ensure success. Others are in the habit of buying the best or the most expensive of everything. The latter can be fatal to a struggling new organization.

◆ *Are you good at managing employees?* If your business has employees (or will have in the future), managing them is an unavoidable part of running the business.

◆ *Do you know enough about getting publicity?* The media receives thousands of press releases and announcements each day, and most are thrown away. Do not count on free publicity to put your name in front of the public to obtain donations.

Advantages of Nonprofit Status

While having a head for business will make starting and running your nonprofit organization easier, there are four main advantages to being a nonprofit organization rather than an ordinary business: the tax exemptions; the ability to receive tax-deductible donations; the ability to qualify for grants; and, the lower costs for such things as postage, advertising, and filing fees. These advantages can increase your chances of success.

Tax Exemption

For many nonprofits, the tax exemptions are the most important benefits. Several exemptions from taxes are available, depending on the type of organization and the state in which it is located.

Income received by a nonprofit is not subject to income tax at either the state or federal level if it successfully applies for and is granted an *exemption*. In most states, nonprofits can get an exemption from paying sales and use taxes on items that the organization purchases. Also, many nonprofits do not have to pay property taxes on the real estate they own. Again, they must apply for, and be granted, the exemption.

Deductibility of Contributions

Perhaps more important than being tax-exempt, contributions made by taxpayers to certain types of nonprofits are *deductible* on the taxpayer's income tax return. This is a big incentive for others to give to an organization. Without this deduction for donors, many nonprofits would not survive. (The laws about soliciting donations are covered in Chapter 7.)

Grants

Being a nonprofit organization makes your group eligible for both private and government grants. There are many large foundations that are required by law to give away a percentage of their assets each year, but they can only do so to qualified nonprofit organizations. (Applying for grants is discussed in Chapter 7.)

Lower Costs

The postal service offers special rates to nonprofit organizations that are much lower than the normal rates. Some newspapers, magazines, radio stations, and other media give discounted advertising rates to nonprofits. In some cases it is even possible for nonprofit organizations to advertise for free. These free advertisements are known as *public service announcements*.

Tax-Exempt Bonds

Some types of nonprofit organizations are able to raise money by issuing tax-exempt bonds, which are similar to municipal bonds. This is usually done by organizations that need to finance multimillion-dollar facilities, like hospitals.

Disadvantages of Nonprofit Status

The benefits of nonprofit status would be useful to nearly all types of businesses and organizations. Many businesses could successfully operate as nonprofits. However, there are also disadvantages that make many types of organizations unable to operate as nonprofits. In recent years, some for-profit businesses complained that nonprofits were competing against them unfairly, so the laws have been changed to make it more difficult for nonprofits to engage in activities that compete with for-profit businesses.

One of the most important things to know about a nonprofit organization is that it is not owned by its founders. Unlike a private business that can be sold after it has grown big and profitable, a nonprofit organization belongs to the public at large. If it dissolves, its assets must be given to another nonprofit organization that has a stated business purpose that is as similar as possible to the dissolved nonprofit's purpose. If its assets are misapplied or used for private benefit by the officers, the state attorney general (or a similar official) can seize them.

Loss of Control

If you are planning to put a lot of money and time into an organization, you should consider whether the advantages are worth the loss of control of the profits. However, there are ways to set up a nonprofit to give yourself *de facto* control, and you are allowed to pay yourself a reasonable salary and set up a pension plan. The limits on these are discussed later in the book.

Limited Purposes

In order to be exempt under the tax laws, a nonprofit organization can only perform certain functions listed in those laws. If it goes outside those limits, the nonprofit may have to pay taxes on some of its income, pay penalties, or lose its exemption entirely.

Lobbying

Most types of tax-exempt, nonprofit organizations are forbidden from contributing to political campaigns and may only do a limited amount of lobbying. (This is discussed in more detail in Chapter 6.)

Public Scrutiny

Another disadvantage is public scrutiny. Because a nonprofit organization is dedicated to the public, its finances are open to public inspection. This means that the public can obtain copies of any nonprofit's tax returns, and can find out its salaries and other expenditures.

Under IRS regulations, you must provide any member of the public who requests it with a copy of your application for tax exemption (Form 1023 or 1024) and copies of your last three years of tax returns (Form 990 or 990EZ). You can charge a reasonable fee for making photocopies. The IRS considers $1 for the first page and 15¢ for each additional page reasonable. You must make the copies available within thirty days of the request. If you willfully refuse to comply, you can face a $5,000 fine and a $20 per day penalty.

Laws that Apply to Nonprofit Organizations

There are three main sets of laws that apply to nonprofit organizations. *State corporation laws* control the formation and operation of the organization. *State charitable solicitation laws* control the activities of the organization if it is soliciting donations from the public. *Federal tax laws* govern which organizations can qualify as tax-exempt and which activities may be undertaken by tax-exempt organizations.

State Laws

State corporation laws cover the formation of the nonprofit corporation. They set the requirements for the articles of organization, the procedures for amendments, and other structural and operational issues.

A summary of each state's laws is included in Appendix B. You can use this summary to get an idea of how your organization can be formed and how it will be regulated. However, you should also obtain copies of the statutes themselves. In running your organization, you will want to be sure not to violate any of them.

State charitable solicitation laws regulate organizations that solicit money from the public and are designed to protect consumers from fraud. There have been numerous cases in which organizations have claimed to be collecting money to fight cancer or feed the hungry, but actually have kept most of the money for themselves.

Not all states regulate charitable solicitation, and each of the states that do have different requirements. To learn more about your state's regulations or exemptions, see Appendix B. (More information on the requirements is in Chapter 7.)

Federal Tax Laws

Federal tax laws are far more important than state laws. The federal tax laws control what a nonprofit may or may not do if it wishes to take advantage of the tax exemptions.

State laws are usually very broad and allow nonprofits wide leeway in their purposes. Nearly any small group that does not intend to distribute its profit to its members could easily fall under the nonprofit law of most states. However, federal tax laws applicable to nonprofits are very strict, and are sometimes contradictory and confusing. Consider the following situations.

- ◆ Because rich donors were setting up nonprofits to hire their family members and avoid estate taxes, a law was passed saying that nonprofits were forbidden to benefit private parties (the *private inurement doctrine*). What about nonprofit social clubs whose sole purpose is to benefit their members? Well, they can only benefit their members and not serve the public.
- ◆ Because the government does not give tax benefits to groups that discriminate, nonprofits are forbidden from discriminating on the basis of race, religion, and so on. What about religious nonprofit organizations? Well, they can discriminate on the basis of religion if they have a good reason.
- ◆ To be sure the government does not subsidize groups that support those who hold office, nonprofits are not allowed to contribute to political campaigns. However, they can set up *political action committees* (PACs) that are also nonprofit organizations, but contribute to political campaigns as their *sole purpose*.

Every year, the *Internal Revenue Service* (IRS) issues new Revenue Rulings, the courts issue new opinions, and Congress usually tinkers with the law. How can you ever hope to comply with such a system? Keep in mind that the people enforcing the law are no more intelligent than you, and in many cases, they are as confused as you—so here is your best strategy.

- Learn as much about the laws as you can, and make a good faith effort to follow them carefully. If you are planning something that might be questionable, ask a tax specialist for an opinion.
- Keep good records.
- If your tax return or activities are questioned, make it clear that you are doing your best to comply and cooperate fully. (However, you should get the best tax advice you can afford to be sure of your rights.)

Other Laws

Other than the specific laws for nonprofits, most laws that apply to other businesses also apply to nonprofits. In most states, for example, the general rules for business corporation procedures apply to nonprofit corporations. Federal election laws apply to nonprofit corporations as well as business corporations.

Permitted Purposes

A nonprofit organization may be formed for any legal purpose under most state laws, as long as it does not pass its profits on to its members. However, in order to qualify for favorable tax treatment and gain other benefits, it must limit its purposes to those allowed in the *Internal Revenue Code* (I.R.C.). The following are some of the most popular purposes allowed by the law.

Section 501(c)(3) Organizations

The best tax treatment is available to nonprofits that qualify under Section 501(c)(3) of the I.R.C. These organizations get both a tax exemption and the ability for their contributors to deduct contributions.

The IRS uses two tests to determine if an organization qualifies under Section 501(c)(3)—the organizational test and the operational test. Under the *organizational test*, the documentation that forms the organization must limit the organization's purpose and activities to those that are permitted. For this reason, it is very important that the articles of incorporation and the bylaws are carefully drafted to pass IRS examination.

Under the *operational test*, the operations or activities must also comply with the law. It is not enough that the paperwork of the organization is correct—the organization must also conduct itself in conformance with those rules.

If the purpose or activities of a nonprofit organization do not qualify for an exemption under Section 501(c)(3), it still may claim an exemption under one of the other subsections of 501(c). The disadvantage is that under most of the other subsections, the income is tax-exempt, but contributions may *not* be deducted on donors' tax returns. Permitted purposes under Section 501(c)(3) include the following.

Religious

Religion is the oldest and broadest category of nonprofit. Because the First Amendment to the Constitution bars the government from making any law that prohibits the free exercise of religion, the government is limited in how much it can regulate religious activities. However, some courts have required newly formed religious groups to be similar to traditional religions, with such things as an established congregation, an organized ministry, regular services, education of the young, and a doctrinal code in order for them to qualify for a tax exemption. This was done to keep people from setting up their own religions just for tax purposes.

Charitable

Under the tax law, the word *charitable* is broader than the normal definition of relieving poverty. Court decisions over the years have allowed all of the following activities to be undertaken by organizations that qualify for Section 501(c)(3) status.

- ◆ *Relieving poverty.* Any activity that gives aid to the poor, such as soup kitchens or homeless shelters, may qualify. However, it must direct its benefit to the public at large and not to any particular person. For example, a group that forms to help a particular family that loses its home in a fire will not qualify for tax-exempt status. To qualify, its purpose would have to be to help all fire victims in a certain area.
- ◆ *Beautifying the community.* Groups that plant trees and clean up highways can qualify for charitable status. The limitation is that they must serve a broad community, such as a city or town. If they only serve a limited number of people, such as a subdivision, they will not qualify.
- ◆ *Lessening the burdens of government.* Groups that help existing government programs, through activities such as improving parks or police facilities, are included as charitable organizations.
- ◆ *Promoting health.* Hospitals, blood banks, clinics, mental health organizations, and groups with similar functions all qualify for charitable status as long as their profits do not go to private individuals.
- ◆ *Promoting social welfare.* Groups that promote social welfare are groups that support civil rights, community alliance, national defense, or similar causes.
- ◆ *Promoting environmental conservation.* Groups that work to preserve national resources may qualify as promoting environmental conservation.

- *Promoting the arts.* Groups that sponsor arts festivals, theater groups, concerts, and programs to encourage young people to develop their talents are covered.
- *Promoting patriotism.* Groups that participate in patriotic displays and inculcate patriotic emotions are considered groups that promote patriotism.
- *Promoting amateur sports.* Groups that support amateur sports, such as little leagues and soccer clubs, but not simply any group that provides athletic facilities or equipment, may qualify as a charitable organization.

Scientific
Scientific research that is theoretical is clearly allowable for charitable nonprofit organizations, but research that is practical and has business applications is not. Testing products is not considered charitable (unless done for public safety), and doing work for one particular company is clearly not allowed.

Testing for Public Safety
Organizations like Underwriters Laboratories, Inc., which test the safety of products, are tax-exempt.

Literary
Literary organizations are exempt if their work is not commercial, but rather promotes the literacy of the community. For example, a publisher that sells books at normal prices will probably not qualify, but one that sells the works of unknown talented people at a discount price may qualify.

Educational
Educational organizations can include libraries and museums as well as traditional schools, colleges, and universities. For the tax exemption, it is important that the school is an objective place of learning rather than a promoter of a particular idea.

Preventing Cruelty to Children or Animals
Organizations like the Society for the Prevention of Cruelty to Animals (SPCA), orphanages, or any group that aids children or animals are included, as long as the group is not limited to any particular child or animal.

Other Types of Organizations
The rationale for other types of tax-exempt organizations is completely different from Section 501(c)(3) organizations. While Section 501(c)(3) organizations are exempt because they are perceived to be doing something beneficial to society, the others are not taxed because they are pooling money to do something that would not be taxed if the money were not pooled.

For example, if a number of people use their money to lobby for better roads or to socialize every Sunday night, there is no tax involved. So, if they put their money together in an organization to do the same thing, there is no reason they should have to pay an extra tax on that money.

The problem arises when these groups try to raise money from outside sources. If a social club charges its members $10 for dinner, but charges outside guests $20 for the same dinner, then the members who pay less are making a *profit* on the arrangement. This type of activity by a nonprofit organization is subject to tax.

Some organizations divide their operations into two or more nonprofit organizations. For example, a Section 501(c)(3) organization may have a *subsidiary* under another 501(c) subsection to perform activities forbidden under Section 501(c)(3) rules.

The following are some of the most common tax-exempt organizations under categories other than Section 501(c)(3).

Civic and Social Welfare Associations

An organization can be formed under Section 501(c)(4) to promote the common good and social welfare of a community. You could use this type of organization if you wanted to do something forbidden to 501(c)(3) organizations, such as lobby for better roads or schools. Because contributions to these organizations are not deductible, you should try to fit your purpose into a Section 501(c)(3) by concentrating on permitted purposes, and only form under Section 501(c)(4) if that is impossible.

Employee Associations

Also under Section 501(c)(4), an association of employees of one employer can be formed if their net earnings are devoted exclusively to charitable, educational, or recreational purposes.

Labor Organizations

A labor or agricultural worker organization can be formed under Section 501(c)(5) if the goal is to improve conditions, production, or efficiency.

Trade Associations

Groups that promote the common interest of a business community or a line of businesses, such as a chamber of commerce or board of real estate, are exempt under Section 501(c)(6). However, the group may not carry on business itself. It may only promote the interests of all businesses in the same field.

The trade association must be involved with only one trade. If it is a group of people from different trades who meet to network, it will not qualify under Section 501(c)(6), though it may be able to qualify as a social club or other type of exempt organization. It must allow competitors in the same field to be members—it cannot support only one faction of an industry.

Social Clubs

A club that is formed solely for pleasure and recreational purposes is exempt under Section 501(c)(7) if most of its income is from member dues and only an insubstantial amount is raised from the public.

With the strict rules that a nonprofit organization cannot give any benefits to its members, it seems anomalous that a group whose sole purpose is to benefit its members could qualify. However, as explained before, there is no reason to tax groups that merely pool their money to do something that would not be taxed if paid for separately.

In order to qualify as a tax-exempt social club, an organization must have a membership that commingles and has shared interests. Some groups that have qualified are fraternities and sororities, lunch and dinner clubs, golf and tennis clubs, gem collectors, and political clubs. One organization that was disallowed an exemption was an auto club, because the IRS found that the interests of the members were too different.

Cemeteries

If a cemetery is not designed to make a profit, but instead to provide plots exclusively for its members, it can be tax-exempt under Section 501(c)(13).

Veterans' Organizations

If 75% of the members of a veterans' organization are past or present members of the armed forces, and most of the rest are relatives of veterans, it can qualify as tax-exempt under Section 501(c)(19).

Prohibited Practices

There are certain activities nonprofit organizations are prohibited from doing. Violation of these rules can cause the loss of tax-exempt status, or even penalties and fines.

Many of these rules were enacted when nonprofit organizations were accused of abusing their status. When one nonprofit opposed the reelection of a United States senator, a law was passed to prohibit the group from political activities. When some rich families began using nonprofit organizations to employ family members, laws were passed to prohibit such arrangements. Every few years, someone does an exposé of abuses at nonprofits, and new laws are proposed to control these organizations. As a nonprofit organization, your group should keep abreast of proposals for changes in the law.

There are big differences in what charitable (Section 501(c)(3)) groups can do and what other nonprofits can do. The limits are much more strict for charitable groups, because the tax deductibility of their income is considered a government subsidy that should go to the good of the community rather than to a few individuals. The following are the major prohibitions for nonprofit organizations.

No Specific Benefit

For nonprofit organizations to qualify as charitable, the focus of their mission must be the community at large, not any individual or small group of individuals. For example, you can get an exemption for a group that wants to aid tornado victims, but not for a group formed to help one specific victim. Similarly, you can get an exemption to clean up an entire community, but not just one subdivision.

Groups that do benefit limited numbers of people, such as social clubs, trade groups, and homeowners associations, can be nonprofit and tax-exempt, but the members' dues are not deductible and their outside income must be limited.

No Private Inurement

Similar to the requirement that the purpose of the nonprofit be to aid the community, the *private inurement doctrine* does not allow private parties to receive *undue profits* from a nonprofit organization.

This means that the organizer and directors cannot get inflated salaries or other unusual financial arrangements. Business dealings between a nonprofit and persons related to it are put under careful scrutiny, and can result in penalties or loss of tax exemption if found to be unreasonable.

Business dealings are allowed between nonprofits and their members and directors, but they should be at commercially reasonable terms. For example, if an organization rents an office from one if its directors, the rent should be documented as fair and reasonable. If the rent is inflated, the organization's tax status is in jeopardy.

In the real world, nonprofits get away with a lot more than the law books would have you believe. Exposés by such publications as *U.S. News & World Report* and the *Philadelphia Inquirer* uncovered nonprofit officers making hundreds of thousands—even millions—of dollars in salaries, guaranteed loans, and numerous other alleged abuses. The expanding IRS regulations in this area are discussed in Chapter 6.

Limited Lobbying

Because of perceived abuses, Congress has put strict restraints on the types of lobbying that can be done by charitable organizations. However, no such limits apply to nonprofit organizations that are not charitable.

Charitable Nonprofits

Charitable nonprofit organizations (those whose contributions are deductible) are prohibited from contributing to political campaigns, and their lobbying cannot be substantial. Private foundations cannot lobby at all, and other charitable organizations must stick to certain limits. The exact limits are determined by applying either the *expenditures test* or the *substantial part test*. (These tests are explained in more detail in Chapter 6.)

Other Nonprofits

Nonprofits that are not charitable (such as social welfare associations, trade associations, social clubs, and labor unions) are free to lobby as long as the lobbying is related to their specific organizational goals. However, if the dues of members are used for lobbying, then that amount may not be deducted as a business expense (or in any other way) by the members.

Political Organizations

Organizations that are formed to support particular political candidates can be nonprofits and give unlimited amounts to campaigns, but they are not allowed to lobby to influence legislation because it is not part of their tax-exempt function, namely supporting particular candidates.

Limited Commercial Activities

Because of complaints by businesses that they cannot compete with tax-exempt organizations that are in the same business, nonprofit organizations are limited in the types of commercial activities in which they can engage. If a nonprofit does engage in a business venture that is unrelated to its purpose, the profits from that venture are taxable. However, if a nontaxable organization has too much taxable income, it may lose its tax-exempt status. For this reason, successful nonprofit groups, such as the National Geographic Society, have to spin off operations that become too profitable.

There are some loopholes nonprofits can use to make money and still avoid paying taxes. These include selling donated items, performing services provided by volunteers, and giving away small items. (For more details about this information, see Chapter 7.)

Chapter 2:
Choosing a Type of Nonprofit Organization

Before forming a nonprofit organization, you should understand the types of structures available so that you can choose the one that will provide the most benefits to the type of organization you are planning.

Association, Trust, or Corporation

A nonprofit organization can organize itself in three ways—as an unincorporated association, a trust, or a corporation. For most groups, a corporation offers the most advantages, but in certain situations, the others may work better.

Association

Any informal group of people who get together for a common purpose—such as a bridge club, Parent Teacher Association, or a ski club—can be considered an *unincorporated association*. Such a group has some legal rights, like the right to open a bank account. However, this structure has some legal liabilities. For example, if the members of a ski club are driving together and get into an accident because of the negligence of the member driving, it is possible that all members of the club could be liable to the person injured, whether or not that person is a club member. For this reason, groups that are involved in risky activities are advised to incorporate.

Small groups of friends who do things together usually do not have to worry, since their auto and homeowners' insurance cover most possible risks. However, if the group expands beyond a small group of friends, starts generating income, or wishes to apply for grants or deductible donations, it should incorporate for the advantages listed under the corporation section.

Trust

A few types of nonprofit organizations are more often formed as *trusts*. For example, charitable gifts made in wills are often set up as charitable trusts. Political committees are also set up as trusts, because federal election laws prohibit corporations from giving money to political campaigns. Multi-employer pension plans must be set up as trusts, as are many other pension plans.

However, for most groups that have members this is not a good entity, since the trustees are not protected against liability. In fact, *trustees* may have a greater exposure to liability because they are held to a higher, *fiduciary* standard. This means that they must be extremely careful in their dealings or they can be personally liable for their mistakes.

Corporation

The corporation is the most common, and usually best, form for a nonprofit organization. Some of the benefits follow. There is a price to pay for these benefits, but it is well worth it. The organization must register with a state and must make periodic filings and disclosures. There are also filing fees, but these are usually small. If professionals are hired to prepare these documents, the cost may be high, but this is not necessary for small groups whose affairs are not complicated.

Protection from Liability

The officers, directors, and members of a nonprofit corporation are protected, in most cases, from liability for the debts and obligations of the corporation. If the corporation incurs debts or if someone is injured by a member of the corporation, the others in the organization normally are not personally liable. There are exceptions to this, however. If the officers or members personally guarantee the debt or if they cause the injury, they are held liable.

Eligibility for Grants

Many government and private programs can only make grants to organizations that are incorporated.

Procedural Rules

When an organization incorporates, it is then governed by state incorporation law. This law usually answers all of the issues that come up in such an organization, such as how many directors there must be, what is a valid *quorum*, and what are the rights of members. If the organization is unincorporated, it must make up its own procedures for all of these issues.

Domestic or Foreign

The first decision that must be made when forming a nonprofit corporation is whether it will be *domestic* (formed in the state in which it is operating) or *foreign* (formed in another state). In nearly all cases, it is best to form a domestic corporation. While the paperwork is about the same, there is an extra registration fee for foreign corporations, and you must hire a registered agent in the state in which the foreign corporation is formed.

Reasons for Incorporating Out-of-State

There are two good reasons to use a foreign nonprofit corporation. First, you may wish to have less than three directors and your state may require three. Many nonprofits have more than three directors because this broadens support and looks better to those providing grants and to the IRS. However, some people who intend to put a lot of their time and money into a new organization are not willing to share the power to make decisions. It may be possible to get friends or relatives to be the additional directors, but if this is not convenient, you could incorporate in a state that allows a single director.

The following states allow a single director in a nonprofit corporation.

- Arizona
- California
- Colorado
- Delaware
- Georgia
- Iowa
- Kansas
- Maryland
- Massachusetts
- Michigan
- Mississippi
- Nevada
- North Carolina
- Oklahoma
- Oregon
- Pennsylvania
- Virginia
- Washington

The second reason to use another state is to have a *stock-based* nonprofit corporation in a state that does not allow it. A stock-based nonprofit corporation is one that is controlled by its stockholders. This keeps the control of the organization to a limited number of persons. Of course, the stockholders cannot receive any dividends or profits of the organization.

Most states do not allow nonprofits to be set up as stock-based, so to form one you need to set up the organization in a state that does. Check with your state to see if a stock-based nonprofit qualifies to do business there.

Membership or Nonmembership

A nonprofit corporation must decide whether to have members, and if it does, if there will be different classes of members, such as voting and nonvoting.

Allowing people to become members of a nonprofit organization may seem like a good way to get support, but because formal members of nonprofits are granted legal rights to control it, many organizations decide against formal membership, at least in the beginning. In most states, formal members have a right to vote on major decisions and to choose directors or officers. This can be time-consuming and costly, and it opens the risk that a splinter group may take over the organization. Consider, for example, if a group of concerned citizens organizes a group to fight the pollution of a chemical plant. If the plant asks all its employees to join the organization, they could become a majority and vote to disband it.

One way to keep control with a membership corporation is to provide that the officers and directors are elected from a slate chosen by a *nominating committee*. This committee can be composed of the founding members and those they approve.

However, the easiest way to keep control of a nonprofit corporation is to set it up as a nonmembership organization. The **BYLAWS** included in this book are for a nonmembership corporation. (see form 6, p.175.) If you wish to have a membership organization, you can use the **ADDENDUM TO BYLAWS** or rewrite the **BYLAWS** to include those sections. (see form 7, p.181.)

As an incentive to support an organization, you can give people an informal membership or list them as *benefactors*, *contributors*, *associates*, or with a similar title. This gives them the feeling of being part of the organization without giving them the power to control its affairs.

Charitable or Noncharitable

The law of nonprofit organizations can be confusing, because there are two meanings for the word *charitable*. One refers to a charity that, for example, aids the poor. The other refers to the broader IRS definition that includes all organizations that can accept tax-deductible contributions. These include educational, religious, scientific, patriotic, and many other types of organizations that are classified under Section 501(c)(3) of the Internal Revenue Code.

If at all possible, you should form your organization to comply with this section, and therefore become a *charitable organization*. To do so, you must draft your *statement of purpose* to fit into the permitted purposes under the law. (This statement is explained in more detail in Chapter 3.)

If you cannot possibly fit your planned activities into a Section 501(c)(3) organization, such as if you plan to do substantial lobbying for new laws or to contribute to political campaigns, you can form a *noncharitable* nonprofit organization under one of the other exemptions. These include:
  ◆ business leagues (trade associations) under Section 501(c)(6);
  ◆ chambers of commerce under Section 501(c)(6);

- civic leagues under Section 501(c)(4);
- employee associations under Section 501(c)(4), (9), or (17);
- labor organizations under Section 501(c)(5);
- lodges under Section 501(c)(10);
- recreational clubs under Section 501(c)(7);
- social clubs under Section 501(c)(7);
- social welfare organizations under Section 501(c)(4); and,
- veterans' organizations under Section 501(c)(19).

Under these sections, an organization can be exempt from paying income taxes, but contributions given to it are not tax-deductible as charitable contributions. However, they might be tax-deductible for another reason. For example, dues to a trade association are usually tax-deductible for businesses in the same trade.

Public Charity or Private Foundation

If you are able to be a charitable organization under Section 501(c)(3), you must determine whether your organization is a *public charity* or a *private foundation*. Every nonprofit should endeavor to avoid private foundation status, since this status can result in some very difficult rules.

Public Charity

All new charitable organizations are presumed to be private foundations unless they can pass certain tests and become public charities. There are three ways to be classified as a public charity— qualifying automatically, passing the *public support test*, or passing the *facts and circumstances test*. These are spelled out in detail in IRS Publication 557 and are summarized below.

Automatic Qualification

A charity automatically qualifies as public if it is one of the following types of organizations:

- a church;
- a school with formal instruction and a regularly enrolled student body;
- a hospital;
- a medical research facility;
- a public safety organization; or,
- an organization that supports one of the above.

Public Support Test

If a charity does not qualify automatically for public charity status, it can qualify if it receives broad public support. For this, the IRS requires an organization to receive at least one-third of its total financial support from public support sources, such as donations from the public.

Facts and Circumstances Test

If a charity cannot pass the public support test, there is a third way to qualify. First, it must receive at least 10% of its funding as public support. Next, it must carry on *bona fide programs* to attract public support on a continual basis. Finally, the IRS will look at the following factors:

- the percentage of public support (10% or more needed);
- the sources of the support (not all from the same family);
- the makeup of the governing body (such as community leaders, government officials, clergy);
- the benefits available to the public (rather than a select group) from the organization; and,
- the makeup of the membership and audience of the organization (a broad audience is better).

An organization does not have to satisfy all of these factors, but the factors will be weighed depending on the nature of the organization.

Private Foundations

If a nonprofit organization cannot qualify for public charity status through any of the above tests, it will be classified as a private foundation. As a private foundation, it must comply with the rules under the I.R.C. It must:

- distribute its income each year so as not to be subject to Section 4942 tax;
- avoid any self-dealing as defined in Section 4941(d);
- avoid retaining business holdings as defined in Section 4943(c);
- refrain from any investments taxable under Section 4944;
- refrain from any expenditures as defined in Section 4945(d); and,
- pay an excise tax on its investment income.

Donors who give to a private foundation can only deduct up to 30% of their adjusted gross income, whereas for a public charity, they can deduct up to 50%.

Private Operating Foundations

If a private foundation can become classified as a *private operating foundation*, it can qualify for donors to be able to deduct up to 50% of their contributions, and it can be relieved of the requirement to distribute funds received from private foundations within one year. To qualify, it must meet the *asset test*, the *support test,* or the *endowment test,* and it must distribute 85% of its income each year.

Under the assets test, 65% or more of assets are devoted directly to exempt activity or a related business, or consist of stock in a corporation that is 80% controlled by the foundation, and at least 85% of assets are devoted to exempt activity or related business. Under the support test, at least 85% of support comes from the general public, not more than 25% comes from one exempt organization, and not more than 50% of support comes from investments. Under the endowment test, at least two-thirds of its minimum investment return is distributed directly for exempt functions. (Minimum investment return is 5% of excess of value of exempt assets over the indebtedness to acquire those assets. For more information, see IRS Publication 557.)

Exempt Operating Foundations

A third possibility for a private foundation is to qualify as an *exempt operating foundation*. As an exempt operating foundation, an organization does not have to pay the excise tax on net investment income. A private operating foundation can qualify as exempt if it has been publicly supported for at least ten years, has a governing body that broadly represents the public, and has no officers and no more than 25% of the governing board as *disqualified individuals* (major donors or their family members). (See IRS Publication 557 for more details.)

Chapter 3:
Start-Up Procedures

The first step in forming a nonprofit corporation, registering with the state, is explained in this chapter. The second step, obtaining your tax exemption, is explained in Chapter 5.

Obtain Forms and Instructions

The first thing to do to form a nonprofit corporation is obtain the forms and instructions that are available from your state's corporate registration office (usually the secretary of state). Some states provide a lot of information, others only the basics. Some are available over the Internet, some by mail. (Refer to your state in Appendix B for more details.)

If you ask for the forms by mail, you should ask for "any and all forms and materials available without charge for forming a new nonprofit corporation." A sample letter is included as form 1 in Appendix C. However, for most states, it is easier to obtain the materials by phone or from the state's website.

You will need the information and forms for state tax exemption from your state's Department of Revenue. The addresses, phone numbers, and websites are in Appendix B. A form request letter is in Appendix C. For some states, you may be able to download the material from the Department of Revenue website. The state tax exemptions are explained in more detail in Appendix B.

If you plan to do charitable solicitation, in most states you will need to obtain information on any registration requirements from the state attorney general's office (in a few states it is a different office). The address, phone number, and basic requirements are listed in Appendix B. (More details on charitable solicitation laws are included in Chapter 7.)

IRS Forms and Instructions

The fastest way to get IRS forms is to download them from the Internet at **www.irs.gov**. However, because they are large booklets, downloading will tie up your line for a long time unless you have a fast connection. Another way to obtain them is to call the IRS forms office at 800-829-1040. (If this does not work in your area, check the federal government pages of your telephone book.) The information you need includes:

- ◆ Publication 557—*Tax-exempt Status for Your Organization*;
- ◆ Package 1023—*Application for Recognition of Exemption under Section 501(c)(3)*;
- ◆ Package 1024—*Application for Recognition of Exemption under sections other than Section 501(c)(3)*;
- ◆ Publication 526—*Charitable Contributions*;
- ◆ Publication 561—*Determining the Value of Donated Property*; and,
- ◆ Publication 598—*Tax on Unrelated Business Income*.

Define Your Purpose

Before forming your nonprofit organization, you should have a clear picture of your purpose and goals. You should then review the permissible purposes under the Internal Revenue Code and decide which type of organization you can be.

You will want to fit your purpose into the requirements for a Section 501(c)(3) organization if at all possible, so that people who contribute money to you can deduct it on their taxes.

If your activities fit into more than one area, you should stress the one that is permitted under Section 501(c)(3).

Example: *If you are starting an organization because you are concerned about pesticides that cause cancer, you should not focus on the fact that you may want to lobby for laws against pesticides that cause cancer. If your primary function is to research pesticides or to educate the public as to which ones may be harmful, you could qualify as a Section 501(c)(3) organization that does scientific research or public education. If you later wanted to lobby, you could do a limited amount within your organization or you could form a separate organization to conduct substantial lobbying.*

If the goal on your application is one that the IRS feels can only be achieved by legislation, they will deny your exemption as a Section 501(c)(3) organization. In such a case, you either have to form a noncharitable organization or redefine your goal.

Example: *A goal such as abolishing nuclear weapons appears to be one that requires legislation. However, if educating the public on the dangers of nuclear proliferation is your goal, then depending on the programs you plan, you may have a better chance to qualify as a charitable organization.*

Review the IRS materials carefully and be sure that your purpose fits into one of the exempt categories. If you find this difficult or feel you may not be successful, you may want to consult with an attorney who specializes in nonprofit organizations. Since this application is one of the most important documents your organization will file, it is worth the investment to get it right.

Choose and Search Your Name

While the activities and accomplishments of your organization will build up a reputation for its name, having a good name to begin with is a good way to appear more trustworthy. At the same time, the *wrong* kind of name (such as sounding like a commercial business) may raise questions with the IRS.

Choosing a Name

In choosing a name, you should use the following guidelines.

Use the Right Suffix

Some states require that certain words or suffixes be a part of the name of a company, such as "Inc." or "Assn." On the state sheets in Appendix B and on the materials from your state, you will find the rules that apply to the corporation's name.

Do Not Use Forbidden Words

Certain words, such as "olympic" or "trust," are not allowed to be a part of an organization's name under many states' laws. Most of these rules can be found either on the state sheets in Appendix B or on the materials from your state.

Do Not Be Too Similar

While there might seem to be some advantage to having your name sound like a similar group, such as the American Cancer Society or the American Red Cross, this leaves you open to a lawsuit by the other organization and possibly legal action by your state's attorney general. You can use words such as "cancer," "heart," or "diabetes" if they relate to your organization's purpose, but do not intentionally make your name sound like another group's name.

Be Sure It Is Not Confusing

Many words in the English language are spelled differently from how they sound. Be sure that the name you choose is easy to spell so that people can locate your phone number or Web address easily.

Searching a Name

Once you have chosen the perfect name, you need to be sure that no one else has established legal rights to it. Many businesses have been forced to stop using their name after spending thousands of dollars in promotions because the name was already in use.

Legal rights can be established by registering a name as a trademark or by merely using the name. Consequently, you cannot be sure no one has rights to a name just by checking registered names. You need to check if anyone is using the name but has not yet registered it.

The following are places you should check.

Federal Trademarks

First, you should check if anyone has registered the name as a federal trademark. To be sure that your use of the name does not violate someone else's trademark rights, you should have a trademark search done of the mark in the *United States Patent and Trademark Office* (PTO). In the past, this required a visit to their offices or the hiring of a search firm for over $100. However, now this can be done on the Internet by going to the United States Patent and Trademark Office website (**www.uspto.gov**) and clicking the "Search" button under "Trademarks."

Yellow Pages

You should search the Yellow Page listings next. With Internet access, you can search all of the Yellow Page listings in the U.S. at a number of sites at no charge. One website, **www.superpages.com**, offers free searches of Yellow Pages for all states at once. You can also use a search engine such as **www.google.com** to see if your company name is used anywhere on the Internet. Since search engines are not always 100% accurate, you should search on at least a few other sites for the state in which you will operate.

Web Addresses

If you have any expectation of having a website some day, you should check if the Web address, or *uniform resource locator* (URL), is available. This can be done at **www.domainname.com**.

As a nonprofit organization, you may use the designation ".org" (rather than ".com" or ".net"), but if you have a clever name you wish to use with ".com," you can use that. If the name you want is already taken in ".org," ".com," and ".net," it may be available in the new designations ".cc" and ".to."

However, because the name is similar to an existing group, you run the risk of being sued and would be better off with a unique name.

Search Services

If you are unable to access the Internet in any way or if you would rather have someone else do the search, you can hire a professional search firm. In addition to a trademark search, they can check other records around the country to give you a more accurate answer as to whether the name is being used anywhere. The cost can range from about $100 to over $800, depending on how thorough the search is and who is doing it. The following are a few firms that do searches. You can call or write to them for a quote.

Government Liaison Services, Inc.
200 North Glebe Road
Suite 321
Arlington, VA 22203
800-624-6564
703-524-8200
Fax: 703-525-8451
www.trademarkinfo.com

Thomson & Thomson
500 Victory Road
North Quincy, MA 02171
800-692-8833
617-479-1600
Fax: 617-786-8273
www.thomson-thomson.com

Blumberg Excelsior Corporate Services, Inc.
4435 Old Winter Garden Road
P.O. Box 2122
Orlando, FL 32802
800-327-9220
407-299-8220
Fax: 407-291-6912
www.blumberg.com

Secretary of State

Finally, you should check with the secretary of state in the state in which you plan to register your corporation to see if the name is available. In some states, this can be done over the phone or on the Internet. In others, you must send a written inquiry.

No matter how thorough your search is, there is no guarantee that there is not a local user somewhere with rights to the mark. If, for example, you register a name and later find out that someone in Tucumcari, New Mexico has been using the name longer than you, that person will still have the right to use the name, but just in his or her local area.

Registering the Name

After you have chosen the name for your new company and you have made sure that it is still available, you should register it before someone else does. You are allowed to reserve a name for a small fee in most states. However, it is usually better to send your **ARTICLES OF INCORPORATION** in as soon as you select a name. (see form 4, p.171.)

By forming your corporation, you have ensured that no other person can register a company with the same name in your state. Nonetheless, this does not stop someone from registering the name with another state or from getting a federal trademark for it.

Trademarks

A federal trademark gives the owner the right to use the name anywhere in the United States and to stop most others from using it. However, it does not eliminate the rights of those who have used the name previously.

Example: *Suppose you form an Italian American social club named Vesuvius Club, do a search, find no one using the same name, and register the name as a trademark. If you later learn that there is a group that has been using the name Vesuvius Club in San Francisco, but they do not have a trademark or telephone listing, you cannot stop them from using it in their area.*

With a federal trademark, you can stop any new clubs from using the name, but not those who used it before you began.

With the Internet reaching into every corner of the world, there is an issue of Internet businesses infringing on the rights of small operators in remote locations. If you plan an operation with a significant Web presence, you may be sued by a small operator somewhere who has used the name before you. If you register a federal trademark and he or she has not, it would work in your favor, but there is now the open legal question of how thorough a business needs to be when doing a search.

One good way to see if anyone is using a name is to perform Web searches on the major search engines (such as Google, Yahoo, Excite, Altavista, Lycos) to see if your desired name is being used anywhere by anyone. If not, you are in good shape. If so, you need to determine if the other use conflicts with your intended use.

Before attempting to register your name, you should know the basics of federal trademarks.

- ◆ A *trademark* is technically the name of a mark applied to goods, while a *service mark* is a mark used with services. A nonprofit organization usually provides services, so it will likely be registering a service mark.
- ◆ Trademarks and service marks are registered according to classes of goods or services. If you plan to use your mark in more than one class, you will need to register (and pay a filing fee of $335) for each class.
- ◆ Your trademark will not be granted until you have actually used the mark. You can file an application indicating your *intent to use* a mark, but you must actually use it before registration is official.
- ◆ In order to qualify for federal registration, you must use your mark in *commerce*, which means in a transaction with people in different states or with a foreign country. The use must be in *good faith*, meaning that you cannot just mail a copy to a relative.
- ◆ You can register your trademark with each state. This is not necessary if you plan to get a federal trademark immediately. However, if you plan to limit your business to one state or do not plan to expand out of state for a number of years, state registration is faster and less expensive than federal registration.

You can get more information from the United States Patent and Trademark Office website at **www.uspto.gov**.

Articles of Incorporation

To create a nonprofit corporation, a document must be filed with the state agency that keeps corporate records—usually the secretary of state. In most states, this document is called the *articles of incorporation*; however, in some states, it may be called the *certificate of incorporation, articles of association*, or *charter*. For simplicity, this document is referred to as the articles of incorporation throughout this book.

Most states provide a blank form for the articles of incorporation, and the IRS provides a sample of what they look for as articles of incorporation. Unfortunately, these two forms are in no way similar. What you will need to do in order to have articles that are acceptable to both your state and the IRS is to combine the requirements of both. This can be done in a few ways.

- ◆ A generic **ARTICLES OF INCORPORATION** form is included in this book. (see form 4, p.171.) It contains the IRS requirements for Section 501(c)(3) organizations and the basic requirements of most states. Check your state material to see if there are any new or additional requirements, and if so, add these to Article 11 of form 4.
- ◆ Also included in this book is an **ADDENDUM TO ARTICLES OF INCORPORATION** form that includes the IRS requirements for Section 501(c)(3) organizations. (see form 5, p.173.) You can use this form as an addendum to your state's form. This will not work for the states that do not provide blank articles of incorporation forms.
- ◆ You can take the requirements from your state's form and the IRS requirements from the addendum, and retype them into a new **ARTICLES OF INCORPORATION** document.

If you are forming an organization that is exempt under a section other than Section 501(c)(3) (e.g., social welfare organizations under Section 501(c)(4) or social clubs under Section 501(c)(7)), you need to use the third option above and retype the material applicable to your type of organization.

NOTE: *Some organizations have special requirements (for example, social clubs must be nondiscriminatory). For more information, see IRS Publication 557.*

If you are forming a private foundation (even though, as explained in Chapter 2, you should try to avoid it), you should obtain IRS Publication 578.

The following is a discussion of the articles included in the **ARTICLES OF INCORPORATION** form in this book. These articles are the common ones on most states' forms.

Article 1: Name of the corporation. Some states require nonprofit corporations to include a suffix like "Inc." or "Assn." at the end of their name, but others do not. Check the state pages in Appendix B for your state's requirements.

Article 2: Address of the corporation. The street address of the principal office, and if different, the mailing address of the corporation, should be provided.

Article 3: Purpose. The first sentence is the *required* language to qualify for Section 501(c)(3) status. After this, you must add the *specific* purpose of your organization. It is important to word this correctly, or your exempt status may be denied by the IRS. Refer to IRS Publication 557 for guidance. If you have trouble drafting your purpose, consider consulting with a specialist in nonprofit law.

Article 4: Directors. Include the number of directors (most states require three, but some allow just one), and their names and addresses.

Article 5: Private inurement and lobbying. This is required by the IRS to prevent the corporation from using its assets for private inurement and from lobbying the government. (see Chapter 6.)

Article 6: Dissolution. This is required by the IRS so that if the corporation dissolves, the assets will go to another qualifying organization.

Article 7: The name of the registered agent and the address of the registered office, along with the agent's acceptance. Each corporation must have a registered agent (in some states called a *statutory agent*) and a registered office. The registered office can be the business office of the corporation if the registered agent works out of that office. It can be the office of another individual who is the registered agent (such as the corporation's attorney), or it can be a professional registered agent's office. In some states, it cannot be a residence unless the address is also a business office of the corporation.

> **Warning:** If you do not comply, you will be unable to maintain a lawsuit and you may possibly be fined.

Article 8: Members. In this section, check the box to designate whether or not the corporation will have members.

Article 9: Duration. In nearly all cases, you want the duration of the corporation to be perpetual rather than for a set number of years.

Article 10: Name and address of the incorporator of the corporation. In some states, this may be any person, even if that person has no future interest in the corporation. There are companies in state capitals that have someone run over to the secretary of state to file corporate articles that are later assigned to the real parties in interest.

Article 11: Additional requirements. Review the state pages in Appendix B and the materials from your state (or the state statute) to determine if any other matters are required to be included in the ARTICLES OF INCORPORATION. If so, include them here. If more than one matter needs to be included, you can designate them Article 12, Article 13, etc.

Execution

In most states, the ARTICLES OF INCORPORATION must be signed and dated by the incorporator in black ink. Typically, the registered agent must sign a statement accepting his or her duties as such. This can be done either as a separate form or on the same form as the ARTICLES OF INCORPORATION.

Filing

The ARTICLES OF INCORPORATION form must be filed with the secretary of state by sending it and the filing fees to the address listed in Appendix B. A duplicate copy must be included in most states. The fees (as available at time of publication) are listed in Appendix B as well. If you wish to receive a certified copy of the articles, which you need for the nonprofit mailing permit, there is an additional cost.

NOTE: *It is possible in some states to file corporate papers by fax or online and to use a credit card for payment.*

The return time for the articles in most states is usually a week or two. If you need to have them back quickly, you might be able to send and have them returned by a courier such as FedEx, Airborne Express, or UPS, with prepaid return. Call your secretary of state for details.

Bylaws

Every corporation must have *bylaws*. This is the document that spells out in detail the corporation's purpose, operating rules, and operational structure. For a nonprofit corporation, they are especially important and must be submitted to the IRS when applying for the tax exemption.

A generic set of BYLAWS is included in this book. (see form 6, p.175.) Read through this set carefully to be sure that everything in it applies to your organization and that there is no conflict with your state laws. If you wish to make any major changes to them (such as powers, voting, or quorum), you should first check your state statutes to be sure that your provisions do not violate any section of the law.

As discussed in Chapter 2, it is not advisable to have formal members. If you decide to, you need to add membership provisions to your BYLAWS. These are included in the ADDENDUM TO BYLAWS. (see form 7, p.181.) Be sure to check the correct box in Article II of the BYLAWS if you use this form.

Taxpayer Identification Number

Prior to opening a bank account, the corporation must obtain a *taxpayer identification number* (formally known as an employer identification number or EIN). This is the corporate equivalent of a Social Security number. You need this number even if you do not expect to hire employees.

The easiest way to obtain your EIN is by filing an online application. In most cases, you get the number immediately, but if there is a problem with your application you may need to phone, fax, or mail your application in. To fill in the SS-4 online, go to the IRS website at **www.irs.gov**, search for "SS-4," link to the online application, and follow the directions.

A copy of the SS-4 is included in this book. You can use this as your worksheet before beginning online. For assistance, call the IRS at 800-829-4933. You can also mail your application in, but it may take weeks before you receive your number.

When you apply for this number, you will probably be put on the mailing list for other corporate tax forms. If you do not receive these, call your local IRS office and request the forms for new businesses. These include Circular E (explains the taxes due), W-4 forms for each employee, the tax deposit coupons, and Form 941 (quarterly return for withholding).

Corporate Supplies

A corporation needs to keep a permanent record of its legal affairs. This includes the original state letter approving your organization, *minutes* of all meetings, lists of members, fictitious names registered, and any other legal matters. The records are usually kept in a ring binder. It is possible to purchase a specially prepared *corporate kit* that has the name of the corporation printed on it and usually contains forms such as minutes and bylaws. However, most of these items are included with this book, so purchasing such a kit might be unnecessary.

Some sources for corporate kits including the following.

Blumberg Excelsior
4435 Old Winter Garden Road
P.O. Box 212
Orlando, FL 32802
800-327-9220
407-299-8220
Fax: 407-291-6912
www.blumberg.com

Corpex
1440 Fifth Avenue
Bay Shore, NY 11706
800-221-8181
631-968-0277
Fax: 800-826-7739
www.corpexnet.com

CorpKit Legal Supplies
46 Taft Avenue
Islip, NY 11751
888-888-9120
Fax: 888-777-4617
www.corpkit.com

Corporate Seal

One thing not included with this book is a *corporate seal*. This must be specially made for each corporation. Most corporations use a metal seal, like a notary's seal, to emboss the paper. This seal can be ordered from an office supply company. Some states now allow rubber stamps for corporate seals. Rubber stamps are cheaper, lighter, and easier to read. These can also be ordered from office supply stores, printers, and specialized rubber stamp companies. The corporate seal should contain the exact name of the corporation, the word "seal," and the year of incorporation.

Organizational Meeting

The real birth of the corporation takes place at the first meeting of the incorporators and the initial board of directors. The officers and board of directors are elected at this meeting. Other business may also take place, such as adopting employee benefit plans.

Usually, minutes, tax, and other forms are prepared beforehand and used as script for the meeting. They are read and voted on during the meeting, and then signed at the end of the meeting.

Agenda

Those items in the following agenda designated with boldface type are forms found in Appendix C of this book. These forms may be torn out of the book, photocopied, or rewritten as necessary to fit your situation.

The agenda for the initial meeting is usually as follows.
1. Sign the **WAIVER OF NOTICE OF ORGANIZATIONAL MEETING.**
2. Note persons present.
3. Present and accept the **ARTICLES OF INCORPORATION** (the copy returned by the secretary of state).
4. Elect the directors.
5. Adopt the **BYLAWS.**
6. Elect the officers.
7. Present and accept the corporate seal.
8. Adopt the **BANKING RESOLUTION.**
9. Adopt the **RESOLUTION TO REIMBURSE EXPENSES.**
10. Adopt any tax resolutions.
11. Adjourn.

Minute Book

After the organizational meeting, set up your *minute book*. The minute book usually contains the following.

◆ Title page ("Corporate Records of _____").
◆ Table of contents.
◆ The letter from the secretary of state acknowledging receipt and filing of the **ARTICLES OF INCORPORATION.**
◆ Copy of the **ARTICLES OF INCORPORATION.**
◆ Copy of any fictitious name registration.
◆ Copy of any trademark registration.
◆ **WAIVER OF NOTICE OF ORGANIZATIONAL MEETING.**
◆ **MINUTES OF ORGANIZATIONAL MEETING.**
◆ **BYLAWS.**
◆ Tax forms:
  • IRS Form SS-4 and taxpayer identification number;
  • IRS Forms 1023 or 1024; and,
  • any state forms.

Bank Account

A corporation needs a bank account. Checks payable to a corporation cannot be cashed by an individual—they must be deposited into a corporate account. Fortunately, some banks have special rates for nonprofit organizations that are very reasonable.

All you should need to open a corporate bank account is a copy of your articles of incorporation, your taxpayer identification number, and perhaps a business license. Some banks, however, want more, and they sometimes do not even know what they want.

Example: *After one individual opened numerous corporate accounts with only his articles, EIN, and business license, he encountered a bank employee who wanted "something certified so we know who your officers are. Your attorney will know what to draw up." He explained that he was an attorney and the president, secretary, and treasurer of the corporation and would write out, sign, and seal whatever they wanted. The bank employee insisted that it had to be a nice certificate signed by the secretary of the corporation and sealed.*

If you have trouble opening the account, you can use the **BANKING RESOLUTION** included with this book, or you can make up a similar form. (see form 13, p.199.)

Licenses

In some states, counties and municipalities are authorized to levy a license fee or tax on the *privilege* of doing business. Nonprofit corporations do not always come under these laws, but some areas have registration provisions to keep track of nonprofits. Check with your town, city, or county clerk to see if registration is required.

County occupational licenses can be obtained from the tax collector in the county courthouse. City licenses are usually available at city hall. Be sure to find out if zoning allows your type of business before buying or leasing property. The licensing departments check the zoning before issuing your license.

If you will be preparing or serving food, you need to check with the local health department to be sure that the premises comply with their regulations. In some areas, if food has been served on the premises in the past, there is no problem getting a license. If food has never been served on the premises, then the property must comply with all the newest regulations. This can be very costly.

Charitable Solicitations

As explained in Chapter 7, if you will be doing charitable solicitations, many states require you to register.

Chapter 4:
The Internet

The Internet has opened up a world of opportunities for businesses. It was not long ago that getting national visibility cost a fortune. Today, a business can set up a Web page for a few hundred dollars, and with some clever publicity and a little luck, millions of people around the world will see it.

This new world has new legal issues and new liabilities. Not all of them have been addressed by laws or by the courts. Before you begin using the Internet, you should know the existing rules and the areas where legal issues exist.

Domain Names

A *domain name* is the address of your website. In recent years, several new *top-level domains* (TLDs) have been created. Top-level domains are the last letters of the *uniform resource locator* (URL), such as ".com," ".org," and ".net." Now you can also register names with the following TLDs.

.biz	.pro
.cc	.aero
.info	.coop
.name	.museum

Dot com is the most popular, as originally, .net was only available to network service providers and .org only to nonprofit organizations. Regulations have eliminated those requirements, but you may wish to use a TLD other than .com to further show your nonprofit status.

Registering a domain name for your organization is a simple process. There are many companies that offer registration services. For a list of those companies, visit the site of the *Internet*

Corporation for Assigned Names and Numbers (ICANN) at **www.icann.org**. You can link directly to any member's site and compare the costs and registration procedures required for the different top-level domains.

One of the best places to register a domain name is **www.registerfly.com**. If your name is taken, they automatically suggest related names that might work for you, and their registration fees are lower than most other sites.

Web Pages

There are many new companies eager to help you set up a website. Some offer turnkey sites for a low, flat rate, while custom sites can cost tens of thousands of dollars. If you have plenty of capital, you may want to have your site handled by one of these professionals. However, setting up a website is a fairly simple process, and once you learn the basics, you can handle most of it in-house.

If you are new to the Web, you may want to look at **www.learnthenet.com** and **www.webopedia.com**, which will familiarize you with the Internet jargon and give you a basic introduction to the Web.

Site Setup

There are seven steps to setting up a website: site purpose, design, content, structure, programming, testing, and publicity. Whether you do it yourself, hire a professional site designer, or employ a college student, the steps toward creating an effective site are the same.

Before beginning your own site, you should look at other sites, especially those of similar nonprofit organizations. Look at the sites of all the organizations that do work similar to yours. Look at hundreds of sites and click through them to see how they work (or do not work).

Site Purpose

To know what to include on your site, you must decide what its purpose will be. Do you want to solicit donations, provide information, seek out those you wish to help, or sell products to raise money for the organization? You might want to do several of these things.

Site Design

After looking at other sites, you can see that there are numerous ways to design a site. It can be crowded, or open and airy; it can have several windows (frames) open at once or just one; and, it can allow long scrolling or just click-throughs.

You will have to decide whether the site will have text only; text plus photographs and graphics; or, text plus photos, graphics, and other design elements, such as animation or JavaScript. Additionally, you will begin to make decisions about colors, fonts, and the basic graphic appearance of the site.

Site Content

You must create the content for your site. For this, you can use your existing promotional materials, new material just for the website, or a combination of the two. Whatever you choose, remember that the written material should be concise, free of errors, and easy for your target audience to read. Any graphics (including photographs) and written materials not created by you require permission. You should obtain such permission from the lawful copyright holder in order to use any copyrighted material. Once you know your site's purpose, look, and content, you can begin to piece the site together.

Site Structure

You must decide how the content (text plus photographs, graphics, animation, and so on) will be structured—what content will be on which page and how a user will link from one part of the site to another. For example, your first page may have the organization name and then choices to click on, such as "our mission," "our services," or "how to help." Have those choices connect to another page containing the detailed information, so that a user can read your mission when he or she clicks on "our mission." Your site could also have an option to click on a link to another website related to yours.

Site Programming and Setup

When you know nothing about setting up a website, it can seem like a daunting task that will require an expert. However, *programming* here means merely putting a site together. There are inexpensive computer programs available that make it very simple.

Commercial programs such as Microsoft FrontPage, Dreamweaver, Pagemaker, Photoshop, MS Publisher, and PageMill allow you to set up Web pages as easily as laying out a print publication. These programs convert the text and graphics you create into HTML, the programming language of the Web. Before you choose Web design software and design your site, you should determine which Web hosting service you will use. Make sure that the design software you use is compatible with the host server's system. The Web host is the provider who will give you space on its server and who may provide other services to you, such as secure order processing and analysis of your site to see who is visiting and linking to it.

If you have an America Online (AOL) account, you can download design software and a tutorial for free. You do not have to use AOL's design software in order to use AOL web hosting services. You are eligible to use this site whether you design your own pages, have someone else do the design work for you, or use AOL's templates. This service allows you to use your own domain name and choose the package that is appropriate for your business.

If you have used a page layout program, you can usually get a simple website up and running within a day or two. If you do not have much experience with a computer, you might consider hiring a college student to set up a website for you.

Site Testing

Some of the website setup programs allow you to thoroughly check your new site to see if all the pictures are included and all the links are proper. There are also websites you can go to that check out your site. Some even allow you to improve your site, such as by reducing the size of your graphics so they download faster. Use a major search engine listed in "Site Publicity" to look for companies that can test your site before you launch it on the Web.

Site Publicity

Once you set up your website, you will want to get people to look at it. *Publicity* means getting your site noticed as much as possible by drawing people to it.

The first thing to do to get noticed is to be sure your site is registered with as many *search engines* as possible. These are pages that people use to find things on the Internet, such as Yahoo and Google. They do not automatically know about you just because you created a website. You must tell them about your site, and they must examine and catalog it.

For a fee, there are services that will register your site with numerous search engines. If you are starting out on a shoestring, you can easily do it yourself. While there are hundreds of search engines, most people use one of the bigger ones. If the services you provide or the type of organization you are has specific niche search engines, you should register with them as well. Most organizations should be mainly concerned with getting on the biggest ones.

By far the biggest and most successful search engine today is Google (**www.google.com**). Some of the other big ones are:

www.altavista.com	www.hotbot.com
www.excite.com	www.lycos.com
www.fastsearch.com	www.metacrawler.com
www.go.com	www.northernlight.com
www.goto.com	www.webcrawler.com

Most of these sites have a place to click to add your site to their system. Some sites charge hundreds of dollars to be listed. If your site contains valuable information that people are looking for, you should be able to do well without paying these fees.

Getting Your Site Known

A *meta tag* is an invisible subject word added to your site that can be found by a search engine. For example, if you are a pest control company, you may want to list all of the scientific names of the pests you control and all of the treatments you have available, but you may not need them to be part of the visual design of your site. List these words as meta tags when you set up your page so people searching for those words will find your site.

Some companies thought that a clever way to get viewers would be to use commonly searched names or names of major competitors as meta tags to attract people looking for those big companies. For example, a small delivery service that has nothing to do with UPS or FedEx might use those company names as meta tags so people looking for them would find the smaller company. While it may sound like a good idea, it has been declared illegal trademark infringement. Today, many companies have computer programs scanning the Internet for improper use of their trademarks.

Once you have made sure that your site is passively listed in all the search engines, you may want to actively promote your site. Newsgroups are places on the Internet where people interested in a specific topic can exchange information. For example, expectant mothers have a group where they can trade advice and experiences. If you have a service that would be great for expectant mothers, that would be a good place for it to be discussed.

Spamming

Sending unsolicited email advertising (called *spam*) started out as a mere breach of Internet etiquette (*netiquette*), but has now become a state and federal crime. The ability to reach millions of people with advertising at virtually no cost was too good for too many organizations to pass up, and this resulted in the clogging of most users' email boxes and near shutdown of some computer systems. Some people ended up with thousands of offers every day.

To prevent this, many states passed anti-spamming laws and Congress passed the CAN-SPAM Act. This law:
   ◆ bans misleading or false headers on email;
   ◆ bans misleading subject lines;
   ◆ requires allowing recipients to opt out of future mailings;
   ◆ requires the email be identified as advertising; and,
   ◆ requires the email include a valid physical address.

Each violation can result in up to an $11,000 fine, and the fines can be raised if advertisers violate other rules such as not harvesting names and not using permutations of existing names. More information can be found on the Federal Trade Commission's website (**www.ftc.gov**).

Advertising

Advertising on the Internet has grown in recent years. At first, small, thin, rectangular ads appeared at the top of websites. These are called *banner ads*. Lately, they have grown bigger, can appear anywhere on the site, and usually blink or show a moving visual.

The fees can be based on how many people view an ad, how many click on it, or both. Some larger companies, such as Amazon.com, have affiliate programs in which they will pay you a percentage of a purchase if a customer comes from your site to theirs and makes a purchase. For sites that have thousands of visitors the ads have been profitable—some sites reportedly make over $100,000 a year.

Legal Issues

Before you set up a Web page, you should consider the many legal issues associated with it.

Jurisdiction

Jurisdiction is the power of a court in a particular location to decide a particular case. Usually, you must be physically present in a jurisdiction or do business there before you can be sued there. Since the Internet extends your organization's ability to reach people in faraway places, there may be instances when you could be subject to legal jurisdiction far from your own state (or country). There are a number of cases that have been decided in this country regarding the Internet and jurisdiction, but very few cases have been decided on this issue outside of the United States.

In most instances, U.S. courts use the pre-Internet test—whether you are present in another jurisdiction or have enough contact with someone in the other jurisdiction. The fact that the Internet itself is not a "place" will not shield you from being sued in another state.

According to the court, there is a spectrum of contact required between you, your website, and consumers or audiences. (*Zippo Manufacturing Co. v. Zippo Dot Com, Inc.*, 952 F. Supp. 1119 (W.D. Pa 1997).) The more interactive your site is with consumers and the more you target an audience in a particular location, the more it becomes possible for someone to sue you outside of your own jurisdiction—so weigh these risks against the benefits when constructing and promoting your website.

The law is not even remotely final on these issues. The American Bar Association, among other groups, is studying this topic in detail. At present, no final, global solution or agreement about jurisdictional issues with websites exists.

One way to protect yourself from the possibility of being sued in a faraway jurisdiction is to state on your website that those using the site or doing business with you agree that "jurisdiction for any actions regarding this site" or your organization is in your home county.

For extra protection, you can have a preliminary page that must be clicked before entering your website. However, this may be overkill for a small nonprofit organization with little risk of lawsuits. If you are in any organization for which you could have serious liability, you should review some similar organizations' sites and see how they handle the liability issue. They often have a place to click for "legal notice" or "disclaimer" on their first page.

You may want to consult with an attorney to discuss the specific disclaimer to use on your website, where it should appear, and whether you should have users of your site actively agree to this disclaimer or just passively read it. However, these disclaimers are not enforceable everywhere in the world. Until there is global agreement on jurisdictional issues, this may remain an area of uncertainty for some time to come.

Libel

Libel is any publication that injures the reputation of another. This can occur in print, writing, pictures, or signs. All that is required for publication is that you transmit the material to at least one other person. When putting together your website, you must keep in mind that it is visible to millions of people all over the planet, and that if you libel a person or company, you may have to pay damages. Many countries do not have the freedom of speech that we do, and a statement that is not libel in the United States may be libelous elsewhere. If you are concerned about this, alter the content of your site or check with an attorney about libel laws in the country you think might take action against you.

Copyright Infringement

It is so easy to copy and borrow information on the Internet that it is easy to infringe copyrights without even knowing it. A *copyright* exists for a work as soon as the creator creates it. There is no need to register the copyright or to put a copyright notice on it. Therefore, practically everything on the Internet belongs to someone.

Some people freely give their works away. For example, many people have created Web artwork (*gifs* and *animated gifs*) that they allow people to copy. There are numerous sites that provide hundreds or thousands of free gifs that you can add to your Web pages. Some require you to acknowledge the source and some do not. You should always be sure that the works are free for the taking before using them.

Linking and Framing

One way to violate copyright laws is to improperly link other sites to yours, either directly or with framing. *Linking* is when you provide a link that takes the user to the linked site. *Framing* occurs when you set up your site so that when you link to another site, your site is still viewable as a frame around the linked-to site.

While many sites are glad to be linked to others, some—especially providers of valuable information—object. Courts have ruled that linking and framing can be a copyright violation. One rule that has developed is that it is usually okay to link to the first page of a site, but not to link to some valuable information deeper within the site. The rationale for this is that the owner of the site wants visitors to go through the various levels of their site (viewing all the ads) before getting the information. By linking directly to the information, you are giving away their product without the ads.

The problem with linking to the first page of a site is that it may be a tedious or difficult task to find the needed page from there. Many sites are poorly designed and make it nearly impossible to find anything.

If you wish to link to another page, the best solution is to ask permission. Email the webmaster or other person in charge of the site, if an email address is given, and explain what you want to do. If they grant permission, be sure to print out a copy of their email for your records.

Privacy

Since the Internet is such an easy way to share information, there are many concerns that it will cause a loss of individual privacy. The two main concerns arise when you post information that others consider private, and when you gather information from customers and use it in a way that violates their privacy.

While public actions of politicians and celebrities are fair game, details about their private lives are sometimes protected by law, and details about persons who are not public figures are often protected. The laws in each state are different, and what might be allowable in one state could be illegal in another. If your site will provide any personal information about individuals, you should discuss the possibility of liability with an attorney.

Several well-known companies have been in the news lately for violations of their customers' privacy. They either shared what the customer was buying or downloading, or looked for additional information on the customer's computer. To let customers know that you do not violate certain standards of privacy, you can subscribe to one of the privacy codes that have been created for the Internet. These allow you to put a symbol on your site guarantying your customers that you follow the code.

The following are the websites of two organizations that offer this service and their fees at the time of this publication.

www.privacybot.com	$100
www.bbbonline.com	$200 to $7,000

COPPA

If your website is aimed at children under the age of 13, or if it attracts children of that age, then you are subject to the federal *Children Online Privacy Protection Act of 1998* (COPPA). This law requires such websites to:

♦ give notice on the site of what information is being collected;

♦ obtain verifiable parental consent to collect the information;

♦ allow the parent to review the information collected;

♦ allow the parent to delete the child's information or refuse to allow the use of the information;

♦ limit the information collected to only that necessary to participate on the site; and,

♦ protect the security and confidentiality of the information.

FTC Rules

Because the Internet is an instrument of interstate commerce, it is a legitimate subject for federal regulation. The *Federal Trade Commission* (FTC) first said that all of its consumer protection rules applied to the Internet, but lately it has been adding specific rules and issuing publications. Many publications for additional information are available from the FTC website at **www.ftc.gov/bcp/menu-internet.htm** or by mail from:

Consumer Response Center
Federal Trade Commission
600 Pennsylvania, NW
Room H-130
Washington, DC 20580

Hiring a Website Designer

If you hire someone to design your website, you should make sure of what rights you are buying. Under copyright law, when you hire someone to create a work, you do not get all rights to that work unless you clearly spell that out in a written agreement.

For example, if your designer creates an artistic design to go on your website, you may have to pay extra if you want to use the same design on your business cards or letterhead. Depending on how the agreement is worded, you may even have to pay a yearly fee for the rights.

If you spend a lot of money promoting your organization, and a logo or design becomes important to your image, you would not want to have to pay royalties for the life of your organization to someone who spent an hour or two putting together a design. Whenever you purchase a creative work from someone, be sure to get a written statement of what rights you are buying. If you are not receiving all rights for all uses for all time, you should think twice about the purchase.

If the designer also is involved with hosting your site, you should be sure you have the right to take the design with you if you move to another host. You should get a backup of your site on a CD in case it is lost or you need to move it to another site.

Chapter 5:
Applying for Tax-Exempt Status

Although it is commonly thought that the Internal Revenue Service grants exemptions to nonprofit organizations, technically, the IRS merely checks to see whether an organization is exempt. The exemption has already been granted by Congress. The IRS's only role is to recognize it.

Having your exemption recognized is an important and somewhat complicated process. You need to read and understand the tax laws to correctly spell out a purpose for your organization that complies with the law.

If you know of any attorneys or accountants who offer low-cost or free services to nonprofit organizations, you should consider using their services.

Charitable Organizations

As explained earlier, under the tax law, the word *charitable* does not only mean charities that help the poor—it means any organization that qualifies to receive tax-deductible donations. If at all possible, you should structure your organization as a charitable organization under IRS Section 501(c)(3). If you cannot (for example, if you plan to do substantial lobbying or to participate in political campaigns), you need to form a noncharitable organization under another section of the I.R.C., as explained in the next section.

Forms

If you sent for the materials mentioned in Chapter 3, you should have all the forms and publications you need, including:

- Package 1023—*Application for Recognition of Exemption*;
- Form 8718—*User Fee for Exempt Organization Determination Letter Request*;

◆ Publication 557—*Tax Exempt Status for Your Organization*; and,
◆ Publication 4220—*Applying for 501(c)(3) Tax-Exempt Status.*

The *Application for Recognition of Exemption* (IRS Form 1023) is the form you need to file to be recognized as an exempt organization. Churches do not need to file the form. Organizations that receive less than $5,000 per year are not required to file, but they should file anyway for the following benefits:

◆ assuring donors of deductibility of donations;
◆ allowing exemption from state taxes;
◆ allowing nonprofit postal rates; and,
◆ guarantying that the information from the form can be used later in other filings, such as state exemption applications or grant applications.

Considering the complexity of the law, the instructions and publications are fairly well written. They guide you through the form, line-by-line, and refer to other sections of the I.R.C. when necessary. If you are preparing your own application, be sure to read the instructions to both Form 1023 and Publication 557 thoroughly before beginning. The following section discusses important issues to consider on the more difficult questions on Form 1023.

How to Fill Out Your Form 1023

The instructions for the Form 1023 are relatively straightforward, considering the subject. You should be sure to read the instructions for each line as you fill it out. Sometimes a word used in the form means something a little different than what you would expect. To help with some of the pitfalls, this section provides some tips for completing the form.

Part I

1. Use your exact corporate name from your articles of incorporation or charter.
2. If you have a specific person in the corporation who should receive all IRS correspondence, you should put his or her name here; otherwise, put "N/A."
3. The IRS prefers a street address, and you should not use a post office box unless you do not have a street address. You should include your nine-digit zip code.
4. Your EIN should have been obtained using Form SS-4, which can be done online, by phone, or by mail. If you have not obtained one yet, you can include the Form SS-4 with this form.
5. Most organizations use a calendar year (January to December) for taxes, but if your operations or your funding sources make a different year better for you, you can choose another date for the end of your taxable year. For example, if the grants you

will be getting are disbursed in August, you might want to have your tax year run from August through July. Your accountant or funding sources may be able to guide you. If you are not sure, you can just use December ("12").

6. Occasionally, the IRS employee examining a form will find some minor discrepancy, and in order to solve it quickly, will call and ask the question, rather than send a letter and wait months for an answer. You should list the person who can best answer such questions—probably the one who prepared this form.

7. Unless you will have an attorney or accountant acting as your representative for your application, you should check "no" to this.

8. If you paid anyone other than the person in question 7 to help you set up your organization, the IRS wants to know. You need to attach a list of names, addresses, and amounts so the IRS can be aware of any insider relationships.

9. Here you list your organization's website and email address. The email address is optional, but usually the more cooperative you are, the more cooperative the IRS is. Your website should be consistent with your organization's purpose and should not contain anything that would harm your chances of approval.

10. If you are a church or if your annual income will be less that $25,000, then you do not have to file Form 990 or 990EZ and you can check "yes" here. Otherwise, check "no." If your income turns out to be more than $25,000 in any year, you will need to start filing Form 990 or 990EZ.

11. This is the date that your articles of incorporation or charter was filed with your state.

12. You would only check "yes" if you are applying for a foreign organization, in which case you need to check with an accountant for guidance on other issues that may come up.

Part II

If you are using this book to form a nonprofit corporation, then you should check "yes" to lines 1 and 5, and check "no" to lines 2, 3, and 4a. Include a copy of your articles of incorporation certified by your secretary of state, and include a copy of your **BYLAWS**. (see form 6, p.175.)

Part III

This part is a checklist to be sure you comply with the *organizational test* of the IRS rules. You should check the box on line 1, and write in the page, article, and paragraph of your articles in which your purpose clause appears. If you use the **ARTICLES OF INCORPORATION** in this book, then you would write "page 1, article 3." (see form 4, p.171.)

Next, you should check box 2a, and on 2b write in "page 1, article 6." (If you retyped the articles and the paragraph comes out on another page, make this change accordingly.)

Part IV

This is the most important part of your application. You need to explain your organization's past, present, and future activities to the IRS, and convince them that your activities fall within the permitted activities for being tax-exempt. You should be sure to read the instructions for Form 1023 and Publication 557 before writing this section.

While there is the temptation to downplay any questionable activities and exaggerate the more appropriate activities, you should be honest in your description, because in an audit you could face losing your exemption and having penalties imposed. If your past or current activities are not appropriate, you should make a written plan on how they will change, so that all of your future activities will be appropriate.

In describing the activities, you should list:
- ◆ exactly what the activity is;
- ◆ when it began or will start;
- ◆ how much time is or will be devoted to it;
- ◆ who performs the activity;
- ◆ how it is or will be funded; and,
- ◆ how the activity furthers the tax-exempt purpose of your organization.

Part V

The IRS has been cracking down in recent years on organizations that are claimed to be started for charitable purposes, but that actually give more benefits to the founders or directors, or to their families. This is the *private inurement doctrine* explained in Chapter 6.

In this section of the form, you must list compensation and other financial arrangements with those who are connected with the organization, such as officers, directors, trustees, employees, and independent contractors. Of course, you are not forbidden from having financial arrangements with those connected with the organization, but you must be sure that they do not receive undue profits from the organization. You need to attach a separate sheet listing the names, qualifications, average hours worked, and duties of the listed persons. You must also list family and business relationships of all of your officers, directors, and trustees to those receiving compensation.

Note that under number 4, you are "recommended" by the IRS to have the practices listed, so you should of course have them. These are included in the **Bylaws** in this book, so if you follow these you can check "yes" to these questions.

For question 5, the IRS has prepared a two-page sample conflict of interest policy, which is included as Appendix A to the instructions for this form. You should adopt this policy and then you can check "yes" to question 5a.

As a newly starting nonprofit organization, you will probably not have any employees or independent contractors receiving more than $50,000 a year, but if you do, you should consult with an accountant who specializes in nonprofits to be sure the arrangement is allowable. Many of the answers regarding these persons require written responses, and these should be prepared by someone knowledgeable about the IRS requirements.

For question 6, the best answers are no. If you need to have non-fixed payments, you should check with an accountant to set up a system that will be allowable.

For question 7, the best answers are no, but if you need to buy assets from insiders (for example, if you bought things ahead of time that you planned to use for the corporation), then you should explain why the price is fair and based on the fair market value.

For 8 again the best answer is no, but if you have any of the listed transactions, you should explain in detail why they are fair. The bottom line is that the IRS does not want you making a profit from the tax-exempt organization. If you are making fair and honest transactions you should be okay. If they are substantial, you should check with a tax expert.

Question 9 is similar to 8, but it is looking for related organizations. Some people try to make a profit on their nonprofit by directing money to their friends, associates, and controlled companies, and this question is looking for those types of transactions.

Part VI

Part VI is concerned with who benefits from your activities. The IRS wants to be sure the benefits are public and not private. Unless you check "no" to these, you should explain how the benefits are open to the community and not just a small group. While only a small number of people may be able to use your services, there should be no limits on who can apply. If any relatives or associates of your insiders benefit from the services, it must not be because of any relationship, but as any member of the public might.

Part VII

If you are starting a new nonprofit you will probably check "no" to question 1, but if you need to check "yes" you should check with a tax expert and complete Schedule G.

You should file this application within twenty-seven months of opening your corporation. If you are later than that and check "no" for 2, you must complete Schedule E.

Part VIII

This part is to be sure you do not violate any of the rules about political activity. If you check "yes" to number 1, your application will be denied. If you check "yes" to 2a or b, you should consult with a tax expert to be sure you are following the rules.

If you will be conducting gambling, you should get a copy of Publication 3079 *Gaming Publications for Tax-exempt Organizations* before answering the questions under number 3.

Question 4 refers to whether you are doing any fundraising unrelated to your tax-exempt purpose. If you are only doing activities related to your purpose, you can check "no". Otherwise, check the boxes for the types of fundraising you are engaged in and attach an explanation of the activities for each. If you check "yes" to 4e, you should consult an expert to be sure you are using the funds for the benefit of the donor. The IRS is doing more audits of this type of activity because of recent abuses.

If you check "yes" to any of questions 5 through 8, you should consult an expert to be sure you can comply with all of the rules and regulations.

For the questions on line 9, if you are claiming an exemption as a child care organization under Section 501(k), you must mainly care for children so that parents can be employed. Be sure to read the instructions for this line.

On line 10, the IRS is concerned with the copyright, patent, and trademark issues, because if the copyrights are not owned by the organization, then a profit is injuring another and the organization may be engaged in a commercial enterprise, both of which raise problems. If these rights will be owned by the organization, then your exemption will more likely be granted.

Line 11 is for abuses in the donation of donated property. Conditions and limitations made by the donors will be a problem.

If you will operate in a foreign country as asked in question 12, you should consult a tax advisor.

For questions 13 through 22, you should read these questions carefully, and if you need to answer "yes" to these, then you should consult a tax expert.

Part IX

Since you are starting a new nonprofit organization, your numbers in this section will be projections. You need projections for the current year and for two succeeding years, so you can leave Column D blank.

Part X

This part of the form asks questions that determine if you are a public charity (good) or a private foundation (not good) as discussed in Chapter 2 of this book. You should carefully read Chapter 2 and the instructions before answering these questions.

Schedules A through H

The schedules only need to be filled in if they apply to your organization. Be sure to carefully read the instruction to each schedule to be sure to give them what they are asking for—but not more or less. In most cases, you are advised to consult with an expert if any of these apply to you.

Schedule A

Schedule A is for churches. If you are claiming to be a church, the more your activities are similar to a traditional church, the more likely you can earn an exemption. If your activities might be considered *nontraditional,* you should consult a professional who has experience in Form 1023.

Schedule B

This is for schools, colleges, and universities, and the main thing they are looking for is a determination that you do not discriminate.

Schedule C

This schedule will help a hospital or medical research organization determine if it is charitable or eligible for public charity status.

Schedule D

This is for a special type of organization that acts as a supporting organization for another nonprofit organization. You will need the services of a professional if this applies to you.

Schedule E

If you have not filed your 1023 in a timely manner (within twenty-seven months of beginning), you will need to request an extension and should have a professional help with this part.

Schedule F

This schedule only applies to housing for elderly, handicapped, or low-income individuals. A specialist can help you be sure that your activities are in compliance with all the regulations.

Schedule G

If you are forming a new nonprofit, you will most likely not be a successor to another group, but if you are, you should consult an expert.

Schedule H

If you will be providing scholarships, loans, or grants, these must be given on a nondiscriminatory basis and not to people connected to the organization or its founders.

While filling out the forms, keep in mind that under the law, they will be public record, and anyone can get a copy of them from the IRS or from you. (There is a penalty if you do not provide copies to those who request them.) Therefore, if there is any information that you need to include on the form but wish to keep private, such as donor lists or trade secrets, you can write "see attachment" in the space for the information on the form. Then write on the attachment "NOT SUBJECT TO PUBLIC INSPECTION," and include the necessary information you wish to be concealed. You should attach a statement of why the information should be withheld from the public.

Noncharitable Organizations

If your organization cannot qualify as a charitable organization under Section 501(c)(3), you will need to apply under a different section of the code and use different IRS forms.

Following are some of the other types of nonprofit organizations that can apply for tax exemption and the code sections that they must qualify under.

◆ Business leagues	Section 501(c)(6)
◆ Chambers of commerce	Section 501(c)(6)
◆ Civic leagues	Section 501(c)(4)
◆ Employee associations	Section 501(c)(4), (9), or (17)
◆ Labor organizations	Section 501(c)(5)
◆ Lodges	Section 501(c)(10)
◆ Recreational clubs	Section 501(c)(7)
◆ Social clubs	Section 501(c)(7)
◆ Social welfare organizations	Section 501(c)(4)
◆ Veterans' organizations	Section 501(c)(19)

All of these organizations use Package 1024 (rather than 1023) to apply for recognition of tax exemption. The questions are similar to those discussed for charitable organizations, but the rules are not as strict. The main concern is that none of the directors or members receive any financial benefits from the organization.

NOTE: *If some of the directors or members receive salaries or rents from the organization, the rates must be reasonable and no higher than what would be paid to a different person.*

Submitting Your Application

The forms should be filed within fifteen months after incorporation in order to have the tax-exempt status apply from the corporation's beginning. If the forms are late, they only apply from the date of filing. However, you can get an extension if you ask before the the end of the fifteen months.

Along with your application, you will need to include **IRS FORM 8718, USER FEE FOR EXEMPT ORGANIZATION DETERMINATION LETTER** (see form 9, p.191), financial statements for the previous three years (or proposed budgets for the next two), and copies of the corporation's articles of incorporation and bylaws. The copy of the articles must be conformed, meaning an exact copy. It is best to send a photocopy of the articles that has been date-stamped or certified by the secretary of state. Otherwise, you may need to include a written declaration certifying its authenticity. The copy of the bylaws need not be signed if it is submitted as an attachment to Form 1023.

Response to Your Application

The response from the IRS can be either yes, maybe, or no. If you have successfully completed the form to the satisfaction of the IRS, your exemption will be granted. If they are not sure your organization qualifies, they may ask for clarification or more information. If it appears that your group does not qualify, they will issue a proposed adverse determination. You have thirty days to appeal this ruling before it becomes final. For information on how to appeal, read IRS Publication 892, *Exempt Organization Appeal Procedures for Unagreed Issues.*

State Tax Exemptions

Most states also exempt many nonprofit organizations from income, property, sales, and other taxes. In most states, the exemption is automatic, either because the organization is formed as a nonprofit or the organization's exemption is recognized by the IRS.

You can find the addresses of the state Departments of Revenue and whether exemption is automatic or not in Appendix B. Also, you should write to the department and ask for the forms necessary for the state exemptions.

Chapter 6:
Protecting Your Nonprofit Status

The rules are strict for nonprofit corporations. If they are broken, tax-exempt status can be lost and you could owe additional taxes and penalties. This chapter explains the most important rules and how to avoid breaking them.

Private Inurement

The *private inurement doctrine* is one of the most important concepts of nonprofit law. It states that the funds and benefits of a nonprofit organization cannot go to any particular persons, but must be used for the approved purpose of the organization. The rule keeps people from using the form of a nonprofit organization to avoid taxes for private transactions.

Example: *If a wealthy individual wants to start a foundation to hire relatives instead of giving them taxable gifts or inheritance, that person cannot use the form of a nonprofit organization.*

The rule does not make sense for organizations such as social clubs or trade associations, whose whole purpose is to give benefits to members rather than to society. For these organizations, the law contorts to say that the members can benefit from the organization, but only if all the members benefit, not just a few. Also, these groups are limited in how much of their funds can come from outside the group. Dues and contributions from members are not taxable, but if the group raises too much money from outsiders, that income may be taxable.

To help you understand what the private inurement doctrine requires, the following are some examples.

Example 1: *A trade association can be formed by apple growers to promote the eating of apples, but it cannot only work to sell its members' apples. It must promote the eating of apples in general.*

Example 2: *A social club can be set up for the benefit of an ethnic group, such as an Italian Americans club, but it cannot give special benefits to some members, such as reduced dues, that are subsidized by other members.*

Example 3: *A scientific organization can be formed to test electrical products for safety, but it cannot work for the interests of just a few manufacturers.*

Example 4: *A museum can be set up to display and sell works of art, but not if its purpose is selling its members' works for their financial gain.*

Excess Benefits Transactions

Besides not having the purpose be to benefit private parties, the actual operations of the group must not give excess profits to private individuals.

Nonprofit organizations are allowed to hire employees, rent property, and pay for services. In most cases, there is no prohibition against hiring, renting from, or buying from their own directors or officers—as long as it is a fair transaction. The salary must not exceed what is fair in the community, the rent must be fair market rent, and the services must not be overpriced compared to other providers of the same services.

Transactions between nonprofits and their directors, officers, and members are looked at carefully by the IRS, so you should keep careful records and be able to back up all transactions.

Example: *If a director rents office space to your organization, you should have evidence of how much rent is charged to others and what other rentals are available to the organization. If the organization pays salaries to employees and officers, you should document how much money those people earned elsewhere and what similar organizations are paying similar employees.*

Excess Benefits Rules

Because of abuses, the IRS has been tightening the rules about private benefits from nonprofits. Rather than costing the organization its exemption as in the past, the IRS now imposes an excise tax on any benefits it deems excessive. The tax can be up to 25% on the recipient and 10% on the organization's members who approved it (up to $10,000 per transaction).

The rules do list some ways that a benefit can be safe from being categorized as excessive, if it is:
♦ clearly spelled out in the organization's records;
♦ based on fair market value or comparable worth; and,
♦ approved by disinterested members of the organization.

The rules are contained in I.R.C. 4958 and the rules implementing it are in IRS Regulations 53-4958-0 through -8.

Lobbying

A basic rule for charitable nonprofit corporations is that if a *substantial part* of the activities consist of *propaganda* or *attempts to influence legislation*, then the tax exemption will be denied or revoked.

Lobbying is considered to be either directly contacting legislators to influence legislation or attempting to influence public opinion on an issue of legislation. It is not considered lobbying if you do a nonpartisan study or analysis, or if you respond to legislative requests for information.

What *substantial* means in the case of lobbying has been a contentious issue for a long time. Two tests exist that can be used by a nonprofit to be sure it does not violate the limit—the *substantial part test* and the *expenditures test*. All charities must pass the substantial part test, unless they elect to use the expenditures test. Churches and related organizations are not allowed to elect the expenditures test.

The expenditures test was devised because the substantial part test was difficult to understand and there were no strict standards to guide the IRS agents. According to the substantial part test, no more than 15% of the organization's expenditures can be for lobbying. However, it is difficult to put a dollar value on many actions of an organization, so it is easy for an organization to err.

Example: *How much money was expended if a group puts one paragraph in their newsletter promoting a legislative issue? Would you include a percentage of the printing, postage, and addressing, as well as the office rent and utilities?*

Although the expenditures test was created to give organizations some certainty, few have used it because the IRS rules require much greater recordkeeping. According to the expenditures test, an organization is allowed to spend 20% of its first $500,000 on exempt purpose expenditures, 15%

of the next $500,000, 10% of the next $1,000,000 and 5% of the rest. However, no group can spend more than $1,000,000 on lobbying. To pass the expenditures test, the organization must file IRS Form 5768 and must use Part VI-A of Schedule A, Form 990 to figure the limits.

Private Foundations
Private foundations under Section 501(c)(3) are not permitted to lobby at all.

Other Nonprofits
Nonprofit organizations that are exempt under provisions other than Section 501(c)(3), such as social welfare organizations and trade associations, do not need to limit lobbying. Therefore, many charitable nonprofit organizations set up noncharitable nonprofit organizations to handle lobbying.

Penalty
The penalty for violating these rules can be a tax on the amounts expended or a complete loss of tax-exempt status.

Further Information
The Nonprofit Lobbying Guide is a book that explains in detail the legislative process and how a nonprofit organization can lobby successfully and legally. It is available for $16 from Independent Sector (call 202-387-5149) or in PDF format for no charge at **www.clpi.org/ CLPI_Publications.aspx**.

Political Campaigning
Political campaigning is strictly controlled for nonprofits. Political campaigning is considered to be supporting of particular candidates for office (as opposed to lobbying, which is supporting legislation). The general rule is that charitable organizations may not do any political campaigning, while noncharitable nonprofits can only do limited campaigning. However, special organizations known as *political action committees* (PACs) can be set up to solely do political campaigning.

Like the rules against lobbying, these rules allow an organization to do nonpartisan voter information campaigns. For example, a group can send out pamphlets listing how legislators voted on particular issues, such as gun control and abortion, and not be considered as supporting any particular candidates. However, the pamphlets are supposed to be written in a nonpartisan manner, without indicating approval or disapproval of either record.

Although the tax law does not impose an absolute ban on political campaigning by nonprofits that are noncharitable, federal election laws severely limit what nonprofit corporations can do.

For this reason, most nonprofit corporations that wish to participate in campaigns set up PACs for political campaigning.

Penalty

The penalty for violating these rules can be a tax on the amounts expended or a complete loss of tax-exempt status.

Conflicts of Interest and Self-Dealing

It is not fatal for an organization to have dealings with its insiders (*disqualified persons* in IRS parlance), but the dealings require careful documentation, and at times can look bad to outsiders. As previously discussed, any transactions with insiders should be documented.

Keep in mind that conflicts of interest and *nepotism* in an organization can have a negative effect on members or contributors. If the person who starts an organization only hires family members and no one else to work for the organization, this may be seen as a conflict of interest to those who make grants or want to join.

In some cases, the salaries in an organization are below normal and few other people are willing to get involved, so a conflict of interest may not occur. However, in a large organization where many people want to be involved, these political problems may result in a loss of support or even in the formation of splinter groups.

> **Warning:** Avoid keeping any conflicts secret. If the organization is dealing with an insider or an insider's family member, do not try to hide it. Explain the person's relationship to the organization and put the transaction in the records.

Sources of Income

There are two main concerns for nonprofit organizations about the sources of income—that new funds do not cause it to lose its public charity status and that not too much of the money is from sources unrelated to its exempt purpose.

Donations

As explained in Chapter 2, a charitable nonprofit organization does not want to be a private foundation. The only way to do this is to pass either the public support test or the facts and circumstances test. Mainly, it must be sure that the income comes from public sources rather than one or two donors. Keep these tests in mind when raising money, since this may mean declining certain donations if they threaten your public charity status.

Fundraising Activities

Both charitable and noncharitable organizations must be careful about how they earn money. If too much comes from improper sources, they may be required to pay tax penalties or completely lose their tax exemption. For charitable organizations, the basic rule is that the money-making activities must be related to the exempt function of the organization. For noncharitable organizations, only a limited amount may be raised from nonmembers.

Checklist for Avoiding Problems

❑ Dealings with insiders
     ❑ Be sure the amount is reasonable
     ❑ Keep detailed documentation
     ❑ Do not hide deals

❑ Lobbying
     ❑ Charitable organization—only insubstantial
     ❑ Set up a separate organization if necessary
     ❑ Noncharitable organizations—okay, but not deductible

❑ Political campaigning
     ❑ No political campaigning
     ❑ Only nonpartisan voter education
     ❑ Set up a PAC for campaigning

❑ Sources of income
     ❑ Watch public support limits
     ❑ Limit unrelated income
     ❑ Pay taxes on unrelated income

Chapter 7:
Raising Money in a Nonprofit Organization

A nonprofit organization cannot operate like a profit-making business—it is limited in the types of profit-making operations it may run. However, it has other possibilities for making money that are not open to profit-making companies.

Applying for Grants

A nonprofit corporation can qualify for grants from both private foundations and government agencies. There are thousands of grants available through various programs, some of which are not claimed by anyone. If you do some research, you may qualify for the fund you need to run your programs.

However, getting a grant is not always easy. If you do not answer the questions correctly or provide the required documentation, you will not get the grant. Writing grant applications has become a profession in itself—as a career, some people compile the information needed for organizations to qualify for grants.

As a new organization, you probably will not want to start using expensive grant-writing services. It will be a good educational experience for you to make some grant applications to learn the process. Grant applications are like tax returns, in that you can better use the services of a professional when you have done it yourself and know what kind of information is needed.

Fortunately, there are many organizations that help individuals and organizations learn how to apply for grants. One of the best is *The Foundation Center*. This organization compiles information about all of the foundations that give grants and makes it available in books, in libraries, and on their website. They have five centers—Atlanta, Cleveland, New York, San Francisco, and

Washington—and sponsor collections of foundation materials in two hundred libraries around the country. To locate their publications, check their website at **www.foundationcenter.org** or visit the largest library near you. Some of their publications include the following.

- ◆ *AIDS Fundraising*
- ◆ *Corporate Foundation Profiles*
- ◆ *The Foundation Directory*
- ◆ *Guide to U.S. Foundations, Their Trustees, Officers, and Donors*
- ◆ *National Directory of Corporate Giving*
- ◆ *National Guide to Funding in Arts and Culture*
- ◆ *National Guide to Funding for Community Development*
- ◆ *National Guide to Funding for the Environment and Animal Welfare*
- ◆ *National Guide to Funding in Health*
- ◆ *National Guide to Funding for Information Technology*
- ◆ *National Guide to Funding for Women and Girls*

For beginners, they have a grant tutorial that explains how to research and apply for grants. It can be found at **www.foundationcenter.org/getstarted/training/online**.

Soliciting Donations

For nonprofit organizations that cannot get grants or are intimidated by the application process, the primary way to gain funds is by soliciting donations from the public. For organizations that qualify under I.R.C. Section 501(c)(3) as charitable, a donation is tax-deductible for the giver. However, if a donor receives something for the donation, then only the amount in excess of the value of the item is deductible.

Example: *If an organization holds a fundraising dinner at $100 a plate, and the value of the dinner is $25, then only $75 of the payment is tax-deductible.*

The IRS requires nonprofits to tell donors what portion of their payment is deductible.

Donations to other nonprofit organizations (such as social welfare, business leagues, and so on) are not deductible unless they are legitimate business expenses. Donations made to an organization (such as a trade association) that are normally deductible as business expenses are limited if the organization engages in lobbying. An organization that engages in lobbying must keep a record of what portion of its budget is used for lobbying and must let members know that this portion is not tax-deductible.

Organizations should keep in mind that besides soliciting immediate gifts from the public, they should also look for bequests in people's wills. People who might only make small donations during their lifetime might be willing to make much greater contributions once they no longer need money. This is especially true of those with large estates and few or no children.

Charitable Solicitation Laws

Because of abuses by some nonprofits in the past, numerous laws regulate the solicitation of money for charitable purposes. Federal, state, and many local governments have acted to protect the public from abuses.

If you will be asking for donations from the public, you need to comply with the laws, or you will face civil or criminal penalties. In many states, your organization must register before it can begin solicitations. If you plan a national solicitation campaign, you need to learn the laws of all fifty states.

Fortunately, there is a movement to simplify the process. A uniform registration form has been proposed and accepted by many states. Also, a great deal of guidance is available to nonprofits, and much of it is free.

Because of our constitutional guarantee of free speech, the regulation of fundraising by nonprofit organizations must be very narrowly drawn. Nonprofits are not considered commercial enterprises, so their regulation cannot be as broad as other areas. However, the regulation that has been allowed is still a substantial burden and requires strict compliance.

Federal Laws

Federal laws concerned with charitable solicitations mostly deal with the tax aspects. The biggest abuse in this area occurs when donors are led to believe that their payments to organizations are deductible when they are not.

Groups to which donations are not deductible are required to state in their solicitation that payments are not deductible as charitable contributions for federal income tax purposes. This rule does not apply to groups whose gross receipts are less than $100,000 a year, or whose solicitations go to less than ten people or are only face-to-face. The penalty can be up to $10,000 if the violation is unintentional or 50% of the money collected if it is intentional.

Although donations to nonqualified groups are not deductible as charitable contributions, in some cases they may be deducted as business expenses.

Example: *A real estate agent may deduct dues to a real estate board.*

However, any part of the dues used to lobby the government is not deductible, and organizations that are exempt under Sections 501(c)(4), (5), and (6) must make their members aware of what amount is not deductible.

For groups to which donations are deductible, there are three rules that must be followed when a donor gets something in exchange for his or her gift.
1. Only an amount in excess of the fair value of the premium is deductible.
2. When the amount is over $75, the donor must be given a written statement indicating what amount is deductible.
3. When a donation is over $250, the donor must be given a written receipt.

See IRS Publications 526 and 557 for more information.

State Laws

The biggest burden on fundraising by nonprofits is that most states require registration and disclosure. Some also require filing fees or bonds that can cost hundreds of dollars. For national organizations, it is a considerable burden to keep track of the laws in all fifty states, send for the filing forms, keep track of all the different deadlines, and compile all the required information. For small nonprofits just starting out, it is practically impossible.

If you are a new organization that needs to raise funds, follow these guidelines. First, find out if you are exempt. Each state has different categories of groups that are exempt. Exempt groups typically include religious organizations, schools, hospitals, and some clubs. Also, most states have a dollar limit, such as $10,000 or $25,000, and you are exempt until your donations reach that level. The dollar limits for each state are included in Appendix B. However, since the laws often change, check to be sure the figures are current. One good place to find information on state requirements is online at **www.rodentia.com/nporegulation/states.html**.

If you do not fit under any of these exemptions, you need to consider registration. If you will be doing most of your fundraising in your own state, you should start by getting the registration information (if registration is required in your state) and by learning the system so you can comply with those regulations. Next, you could expand your fundraising into the states that do not have registration requirements. The following states do not have registration requirements.
- Delaware
- Hawaii
- Idaho
- Indiana
- Iowa
- Montana

◆ Nebraska
◆ Nevada
◆ South Dakota (telephone solicitors must register)
◆ Texas
◆ Vermont
◆ Wyoming

Your next step could be to start registering on a state-by-state basis. If your potential donors are concentrated in a few states, then of course, those are the best ones to start with. If not, you could start with the states with the simplest or cheapest registration, or the states with the highest population.

Just as there is a big difference in what each state requires, there is a difference in how seriously each state keeps track of registrations. Some states demand strict compliance and have teams of attorneys investigating nonprofit compliance, while others just pile the registration forms in a warehouse. If you find that strict compliance is not possible because of your group's limited resources, the following are some things to consider.

Mail Solicitations

The United States Supreme Court has ruled that states do not have the right to require companies to collect sales taxes if they do not do business in that state. Mailing catalogs to and placing advertisements in a state is not considered doing business. Some have argued that merely mailing charitable solicitations to people in a state is not enough to require registration in that state, but there has not yet been a definitive court ruling on this.

Your group could take the position that sending a few solicitations by mail to a state is not enough to require your registration. Most likely, your letters will not be brought to the attention of the regulators anyway. However, if they do find out about it and decide that you should have registered, you may have to pay legal fees to resolve the matter. If your promotional materials are honest and you use the funds legitimately, you will be in much better position than if your materials are misleading or your promotion a scam.

Internet Solicitations

The Internet has added new legal issues to the matter of charitable solicitations. A few courts have ruled that anyone who has a website is legally *doing business* every place that can view the site. This has lead to some conclusions that might seem ridiculous, since a New York website owner can be guilty of violating a German obscenity law.

If this rationale is accepted, the strictest law of any town on the planet controls every site on the Internet. Therefore, states that insist that anyone with a website comes under its jurisdiction are most likely wrong and soliciting funds on your website should not bring you under the jurisdiction of all fifty states. However, keep in mind that the law is not yet clear on this point and some states insist that all websites are under their jurisdiction.

If you are registered in some states and not others, you could put a disclaimer on your website that it is only intended for residents of those states. This should protect you, but since the law is new and still in flux, no one can be sure in every case.

Uniform Registration Statement

Because the different registration requirements of the different states create such a burden on interstate nonprofit organizations, many states have attempted to standardize the process. Instead of a different form with different requirements for each state, they have proposed a *Uniform Registration Statement* (URS) that could be used for all states.

Not all states have agreed to this since it has to go through hearings in each state legislature. However, many states have agreed, and in time, there may be just one form for all states.

At the time of this publication, the following states and districts have agreed to accept the URS.

◆ Alabama	◆ Maryland	◆ Ohio
◆ Arizona	◆ Massachusetts	◆ Oklahoma
◆ Arkansas	◆ Michigan	◆ Oregon
◆ California	◆ Minnesota	◆ Pennsylvania
◆ Connecticut	◆ Mississippi	◆ Rhode Island
◆ District of Columbia	◆ Missouri	◆ South Carolina
◆ Georgia	◆ New Hampshire	◆ Tennessee
◆ Illinois	◆ New Jersey	◆ Utah
◆ Kansas	◆ New Mexico	◆ Virginia
◆ Kentucky	◆ New York	◆ Washington
◆ Louisiana	◆ North Carolina	◆ West Virginia
◆ Maine	◆ North Dakota	◆ Wisconsin

In addition to the URS, supplemental forms are required in Arkansas, District of Columbia, Georgia, Mississippi, North Dakota, Tennessee, Utah, Washington, and West Virginia. An excellent source of information on the state requirements, as well as copies of the forms, can be found at **www.multistatefiling.org**.

Alaska, Colorado, and Florida require registration, but do not yet accept the URS. The following states do not require registration: Delaware, Hawaii, Idaho, Indiana, Iowa, Montana, Nebraska, Nevada, South Dakota, Texas, Vermont, and Wyoming.

Local Laws

Besides the state laws, numerous cities and towns have their own charitable solicitation laws. While many of these only apply to in-person, door-to-door, or telephone solicitors, some expect every group conducting a national campaign to register.

If you are conducting a local fundraising campaign, check with the clerk of any city or town in which you will be operating. Checking with every town in the nation is clearly beyond the ability of most new groups. When you grow, you may need to hire a professional fundraiser who can keep track of such compliance.

Constitutional Issues

Regulating charitable solicitations raises some serious constitutional issues, most importantly, free speech. While states have argued that soliciting money is a commercial activity that is subject to regulation, the United States Supreme Court has held that asking for money for charitable causes is *not* commercial speech, but is a highly protected form of free speech.

Whereas most laws only need to be reasonable to be valid, any laws that regulate charitable fundraising must be as limited as possible to achieve only a legitimate and narrow governmental interest. The government cannot use broad formulas, such as percentages of net proceeds that go to charity, to limit solicitations, and they cannot require lengthy disclosures to be made during verbal solicitations.

If you feel that a regulation violates your constitutional rights, you can ignore it. However, keep in mind that if someone complains, and you are investigated and charged with violating the law, you will need to take the time and money to defend yourself or face the penalties.

States have been able to regulate trespassing, gambling, fraud, and disclosure. Laws on these subjects that affect charitable solicitors will usually be upheld.

Unrelated Business Income

To keep nonprofit organizations from competing unfairly with profit-making businesses, there are strict limits on how much unrelated income such groups can earn. Violation of the limits can result in tax penalties or loss of tax-exempt status. In all cases, unrelated business income is taxed and a separate tax form must be filed for the taxable income.

There are some exemptions for nonprofits that allow income to be raised without penalty. An organization cannot regularly operate an unrelated trade or business. However, if an organization operates a business only sporadically, such as hosting an annual fund drive, the income is exempt. Also, if the business is related to its exempt function, such as a cafeteria in a hospital or a bookstore in a school, then the business is exempt.

Exempt Activities

Besides the exemptions for related and sporadic income sources, nonprofit organizations can earn some exempt types of income without penalty. These include:

◆ activities carried on primarily for the benefit of the members, employees, patients, students, or officers of the organization;

◆ activities done by volunteers, such as a car wash or carnival;

◆ renting out the organization's list of donors;

◆ selling items donated to the organization, such as a baked goods, books, or clothing;

◆ low-cost items given for donations, such as address labels, Christmas seals, or greeting cards;

◆ trade shows about the organization's exempt function;

◆ interest, dividends, and royalties;

◆ rents; and,

◆ profits on sale of property owned by the organization.

Associate Members

In recent years, the IRS has penalized organizations that have different classes of members. Typically, a tax-exempt group has regular members and associate members who do not usually participate in the group in the same manner as regular members, but who get many of the same benefits. Currently, the IRS says that if the rights and participation between different classes of members are too different, then the associates' member dues are unrelated business taxable income. (For guidance, see IRS Revenue Procedure 95-21.)

Affinity Programs

A nonprofit can also earn extra income by endorsing certain products to its members, such as car rental companies or long-distance carriers, and can earn a percentage of the income generated. Some groups sponsor their own credit cards, with the symbols of their organization appearing on the card.

Such arrangements can either be unrelated business taxable income or exempt royalty income, depending on how the deal is structured. If it is a passive arrangement in which the group receives a royalty for use of its logo, the income is not taxable. If the members of the group must materially participate, such as by promoting the products, the income is then taxable. (For guidance, see IRS Revenue Ruling 81-178 (1981-2 C.B. 135).)

Corporate Sponsorship

Income received from corporations for sponsoring events run by nonprofit corporations may or may not be taxable, depending on whether the corporate sponsor is *promoted* or merely *identified* at the event. Displaying a brand, logo, or name of a sponsor; listing products or services; or, giving addresses or phone numbers is considered identification. However, promoting products, giving prices or discounts, and suggesting people buy the products are considered promotions, and any money received for them is taxable. (For guidance, see IRS Proposed Regulation 1.513-4.)

Bequests

One source of funding for many nonprofits is gifts people leave in their wills, which are called *bequests*. Of course, this is something that does not produce immediate income, but rather something that must be developed over the years to provide funding in the future.

The simplest way to promote such gifts is to include in your fundraising materials a plea to "remember us in your will," and be sure to list the exact legal name of your organization. If someone leaves a bequest to a name that is not exactly your organization's name, another organization might claim it or the family might contest it as being too vague.

Larger organizations devote considerable resources to courting bequests, and have employees who can sit down with potential donors to plan for the gift. Sometimes large donors may want to have a program or building named after themselves.

Endowments

An *endowment* is a fund that is built up so that the income can be used for expenses. Some grants and bequests you receive might be required to be part of an endowment. If so, you need to set up an investment account to hold your endowments. If there is not enough to provide much current income, you might want to let it build up for several years.

Chapter 8:
Locating Your Organization

Your organization may be one that needs an actual place to provide the services you offer, or you may grow to need additional people to help you fulfill your purpose. This chapter provides a few guidelines when you need to have a physical location to conduct your organization's business.

Choosing a Retail Site

For most types of retail stores, the location is of prime importance. Things to consider include how close it is to your potential customers, how visible it is to the public, and how easily accessible it is to both autos and pedestrians. The attractiveness and safety of the site should also be considered. Depending on the services you provide, a location near the people you seek to help is the best course of action.

Leasing a Site

A lease of space can be one of the biggest expenses of a small organization, so you should do a lot of homework before signing one. There are a lot of terms in a commercial lease that can make or break your organization. The most critical terms are discussed in the following pages.

Zoning

Before signing a lease, you should be sure that everything your organization needs to do is allowed by the zoning of the property. Check the city and county zoning regulations.

Signs

Business signs are regulated by zoning laws, sign laws, and property restrictions. If you rent a hidden location with no possibility for adequate signage, your chances of reaching the people who your organization is meant to help are less than with a more visible site or much larger sign.

ADA Compliance

The *Americans with Disabilities Act* (ADA) requires that reasonable accommodations be made to make businesses accessible to the disabled. When a business is remodeled, many more changes are required than if no remodeling is done. Be sure that the space you rent complies with the law, or that the landlord will be responsible for compliance. Be aware of the full costs you will bear.

Expansion

As your organization grows, you may need to expand your space. The time to find out about your options is before you sign the lease. Perhaps you can take over adjoining units when those leases expire.

Renewal

Location is a key to success for some organizations. Therefore, you should have a renewal clause on your lease. Usually, this allows an increase in rent based on inflation.

Guarantee

Most landlords of commercial space will not rent to a small organization without a personal guarantee of the lease. This is a very risky thing for a nonprofit business owner to do. The lifetime rent on a long-term commercial lease can be hundreds of thousands of dollars, and if your organization fails, the last thing you want to do is be personally responsible for five years of rent.

Where space is scarce or a location is hot, a landlord can get the guarantees he or she demands, and there is nothing you can do about it (except perhaps set up an asset protection plan ahead of time). However, where several units are vacant or the commercial rental market is soft, often you can negotiate out of the personal guarantee. If the lease is five years, maybe you can get away with a guarantee of just the first year.

Checking Governmental Regulations

When looking for a site for your business, you should investigate the different governmental regulations in your area. For example, a location just outside the city or county limits might have a lower licensing fee, a lower sales tax rate, and less strict sign requirements.

Chapter 9:
Running a Nonprofit Organization

Because of the stringent rules for nonprofits, they must be much more careful in following the correct procedures in their day-to-day operations. This chapter explains the important rules.

Day-to-Day Activities

On a day-to-day basis, there are not many differences between running a nonprofit corporation and running any other type of business or corporation. Most importantly, you must remember the prohibitions explained in Chapter 1. Make sure that everyone in the organization is aware of these.

The prohibition on mixing personal and business matters in a for-profit corporation is even stronger in a nonprofit. Do not write corporation checks for your personal expenses, even if you pay them back quickly. Do not do favors for relatives with corporation assets. Treat the corporation as if you are responsible for taking care of it for someone else.

Another important thing to remember is to *always* refer to the corporation as a corporation. *Always* use the complete corporate name, including designations such as "Inc." or "Assn." *Always* sign corporate documents with your corporate title.

> **Warning:** If you do not use the complete corporate name and your title, you may lose your protection from liability. Several times people have forgotten to put the word *president* after their name when entering into contracts for the corporation. As a result, they were determined to be personally liable for the contract.

As explained in Chapter 1, you should obtain a copy of your state's nonprofit corporation laws and become familiar with them. Some states have specific requirements that must be complied with, and you are expected to know what is required of your organization.

Corporate Records

The laws that records must be kept on are slightly different in each state. You should review your state statute and make a list of which records are required, and then keep those records together with the list. The following are some typical rules.

Articles and Bylaws

Copies of the articles of incorporation, bylaws, and any revisions of these must be kept on hand by the corporation.

Minutes

A corporation must keep minutes of the proceedings of its board of directors, its members (if any), and any committees. The minutes should be in writing. Some states allow minutes to be kept in forms other than writing, provided they can be converted into written form within a reasonable time, so they can be kept in a computer or even on a videotape. However, it is always best to keep a duplicate copy or at least one written copy. Accidents can easily erase magnetic media. Blank forms that can be used for **MINUTES** are included in Appendix C.

Finances

A nonprofit corporation must keep accurate financial records, especially if it is engaged in charitable solicitations. These records usually include records of all receipts and disbursements, as well as tax returns and any other financial reports that are filed.

Members

If the corporation has members, it must usually keep accurate records of the names and addresses of the members. Some states require the records to be in alphabetical order.

Meetings

The corporation must hold an annual meeting of the board of directors. If there are formal members, they must have a meeting as well. Usually, the members elect directors, and the directors, in turn, elect officers. Minutes of these meetings must be kept with the corporate records. Forms for the **MINUTES OF ANNUAL MEETING OF DIRECTORS** are included in Appendix C. (see form 15, p.203.) You can use these forms as master copies to photocopy each year. All you need to change is the date, unless the officers or directors change, or you need to take some other corporate action.

Annual Reports

Most states require that each corporation file an annual report. Some states require only one report every two years. Fortunately, the report is a simple, often one-page form that is sent to the corporation by the secretary of state, and may simply need to be signed and dated. It contains the taxpayer identification number, officers' and directors' names and addresses, the registered agent's name, and the address of the registered office. It must be signed and returned with the required fee by the date specified. If it is not, the corporation is dissolved after notice is given.

Charitable Solicitation

Most states that require registration for charitable solicitation also require annual reports, and some require detailed financial reports. The state pages in Appendix B tell whether an annual report is required and provide the address you can write to for more information.

Bookkeeping and Accounting

It is beyond the scope of this book to explain all the intricacies of setting up an organization's bookkeeping and accounting systems. However, it is important to realize that if you do not set up an understandable bookkeeping system, your organization will undoubtedly fail.

Without accurate records of where your income is coming from and where it is going, you will be unable to increase your services, lower your expenses, obtain needed financing, or make the right decisions in all areas of your organization. The time to decide how you will handle your bookkeeping is when you start your organization—not a year later when it is tax time.

Initial Bookkeeping

If you do not understand business taxation, you should pick up a good book on the subject. The most important thing to do is to set up your bookkeeping so that you can easily fill out your monthly, quarterly, and annual tax returns. The best way to do this is to get copies of the returns—not the totals that you will need to supply—and set up your bookkeeping system to group those totals.

For example, for a nonprofit organization, you will use Form 990 to report revenue and expenses to the IRS at the end of the year. Use the categories on that form to sort your expenses. To make your job especially easy, every time you pay a bill, put the category number on the check.

Accountants

Most likely, your new business will not be able to afford hiring an accountant right away to handle your books. Do not be discouraged—doing them yourself will force you to learn about business accounting and taxation. The worst way to run a business is to know nothing about the tax laws and turn everything over to an accountant at the end of the year to find out what is due.

You should know the basics of tax law before making basic decisions, such as whether to buy or rent equipment or premises. You should understand accounting so you can time your financial affairs appropriately. If your organization needs to buy supplies, inventory, or equipment, and provides goods or services throughout the year, you need to at least have a basic understanding of the system within which you are working.

Once you can afford an accountant, you should weigh the cost against your time and the risk that you will make an error. Even if you think you know enough to do your organization's tax return, you should still take it to an accountant one year to see if you have been missing any deductions. You might decide that the money saved is worth the cost of the accountant's services.

Tax Returns

Most nonprofit corporations are required to file a Form 990 tax return each year. If the income is below $100,000 and assets below $250,000, then Form 990EZ can be filed. If the income is less than $25,000 or the corporation is a church, school, or related organization, it may be exempt from filing. Check the instructions for the latest Form 990 to see if you qualify as exempt.

If your organization is a private foundation or has unrelated business income, you may need to file Form 990-PF or 990-T. If a charitable organization makes a political contribution of over $100, it must file Form 1120-POL. Check the instructions for these forms or Publication 598 if these situations apply to you.

In some cases, nonprofit corporations must file *interim tax returns*. If a charitable nonprofit organization receives a donation of certain types of property and sells or disposes of it within two years, the organization must file Form 8282 with the IRS and give a copy to the donor. Also, Form 8300 must be filed if more than $10,000 in cash is received.

All organizations that have employees must make regular deposits of taxes withheld (quarterly or more, often depending on the amount) and Form 941 must be filed quarterly reporting these deposits.

State

Some states require annual filings by nonprofits, some waive them once they are exempt, and others just want copies of the federal return. The addresses and phone numbers of state revenue offices are listed in Appendix B, and you should determine what your state requires.

Employment Requirements

If you will be paying wages to anyone—even yourself—you will need to comply with all of the employer reporting and withholding laws of both your state and the federal government. The following is a summary of most of the requirements.

- ◆ *New hire reporting.* To improve the enforcement of child support payments, all employers must report the hiring of each new employee to an agency in the state.
- ◆ *Employment eligibility.* To combat the hiring of illegal immigrants, employers must complete the Department of Justice Form I-9 for each employee.
- ◆ *Federal tax withholding.* Social Security and income taxes must be withheld from employees' wages and deposited to an authorized bank quarterly, monthly, or more often, depending on the amount. The initial step is to obtain a Form W-4 from each employee upon hiring. (This same form can also be used to fulfill the new hire reporting law discussed above.)
- ◆ *State withholding.* In states that have income taxes, there is usually a withholding and reporting requirement similar to the federal one.
- ◆ *Local withholding.* In cities that have income taxes, there is usually a withholding and reporting requirement similar to the federal one.
- ◆ *Unemployment compensation.* Employers must pay taxes on employee wages to the state and federal governments regularly. Also, employers must submit reports both quarterly and annually.
- ◆ *Workers' compensation.* Depending on the number of employees and the type of work, the state may require that the employer obtain workers' compensation insurance.

Employees

There are many instances when you may need to hire people to help you get things accomplished. The hiring of an employee is a risky endeavor. As can be seen from the summary at the start of this section, there are numerous governmental laws and regulations that cover hiring, and failure to comply can result in financial penalties. For example, if someone does not have the legal right to work in this country, you can be fined for hiring him or her.

For these reasons, you should thoroughly check the background of anyone you hire. An **APPLICATION FOR EMPLOYMENT** can be used to get references and other information from a candidate. (see form 19, p.211.) While former employers may be afraid to say anything negative about a person, a glowing review can work well in the applicant's favor.

Background Checks

To check an applicant's background, you can use an *authorization to release employment information, verification of education,* and *verification of licensure.* These forms are signed by the applicant, and grant you permission to obtain the information you need. The **AUTHORIZATION TO**

RELEASE EMPLOYMENT INFORMATION can be used to check on employees for any type of job. (see form 20, p.213.) The VERIFICATION OF EDUCATION and VERIFICATION OF LICENSURE would only be necessary if the applicant's education or license was important to the job. (see form 21, p.215 and form 22, p.217.) However, you might check these things just to see if the employee was honest on the application.

To confirm an employee's legal status, you should use FORM I-9. (see form 21, p.219.) This shows you which documentation is adequate to check eligibility to work. If the applicant uses fake identification, you are not liable for hiring him or her, as long as you made an honest effort to be sure he or she produced the documentation required by law. This form should not be used until you have decided to hire a person.

Employer Identification Number

If you hire someone for more than a few hours work, you are required to register with the state and federal government to withhold taxes. Before you hire someone, you must obtain an employer identification number using **IRS FORM SS-4**. (see form 8, p.183.) Once you hire someone, you must have them complete **IRS FORM W-4** in order to calculate his or her withholding of income taxes.

Most states have their own registration and reporting requirements. Contact your state department of revenue for forms and applications.

Withholding, Social Security, and Medicare Taxes

If you need basic information on business tax returns, the IRS publishes a rather large booklet that answers most questions and is available free of charge. Call or write them and ask for Publication No. 334. If you have any questions, look up their toll-free number in the phone book under "United States Government/Internal Revenue Service." If you want more creative answers and tax-saving information, you should find a good local accountant. To get started, you will need to be familiar with the following:

- ◆ Employee's Withholding Allowance Certificate;
- ◆ federal tax deposit coupons;
- ◆ electronic filing;
- ◆ employer's quarterly tax return;
- ◆ wage and tax statement; and,
- ◆ earned income credit.

Employee's Withholding Allowance Certificate

You must have each employee fill out an *Employee's Withholding Allowance Certificate* (IRS Form W-4) to calculate the amount of federal taxes to be deducted and to obtain their Social Security numbers. (The number of allowances on this form is used with IRS Circular E, Publication 15, to figure out the exact deductions.)

Federal Tax Deposit Coupons

After taking withholdings from employees' wages, you must deposit them at a bank that is authorized to accept such funds. If at the end of any month you have over $1,000 in withheld taxes, including your contribution to FICA (Social Security and Medicare), you must make a deposit prior to the 15th of the following month. If on the 3rd, 7th, 11th, 15th, 19th, 22nd, or 25th of any month you have over $3,000 in withheld taxes, you must make a deposit within three banking days.

Electronic Filing

Each year, the IRS requires a few more forms to be filed electronically or over the telephone. When you receive your paper filing forms from the IRS, they will include your options for filing electronically or by telephone. In some cases, electronic filing may save time, but if your business is small and most of your numbers are zeros, it may be faster to mail in the paper forms.

Employer's Quarterly Tax Return

Each quarter, you must file Form 941, reporting your federal withholding and FICA taxes. If you owe more than $1,000 at the end of a quarter, you are required to make a deposit at the end of any month that you have $1,000 in withholding. The deposits are made to the Federal Reserve Bank or an authorized financial institution on Form 501. Most banks are authorized to accept deposits. If you owe more than $3,000 for any month, you must make a deposit at any point in the month in which you owe $3,000. After you file Form SS-4, the 941 forms will be sent to you automatically if you checked the box saying that you expect to have employees.

Wage and Tax Statement

At the end of each year, you are required to issue a W-2 Form to each employee. This form shows the amount of wages paid to the employee during the year, as well as the amounts withheld for taxes, Social Security, Medicare, and other purposes.

Earned Income Credit

Persons who are not liable to pay income tax may have the right to a check from the government because of the earned income credit. You are required to notify your employees of this. You can satisfy this requirement with one of the following:

- ◆ a W-2 Form with the notice on the back;
- ◆ a substitute for the W-2 Form with the notice on it;

◆ a copy of Notice 797; or,

◆ a written statement with the wording from Notice 797.

A Notice 797 can be downloaded from the IRS website at **www.irs.gov/pub/irs-pdf/n797.pdf**.

At the end of each year, you must file Form 940 or Form 940EZ. This is your annual report of federal unemployment taxes. You will receive an original form from the IRS.

Independent Contractors

Independent contractor is a legal term for a person who works for you but is not your employee. You pay him or her to do a job, but he or she is an independent business that takes care of his or her own taxes and insurance.

You cannot just avoid all employment laws by calling your workers independent contractors. There are rules and regulations detailing when a person can and cannot be an independent contractor. The most important rule is that workers cannot be independent contractors if you control how and when they do their work. If you just hire them to do a job and let them do it in their way at their time, then they can be considered independent contractors. However, if you supervise, give them the tools to use, and tell them when to show up, they will most likely be considered employees.

A list of factors to be considered follows. A *yes* answer to all or most of the following questions will likely mean that the person hired is an independent contractor rather than an employee. For more certainty, use **IRS FORM SS-8**. (see form 24, p.221.)

◆ Does the person hired exercise independent control over the details of the work, such as the methods used to complete the job?

◆ Is the person hired in a business different from that of the person hiring? (For example, a plumber is hired by a lawyer.)

◆ Does the person hired work as a specialist without supervision by the person hiring?

◆ Does the person hired supply his or her own tools?

◆ Is the person hired for only a short period of time rather than consistently over a relatively long period?

◆ Does the job require a relatively high degree of skill?

◆ Is the person paid by the job rather than by the hour?

Contractor Agreement

Contracts with independent contractors do not have to be in writing; however, having these in writing is often very important. For one thing, an employment contract in writing is an opportunity to state clearly that you intend it to be an independent contractor arrangement. Also, since by definition you have relatively little control over the way an independent contractor does the work, the writing may be your last chance to influence important matters, like exactly what the job is and when it must be completed.

NOTE: *It is often tempting to use the word **employer** in these contracts; however, it is not appropriate since the independent contractor is not **employed** (and you do not want the IRS thinking otherwise).*

Form 1099 Miscellaneous

If you pay at least $600 to a person other than an employee (such as an independent contractor), you are required to file a Form 1099-MISC for that person. Along with the 1099s, you must file a Form 1096, which is a summary sheet of all the 1099s you issued.

Many people are not aware of this law and fail to file these forms, but they are required for such things as services, royalties, rents, awards, and prizes that you pay to individuals (but not corporations). The rules for this are quite complicated, so you should either obtain Package 1099 from the IRS or consult your accountant.

NOTE: *For more information on employment and labor laws, see Chapter 10.*

Unemployment Compensation Tax

You must pay federal unemployment taxes if you paid wages of $1,500 in any quarter, or if you had at least one employee for twenty calendar weeks. The federal tax amount is 0.8% of the first $7,000 of wages paid each employee. If more than $100 is due by the end of any quarter (if you paid $12,500 in wages for the quarter), then Form 508 must be filed with an authorized financial institution or the Federal Reserve Bank in your area. You will receive Form 508 when you obtain your employer identification number.

Insurance

There are few laws requiring you to have insurance, but if you do not have insurance you may face liability that may ruin your business. You should be aware of the types of insurance available and weigh the risks of a loss against the cost of a policy.

Be aware that there can be a wide range of prices and coverage in insurance policies. You should get at least three quotes from different insurance agents and ask each one to explain the benefits of his or her policy.

Workers' Compensation

In most states, if you have four or more employees, you are required by law to carry workers' compensation insurance. It protects you if an employee is injured while on the job.

To protect yourself from litigation, you may wish to carry workers' compensation insurance even if you are not required to have it. This insurance can be obtained from most insurance companies, and at least for low-risk occupations, it is not expensive. Failure to provide workers' compensation insurance when required is considered serious. If a person is injured on a job, even if another employee caused it or the injured person contributed to his or her own injury, you may be required to pay for all resulting losses.

Hazard Insurance

One of the worst things that can happen to your organization is a fire, flood, or other disaster. Losses after such an event have caused many organizations to close. The premium for such insurance is usually reasonable and could protect the organization from failure.

Automobile Insurance

If you or any of your employees will be using an automobile for business purposes, be sure that such use is covered. Sometimes, a policy may contain an exclusion for business use. Check to be sure your liability policy covers you if one of your employees causes an accident while running a business errand.

Health Insurance

While new organizations can rarely afford health insurance for their employees, the sooner they can obtain it, the better chance they will have to find and keep good employees. As the person running the organization, you will certainly need health insurance for yourself (unless you have a working spouse who can cover the family), and you can sometimes get a better rate if you purchase a small business package.

Employee Theft

If you fear employees may be able to steal from the organization, you may want to have them *bonded*. This means that you pay an insurance company a premium to guarantee employees' honesty, and if they cheat you, the insurance company pays you damages. This can cover all existing and new employees.

Training

Many training programs and manuals are available to nonprofit organizations, so if you, your board of directors, or your officers are unfamiliar with nonprofits, consider this training. Many of the resources listed in Appendix A sponsor programs, publish manuals, and have educational websites. Because the rules for nonprofits are different from those of for-profit businesses, you should encourage everyone in your group to learn as much as possible.

Chapter 10:
Employment and Labor Laws

Congress and the states have heavily regulated the actions that employers can take with regard to hiring and firing, improper employment practices, and discrimination. Because the penalties can be severe, educate yourself on the proper actions to take and consult a labor and employment lawyer (if necessary) prior to making important employee decisions.

Hiring and Firing Laws

For small organizations, there are not many rules regarding who you may hire or fire. The ancient law that an employee can be fired at any time (or may quit at any time) still prevails. In certain situations and as you grow, however, you will come under a number of laws that affect your hiring and firing practices.

One of the most important things to consider when hiring someone is that if you fire him or her, that fired employee may be entitled to unemployment compensation. If so, your unemployment compensation tax rate will go up and it can cost you a lot of money. Therefore, you should only hire people you are sure you will keep, and you should avoid situations where your former employees can make claims against your organization.

One way this can be done is by hiring only part-time employees. The drawback to this is that you may not be able to attract the best employees.

A better solution is to screen applicants to begin with and only hire those who you feel certain will work out. Of course, this is easier said than done. Some people interview well, but then turn out to be incompetent at the job.

The best record to look for is someone who has stayed a long time at each of his or her previous jobs. Next best is someone who has not stayed as long (for good reasons), but has always been employed. The worst type of hire would be someone who is or has been collecting unemployment compensation.

The reason those who have collected compensation are a bad risk is that if they collect in the future, even if it is not your fault, your employment of them could make you chargeable for their claim. For example, say you hire someone who has been on unemployment compensation and he or she works out well for a year, but then quits to take another job, and is fired after a few weeks. In this situation, you would be chargeable for most of his or her claim, because the last five quarters of work are analyzed. Look for a steady job history.

Often, the intelligence of an employee is more important than his or her experience. An employee with years of typing experience may be fast, but unable to figure out how to use your new computer, whereas an intelligent employee can learn the equipment quickly and eventually gain speed. Of course, common sense is important in all situations.

The bottom line is that you cannot know if an employee will be able to fill your needs from a résumé and interview. Once you have found someone who you think will work out, offer that person a job with a ninety-day probationary period. If you are not completely satisfied with the employee after the ninety days, offer to extend the probationary period for ninety additional days rather than end the relationship immediately. Of course, all of this should be in writing.

Background Checks

Beware that a former boss may be a good friend or even a relative. It has always been considered acceptable to exaggerate on résumés, but in recent years, some applicants have been found to be completely fabricating sections of their education and experience. Thoroughly checking references is important.

Polygraph Tests

Under the federal *Employee Polygraph Protection Act*, you cannot require an employee or prospective employee to take a polygraph test unless you are in the armored car, guard, or pharmaceutical business.

Drug Tests

Under the *Americans with Disabilities Act* (ADA), drug testing can only be required of applicants who have been offered jobs conditioned upon passing the drug test.

Firing

In most cases, unless you have a contract with an employee for a set time period, you can fire him or her at any time. This is only fair, since the employee can quit at any time. This type of employment is called *at will*. You should make it clear when offering a job to someone that, upon acceptance, he or she will be an at-will employee. The exceptions to this are if you fired someone based on illegal discrimination, for filing some sort of health or safety complaint, or for refusing your sexual advances.

New Hire Reporting

In order to track down parents who do not pay child support, a federal law was passed in 1996 that requires the reporting of new hires. The *Personal Responsibility and Work Opportunity Reconciliation Act of 1996* (PRWORA) provides that such information must be reported by employers to their state government.

Within twenty days of hiring a new employee, an employer must provide the state with information about the employee, including the name, Social Security number, and address. This information can be submitted in several ways, including mail, fax, magnetic tape, or over the Internet. There is a special form that can be used for this reporting; however, an employer can simply use the Employee's Withholding Allowance Certificate (IRS Form W-4) for this purpose. Since this form must be filled out for all employees anyway, it would be pointless to use a separate form for the new hire reporting.

Employment Agreements

To avoid misunderstanding with employees, you should use an employment agreement or an employee handbook. These can spell out in detail the policies of your company and the rights of your employees. These agreements can protect your trade secrets and spell out clearly that employment can be terminated at any time by either party.

Make sure that your agreement is fair and clear, because you have the upper hand in this situation and you would not want a court to find that you abused that bargaining power with an unreasonable employee agreement.

If having an employee sign an agreement is awkward, you can usually obtain the same rights by putting the organization's policies in an employee manual. Each existing and new employee should be given a copy along with a letter stating that the rules apply to all employees, and that by accepting or continuing employment at your organization, they agree to abide by the rules. Having an employee sign a receipt for the letter and manual is proof that he or she received it.

One danger of an employment agreement or handbook is that it may be interpreted to create a long-term employment contract. To avoid this, be sure that you clearly state in the agreement or handbook that the employment is at will and can be terminated at any time by either party.

Some other things to consider in an employment agreement or handbook are:
- what the salary and other compensation will be;
- what the hours of employment will be;
- what the probationary period will be;
- that the employee cannot sign any contracts binding the employer; and,
- that the employee agrees to arbitration rather than filing a lawsuit if serious disagreements arise.

Temporary Workers

A way to avoid the hassles of hiring employees is to get workers from a temporary agency. In this arrangement, you may pay a higher amount per hour for the work, but the agency will take care of all of the tax and insurance requirements. Since these can be expensive and time-consuming, the extra cost may be well worth it.

Whether or not temporary workers will work for you depends upon the type of organization you are in and tasks you need performed. For a job such as executive manager, you would probably want someone who will stay with you long-term and develop relationships with donors, but for delivering food to shelters, temporary workers might work out well.

Another advantage of temporary workers is that you can easily stop using those who do not work out well for you. Conversely, if you find one who is ideal, you may be able to hire him or her on a full-time basis.

Discrimination Laws

There are numerous federal laws forbidding discrimination based upon race, sex, pregnancy, color, religion, national origin, age, or disability. The laws apply to both hiring and firing, and to employment practices such as salaries, promotions, and benefits. Most of these laws only apply to an employer who has fifteen or more employees for twenty weeks of a calendar year, or has federal contracts or subcontracts. Therefore, you most likely will not be required to comply with the law immediately upon starting your organization. However, there are similar state laws that may apply to your organization that have a lower employee threshold.

One exception to the fifteen or more employees rule is the *Equal Pay Act*. This act applies to employers with two or more employees, and requires that women be paid the same as men in the same type of job.

Employers with fifteen or more employees are required to display a poster regarding discrimination. This poster is available from the Equal Employment Opportunity Commission on their website at **www.dol.gov/esa/regs/compliance/posters/eeo.htm**. Employers with one hundred or more employees are required to file an annual report with the EEOC.

Discriminatory Interview Questions

When hiring employees, some questions are illegal or inadvisable to ask. The following data should not be collected on your employment application or in your interviews, unless the information is somehow directly tied to the duties of the job.

◆ Do not ask about an applicant's citizenship or place of birth. However, after hiring an employee, you must ask about his or her right to work in this country.

◆ Do not ask a female applicant her maiden name. You can ask if she has been known by any other name in order to do a background check.

◆ Do not ask if applicants have children, plan to have them, or have child care. You can ask if an applicant will be able to work the required hours.

◆ Do not ask if the applicant has religious objections for working Saturday or Sunday. You can mention if the job requires such hours and ask whether the applicant can meet this job requirement.

◆ Do not ask an applicant's age. You can ask if an applicant is age 18 or over, or if it is a liquor-related job, you can ask if the applicant is age 21 or over.

◆ Do not ask an applicant's weight.

◆ Do not ask if an applicant has AIDS or is HIV-positive.

◆ Do not ask if the applicant has filed a workers' compensation claim.

◆ Do not ask about the applicant's previous health problems.

◆ Do not ask if the applicant is married or whether the spouse would object to the job, hours, or duties.

◆ Do not ask if the applicant owns a home, furniture, or a car, as it is considered racially discriminatory.

◆ Do not ask if the applicant was ever arrested. You can ask if the applicant was ever convicted of a crime.

ADA

Under the *Americans with Disabilities Act* (ADA), employers who do not make reasonable accommodations for disabled employees will face fines of up to $100,000, as well as other civil penalties and civil damage awards.

The ADA currently applies to employers with fifteen or more employees. Employers who need more than fifteen employees might want to consider contracting with independent contractors to avoid problems with this law, particularly if the number of employees is only slightly larger than fifteen.

For more information on how this law affects your business, see the U.S. Department of Justice website at **www.usdoj.gov/crt/ada/business.htm**.

Records

To protect against potential claims of discrimination, all employers should keep detailed records showing reasons for hiring or not hiring applicants, and for firing employees.

Sexual Harassment

As an employer, you can be liable for the acts of your employees. One of the latest types of acts that employers have been held liable for is sexual harassment of customers, employees, and others. While you cannot control every act of every employee, if you indicate to employees that such behavior is unacceptable and set up a system to resolve complaints, you will do much to protect yourself against lawsuits.

The EEOC has held the following in sexual harassment cases.
- The victim as well as the harasser may be a woman or a man.
- The victim does not have to be of the opposite sex.
- The harasser can be the victim's supervisor, an agent of the employer, a supervisor in another area, a coworker, or a nonemployee.
- The victim does not have to be the person harassed, but could be anyone affected by the offensive conduct.
- Unlawful sexual harassment may occur without economic injury to or discharge of the victim.
- The harasser's conduct must be unwelcome.

Some of the actions that have been considered harassment are:
- displaying sexually explicit posters in the workplace;
- requiring female employees to wear revealing uniforms;
- rating the sexual attractiveness of female employees as they pass male employees' desks;
- continued sexual jokes and innuendos;
- demands for sexual favors from subordinates;
- unwelcome sexual propositions or flirtation;
- unwelcome physical contact; and,
- whistling or leering at members of the opposite sex.

Some things an organization can do to protect against claims of sexual harassment include the following.

◆ Distribute a written policy against all kinds of sexual harassment to all employees.

◆ Encourage employees to report all incidents of sexual harassment.

◆ Ensure there is no retaliation against those who complain.

◆ Make clear that your policy is zero tolerance.

◆ Explain that sexual harassment includes both requests for sexual favors and a work environment that some employees may consider hostile.

◆ Allow employees to report harassment to someone other than their immediate supervisor, in case that person is involved in the harassment.

◆ Promise as much confidentiality as possible to complainants.

Wage and Hour Laws

The *Fair Labor Standards Act* (FLSA) applies to all employers who are engaged in interstate commerce or in the production of goods for interstate commerce (anything that will cross the state line), and all employees of hospitals, schools, residential facilities for the disabled or aged, or public agencies. It also applies to all employees of enterprises that gross $500,000 or more per year.

While many small businesses might not think they are engaged in interstate commerce, the laws have been interpreted so broadly that nearly any use of the mail, interstate telephone service, or other interstate services, however minor, is enough to bring a business under the law.

Minimum Wage

The federal wage and hour laws are contained in the federal Fair Labor Standards Act. In 1996, Congress passed and President Clinton signed legislation raising the minimum wage to $5.15 an hour beginning September 1, 1997. Many states and some local communities have higher minimum wage requirements that you may have to pay, depending on your location.

Exempt Employees

While nearly all businesses are covered, certain employees are exempt from the FLSA. Exempt employees include those who are considered executives, administrators, managers, professionals, computer professionals, and outside salespeople.

Whether or not one of these exceptions applies to a particular employee is a complicated legal question. Thousands of court cases have been decided on this issue, but they have given no clear answers. In one case, a person could be determined to be exempt because of his or her duties, but in another, a person with the same duties could be found not exempt.

One thing that is clear is that the determination is made on the employee's function, and not just the job title. You cannot make a secretary exempt by calling him or her a manager if most of his or her duties are clerical. For more information, see the Department of Labor website **www.dol.gov/ esa/whd/flsa**.

You can obtain information on the Department of Labor's Employment Law Guide online at **www.dol.gov/asp/programs/guide/main.htm**.

Overtime

The general rule is that employees who work more than forty hours a week must be paid time-and-a-half for hours worked over forty. However, there are many exemptions to this general rule based on salary and position. These exceptions were completely revised in 2004, and an explanation of the changes, including a tutorial video, is available at **www.dol.gov/esa**. For answers to questions about the law, call the Department of Labor at 866-4-USA-DOL (866-487-2365).

Benefit Laws

There are no laws requiring an organization to provide any types of special benefits to employees. Such benefits are given to attract and keep good employees. With pension plans, the main concern is if you do start one, it must comply with federal tax laws.

There are no federal laws that require employees be given holidays off. You can require them to work Thanksgiving and Christmas, and can dock their pay or fire them for failing to show up. Of course, you will not have much luck keeping employees with such a policy.

Holidays

Most companies give full-time employees a certain number of paid holidays, such as: New Year's Day (January 1); Memorial Day (last Monday in May); Fourth of July; Labor Day (first Monday in September); Thanksgiving (fourth Thursday in November); and Christmas (December 25). Some employers include other holidays such as Martin Luther King Jr.'s birthday; President's Day; and Columbus Day. If one of the holidays falls on a Saturday or Sunday, many employers give the preceding Friday or following Monday off. Certain states have additional holidays that are traditionally granted.

Sick Days

There is no federal law mandating that an employee be paid for time that he or she is home sick. The situation seems to be that the larger the organization, the more paid sick leave is allowed. Part-time workers rarely get sick leave, and in a small organization, sick leave is usually limited for the simple reason that they cannot afford to pay for time that employees do not work.

Family and Medical Leave Law

To assist business owners in deciding what type of leave to offer their employees, Congress passed the *Family and Medical Leave Act of 1993* (FMLA). This law requires that an employee be given up to twelve weeks of unpaid leave when:

◆ the employee or employee's spouse has a child;

◆ the employee adopts a child or takes in a foster child;

◆ the employee needs to care for an ill spouse, child, or parent; or,

◆ the employee becomes seriously ill.

The law only applies to employers with fifty or more employees. Also, the top 10% of an employer's salaried employees can be denied this leave because of the disruption in business their loss could cause.

Child Labor Laws

The Fair Labor Standards Act also contains rules regarding the hiring of children. The basic rules are that children under 16 years old may not be hired at all except in a few jobs, such as acting and newspaper delivery, and those under 18 may not be hired for dangerous jobs. Children may not work more than three hours a day or eighteen hours a week in a school week, or more than eight hours a day or forty hours a week in a nonschool week. If you plan to hire children, you should check the Fair Labor Standards Act, which is in United States Code (U.S.C.), Title 29, and the related regulations, which are in the Code of Federal Regulations (C.F.R.), Title 29. Most states have additional child labor laws. You should familiarize yourself with your state's law.

Immigration Laws

There are strict penalties for any business that hires aliens who are not eligible to work. You must verify both the identity and the employment eligibility of anyone you hire by using the EMPLOYMENT ELIGIBILITY VERIFICATION (FORM I-9). (see form 23, p.219.) Both you and the employee must fill out the form, and you must check an employee's identification cards or papers. Fines for hiring illegal aliens range from $250 to $2,000 for the first offense, increasing up to $10,000 for the third offense. Failure to maintain the proper paperwork may result in a fine of up to $1,000. The law does not apply to independent contractors with whom you may contract, and it does not penalize you if the employee used fake identification.

There are also penalties that apply to employers of four or more persons for discriminating against eligible applicants because they appear foreign or because of their national origin or citizenship status.

For more information, call 800-357-2099. For the *Handbook for Employers and Instructions for Completing Form I-9*, check the United States Citizenship and Immigration Services (USCIS) website at **www.uscis.gov**.

Foreign Employees

If you wish to hire employees who are foreign citizens and are not able to provide the proper documentation, they must first obtain a work visa from USCIS.

Work visas for foreigners are not easy to get. Millions of people around the globe would like to come to the U.S. to work, but the laws are designed to keep most of them out to protect the jobs of American citizens.

Whether or not a person can get a work visa depends on whether there is a shortage of U.S. workers available to fill the job. For jobs requiring few or no skills, it is practically impossible to get a visa. For highly skilled jobs (such as nurses and physical therapists) and for those of exceptional ability (such as Nobel Prize winners and Olympic medalists), obtaining a visa is fairly easy.

There are several types of visas, and different rules for different countries. For example, NAFTA has made it easier for some types of workers to enter the U.S. from Canada and Mexico. For some positions, the shortage of workers is assumed by the USCIS. For others, a business must first advertise a position available in the United States. Only after no qualified persons apply can it hire someone from another country.

The visa system is complicated and subject to regular change. If you wish to hire a foreign worker, you should consult with an immigration specialist or a book on the subject.

Hiring Off the Books

Because of the taxes, insurance, and red tape involved with hiring employees, some new organizations hire people *off the books*. They pay employees in cash and never admit they are employees. While the cash paid in wages would not be deductible, they consider this a smaller cost than compliance. Some even use off-the-books receipts to cover it.

Except when your spouse or child is giving you some temporary help, this is a terrible idea. Hiring people off the books can result in civil fines, loss of insurance coverage, and even criminal penalties. It may be more costly and time-consuming to comply with the employment laws, but if you are concerned with long-term growth with less risk, compliance is the wiser way to go.

Federal Contracts

Companies that do work for the federal government are subject to the following laws.

- ◆ The *Davis-Bacon Act* requires contractors engaged in U.S. government construction projects to pay wages and benefits that are equal to or better than the prevailing wages in the area.
- ◆ The *McNamara-O'Hara Service Contract Act* sets wages and other labor standards for contractors furnishing services to agencies of the U.S. government.
- ◆ The *Walsh-Healey Public Contracts Act* requires the Department of Labor to settle disputes regarding manufacturers supplying products to the U.S. government.

Miscellaneous Laws

In addition to the broad categories of laws affecting organizations, there are several other federal (and state) laws that you should be familiar with, including laws that regulate affirmative action, layoffs, unions, and informational posters.

Affirmative Action

In most cases, the federal government does not tell employers who they must hire. The only situation in which a small organization would need to comply with affirmative action requirements would be if it accepted federal contracts or subcontracts. These requirements could include hiring minorities or veterans of the conflict in Vietnam.

Layoffs

Organizations with one hundred or more full-time employees at one location are subject to the *Worker Adjustment and Retraining Notification Act.* This law requires a sixty-day notification prior to certain layoffs and has other strict provisions.

Unions

The *National Labor Relations Act of 1935* gives employees the right to organize a union or to join one. (29 U.S.C. Secs. 151, et seq.) There are things employers can do to protect themselves, but you should consult a labor attorney or a book on the subject before taking action that might be illegal and result in fines.

Poster Laws

Poster laws require certain posters to be displayed to inform employees of their rights. Not all businesses are required to display all posters, but the following list should be of help.

◆ All employers must display the wage and hour poster available from the U.S. Department of Labor at **www.dol.gov/esa**.

◆ Employers with fifteen or more employees for twenty weeks of the year must display the sex, race, religion, and ethnic discrimination poster, as well as the age discrimination poster, available from the EEOC at **www.eeoc.gov/publications.html**.

◆ Employers with federal contracts or subcontracts of $10,000 or more must display the sex, race, religion, and ethnic discrimination poster, plus a poster regarding Vietnam Era Veterans (available from the local federal contracting office).

◆ Employers with government contracts subject to the *Service Contract Act* or the *Public Contracts Act* must display a notice to employees working on government contracts available from the Employment Standards Division at **www.dol.gov/esa/whd**.

Glossary

A

acceptance. Agreeing to the terms of an offer and creating a contract.

affirmative action. Hiring an employee to achieve a balance in the workplace, and to avoid existing or continuing discrimination based on minority status.

alien. A person who is not a citizen of the country in which he or she resides.

annual report. A document filed by a corporation or limited liability company each year that usually lists its officers, directors, and registered agent.

articles of incorporation. The document that demonstrates the organization of a corporation.

articles of organization. The document that demonstrates the organization of a limited liability company.

association. A group of individuals united—but not incorporated—for a purpose.

B

bait advertising. Offering a product for sale with the intention of selling another product.

blue sky laws. Laws governing the sales of securities.

bulk sales. The sale of substantially all of a company's inventory.

bylaws. Rules governing the conduct and affairs of a corporation.

C

C corporation. A corporation that pays taxes on its profits.

certificate of incorporation. *See articles of incorporation.*

charitable. Qualifying under the tax laws to allow donors to deduct donations.

collections. The collection of money owed to a business.

common law. Laws that are determined in court cases rather than statutes.

common stock. The basic ownership shares of a corporation.

consideration. The exchange of value or promises in a contract.

contract. An agreement between two or more parties.

copyright. Legal protection given to original works of authorship.

corporation. An organization recognized as a person in the law that is set up to conduct a business owned by shareholders, and run by officers and directors.

D

deceptive pricing. Pricing goods or services in a manner intended to deceive the customers.

discrimination. The choosing among various options based on their characteristics. It is illegal to use discriminatory hiring practices.

distributions. Money paid out to owners of a corporation or limited liability company.

domain name. The address of a website.

E

employee. A person who works under another person's control and direction.

employer identification number. Number issued by the Internal Revenue Service to identify taxpayers.

endorsements. Positive statements about goods or services.

estate planning. Preparing such documents as a will, trust, and other arrangements to control the passing of one's property at death.

excise tax. A tax paid on the sale or consumption of goods or services.

exemption. The ability to sell certain limited types of securities without full compliance with securities registration laws.

express warranty. A specific guarantee of a product or service.

F

fictitious name. The name a business uses that is not its personal or legal name.

G

general partnership. A business that is owned by two or more persons.

goods. Items of personal property.

grant. Money given away to attempt to accomplish a specific purpose.

guarantee. A promise of quality of a good or service.

I

implied warranty. A guarantee of a product or service that is not specifically made, but can be implied from the circumstances of the sale.

independent contractor. A person who works for another as a separate business, not as an employee.

intangible property. Personal property that does not have physical presence, such as ownership interest in a corporation.

intellectual property. Legal rights to the products of the mind, such as writings, musical compositions, formulas, and designs.

L

liability. The legal responsibility to pay for an injury.

limited liability company. An entity recognized as a legal person that is set up to conduct a business owned and run by members.

limited liability partnership. An entity recognized as a legal person that is set up to conduct a business owned and run by professionals, such as attorneys or doctors, and is taxed as a partnership.

limited partnership. A business that is owned by two or more persons, of which one or more is liable for the debts of the business, and one or more has no liability for the debts.

limited warranty. A guarantee covering certain aspects of a good or service.

M

management agreement. A contract controlling the operation of a limited liability company in which the company is run by its managers.

membership agreement. A contract controlling the operation of a limited liability company in which the company is run by its members.

merchant. A person who is in business.

merchant's firm offer. An offer by a business made under specific terms.

minutes. Records of the proceedings of corporate meetings.

N

nonprofit corporation. An entity recognized as a legal person that is set up to run an operation in which none of the profits are distributed to controlling members.

O

occupational license. A government-issued permit to transact business.

offer. A proposal to enter into a contract.

operating agreement. A contract among members of a limited liability company, spelling out how the company will be run.

option. The right to buy stock at a future date, usually at a predetermined price.

organizational meeting. The meeting of the founders of a corporation or limited liability company, during which the company is structured and prepared to begin business.

overtime. Hours worked in excess of forty hours in one week, or eight hours in one day.

P

partnership. A business formed by two or more persons.

par value. A value given to newly issued stock. This used to have legal significance, but now usually does not relate to anything except taxation in some states.

patent. Protection given to inventions, discoveries, and designs.

personal property. Any type of property other than land and the structures attached to it.

piercing the corporate veil. When a court ignores the structure of a corporation and holds its owners responsible for its debts or liabilities.

political action committee (PAC). An organization formed to aid political campaigns.

private foundation. A nonprofit organization that does not qualify as a public charity.

private inurement. Benefiting a private person rather than the public.

professional association. An entity recognized as a legal person that is set up to conduct a business of professionals, such as attorneys or doctors, and is taxed as a corporation.

promoters. Persons who start a business venture and usually offer interests for sale to investors.

proprietorship. A business that is owned by one person.

R

real property. Land and the structures attached to it.

registered agent. The person authorized to accept legal papers for a corporation or limited liability company.

resident agent. *See registered agent.*

resident alien. A person who is not a citizen of a country, but who may legally reside and work there.

S

S corporation. A corporation in which profits are taxed to shareholders.

sale on approval. Selling an item with the agreement that it may be brought back and the sale cancelled.

sale or return. An agreement whereby goods are to be purchased or returned to the vendor.

Section 501(c)(3) organization. An organization that has been granted tax-exempt status under Section 501(c)(3) of the Internal Revenue Code.

securities. Interests in a business, such as stocks or bonds.

service mark. A name or symbol used to identify the source of a service.

sexual harassment. Activity that causes an employee to feel or be sexually threatened.

shareholder agreement. A contract among the owners of a corporation that spells out their rights.

shares. Units of stock in a corporation.

statute of frauds. Law that requires certain contracts to be in writing.

stock. Ownership interests in a corporation.

sublease. An agreement to rent premises from an existing tenant.

T

tangible property. Physical personal property, such as desks and tables.

tax-deductible. Contributions that donors can deduct from their taxable income.

tax-exempt. Money received on which no tax needs to be paid.

trademark. A name or symbol used to identify the source of goods.

trade secret. Commercially valuable information or process that is protected by being kept a secret.

transferability. The ability to sell shares of stock in a corporation.

trust. Arrangement in which property is held and used for a specific purpose.

U

unemployment compensation. Payments to a former employee who was terminated from a job for a reason not based on his or her fault.

usury. Charging an interest rate higher than what is allowed by law.

W

withholding. Money taken out of an employee's salary for the government.

Z

zoning. Governmental regulation controlling the use of real property.

Appendix A:
Resources for Nonprofit Organizations

This appendix includes organizations, websites, and books that offer useful information to nonprofit organizations.

Organizations

Accounting Aid Society
18145 South Mack Avenue
Detroit, MI 484224
313-647-9620
www.accountingaidsociety.org

Alliance of Nonprofit Mailers
1211 Connecticut Avenue, NW
#620
Washington, DC 20036
202-462-5132
www.nonprofitmailers.org

Aspen Washington, D.C.
One Dupont Circle, NW
#700
Washington, DC 20036
202-736-5800
www.aspeninst.org

Boardsource
1828 L Street, NW
#900
Washington, DC 20036
800-883-6262
www.boardsource.org

The Foundation Center
79 Fifth Avenue
New York, NY 10003
212-620-4230
www.fdncenter.org

National Council of
Nonprofit Associations
1030 15th Street, NW
Suite 870
Washington, DC 20005
202-962-0322
www.ncna.org

Websites

Center for Excellence in Nonprofits
     www.cen.org
Compass Point Nonprofit Services
     www.compasspoint.org
Council on Foundations
     www.cof.org
Don Kramer's Nonprofit Issues (*online newsletter*)
     www.nonprofitissues.com
Internal Revenue Service Charities Site
     www.irs.ustreas.gov/charities
The Nonprofit Resource Center
     www.not-for-profit.org
Thompson & Thompson, P.C. (*nonprofit tax issues*)
     www.taxexemptlaw.com
University of Wisconsin—Madison (*resources for starting a nonprofit*)
     www.library.wisc.edu/libraries/Memorial/grants/npweb.htm

Books

The following books provide detailed information on all aspects of nonprofit organization law. If you have a specific question, you may find the answer in one of these titles. However, some of them cost over $100, so you might want to review them at a law library if you are on a limited budget.

The Legal Answer Book for Nonprofit Organizations, Hopkins, Bruce R., Wiley, John, & Sons, Inc., 1996

Nonprofit Corporations, Organizations & Associations, Oleck, Howard L. and Stewart, Martha E., Prentice Hall

Nonprofit Enterprises: Law and Taxation, Phelan, Marilyn E., Callaghan

Nonprofit Law Dictionary, Hopkins, Bruce R., Wiley, John, & Sons, Inc.

Parliamentary Law and Practice for Nonprofit Organizations, Oleck, Howard L. & Green, Cami, ALI-ABA, 1994

The Second Legal Answer Book for Nonprofit Organizations, Hopkins, Bruce R., Wiley, John, & Sons, Inc., 1999

The following books are available from *The Foundation Center*:

The 21ˢᵗ Century Nonprofit

America's Nonprofit Sector: A Primer

Best Practices of Effective Nonprofit Organizations

The Board Member's Book

The Handbook on Private Foundations

The Nonprofit Entrepreneur

Promoting Issues and Ideas

Appendix B:
State-by-State Nonprofit Laws and Addresses

The following pages contain a listing of each state's nonprofit corporation laws and fees. Because the laws are constantly being changed by state legislatures, you should call before filing your papers to confirm the fees and other requirements. The phone numbers are provided for each state.

In the continued growth of the World Wide Web, more and more state corporation divisions are making their fees and procedures available online. Some states have downloadable forms available, and some even allow you to search their entire database from the comfort of your home or office.

The best websites at the time of publication of this book are included for each state. However, the sites change constantly, so you may need to look a little deeper if your state's site has changed its address.

· · · · ·

Acknowledgment

Special thanks must be given to my wife, Alexandra Schiller Warda, who helped me completely update this appendix.

Alabama

INCORPORATION:
Secretary of State
Corporations
P.O. Box 5616
Montgomery, AL 36103
334-242-5324
Fax: 334-240-3138
www.sos.state.al.us/business/corporations.cfm

What must be filed:
You need to file the original and two copies of the Articles of Corporation in the county where the corporation's registered office is located.

Name requirements:
The corporate name shall not be the same as, or deceptively similar to, the name of any other corporation existing in Alabama. The name may not contain a word or phrase that indicates it is organized for a purpose other than contained in the Articles of Incorporation.

Directors requirements:
Your corporation must be have at least three directors. You have to fix the number of directors by the bylaws. The directors may be divided in classes and the terms of the different classes need not to be uniform.

Articles requirements:
The minimum requirements for the Articles are as follows:
- the name of the corporation
- the period of duration
- the purpose of the corporation
- any provisions for the regulation of the internal affairs (including final liquidation)
- local and mailing address
- number of the directors constituting the initial board of directors and names and addresses of the initial directors
- name and address of each incorporator

Filing fees:
The Judge of Probate filing fee is $25 and the Secretary of State's fee is $20. Both fees are payable to the Judge of Probate.

Reports:
You have to file an annual report between January 1 and March 15.

Statute: Alabama Code 10-3A-1 to 225

TAXES:
Alabama Department of Revenue
Corporate Section
50 North Ripley Street
Montgomery, AL 36132
334-242-1170
www.ador.state.al.us

Automatic exemption: No

CHARITABLE SOLICITATION:
Office of Attorney General
Consumer Protection Section
11 South Union Street
Montgomery, AL 36130
205-242-7334
www.ago.state.al.us/consumer_charities.cfm

Statute: Alabama Code 13A-9-70, et seq.

Exemption: Less than $25,000, provided that all fundraising functions are carried out by volunteers

Annual filing: Yes

Accept URS: Yes

Alaska

INCORPORATION:

Department of Community and Economic Development
Division of Banking, Securities and Corporations
Corporations Section
P.O. Box 110808
Juneau, AK 99811
907-465-2530
Fax: 907-465-3257
www.commerce.state.ak.us/occ

What must be filed:

Print or type your documents in dark, legible print and file two copies of the Articles of Incorporation. Computer print must be high resolution, laser print quality, suitable for microfilming. Make sure your documents bear the original signatures and are both notarized. Enclose the filing fee. One copy will be returned to you for your records. Paper must be no larger than 8 by 11 inches.

Name requirements:

The corporate name may not contain a word or phrase that indicates or implies that it is organized for a purpose other than one or more of the purposes contained in your Articles of Incorporation.

Directors requirements:

Your nonprofit corporation must have at least three initial directors. The number of directors has to be fixed by the Bylaws later on but the initial board of directors shall be fixed by the Articles of Incorporation.

The directors do not have to be residents of Alaska or members of the corporation, unless the Articles or Bylaws require so. The director's default term is one year.

Articles requirements:

You must state the names, telephone numbers, and addresses of your initial (first) board of directors in Article 6. In Alaska there must be at least three incorporators who must be natural persons at least 19 years old. Enter the names and (business) addresses of these incorporators in Article 7. Make sure that your Articles are notarized. The Articles should contain a statement that they are being filed under the provisions of the Alaska Nonprofit Corporation Act (AS 10.20).

Include in the Articles the following:
- the name of the corporation
- the period of duration, which may be perpetual
- the purpose or purposes for which the corporation is organized
- any provisions for the regulation of the internal affairs (including final liquidation)
- physical address of its initial registered office and the name of its initial registered agent
- number of the directors constituting the initial board of directors and names and addresses of persons who are to serve as the initial directors
- the name and address of each incorporator

Filing fees:

$50, payable to the State of Alaska Department of Commerce and Economic Development.

Reports: You have to file an annual report by July 2.

Statute: Alaska Statutes, Section 10.06.208-210

TAXES:

Alaska Department of Revenue
P.O. Box 110420
Juneau, AK 99811
907-465-2322
www.revenue.state.ak.us

Automatic exemption: Yes

CHARITABLE SOLICITATION:

Department of Law—Civil Division
Fair Business Practices Section
1031 West 4th Avenue
Suite 200
Anchorage, AK 99501
907-276-8554
www.law.state.ak.us

Statute: Alaska Statutes, Title 45, Chapter 68

Exemption: First $5,000 or 10 or less donors

Annual filing: No

Accept URS: No

Arizona

INCORPORATION:

Corporations Division
Arizona Corporation Commission
1300 West Washington Street
Phoenix, AZ 85007
www.cc.state.az.us/corp/index.htm

Corporate Records Section:
602-542-3026
800-345-5819 (in-state only)
Fax: 602-542-3414

Corporate Filing Section:
602-542-3026
Fax: 602-542-4990

Tucson Office:
Tucson Corporations Division
400 West Congress Street
Suite 221
Tucson, AZ 85701
520-628-6560
Fax: 520-628-6614

What must be filed:

Complete your Articles and file the original and two copies. Also fill in the Certificate of Disclosure and attach it to your Articles. Enclose the filing fee. After filing your Articles must be published within 60 days in a newspaper of general circulation in the county of the place of business in Arizona. There must be three consecutive publications of a copy of the approved Articles. Within 90 days of filing an affidavit evidencing the publication must be filed with the Commission.

Name requirements:

Check your corporate name with the Commission prior to filing your documents by calling 602-542-3026 in Phoenix or 520-628-6560 in Tucson or on the website: www.cc.state.az.us/corp/filings/namesearch.htm. A name may be formally reserved for a $10 fee for 120 days.

Directors requirements:

Your corporation must have one director. The names and addresses of the initial directors must be entered in Article 9.

Articles requirements:

Enter one of the specific valid purposes for which a nonprofit corporation may be formed in Article 3.

In Article 5 and 6 you must enter the applicable Section number of of the IRS code under which your corporation plans to organize. Contact your local IRS office to obtain these numbers.

In Article 8 enter the name and business address of your initial statutory agent. This statutory agent has to sign the Articles on the bottom of the page.

Also complete your Certificate of Disclosure that has to be filed with your Articles. It contains information about your officers, directors, and anyone involved in the corporation.

Filing fees:

$40, payable to the Arizona Corporation Commission. For expedited service, add an extra $35.

Reports:

The annual report must be filed by April 15 (or by the 15th day of the 4th month of the corporation's fiscal year if a different fiscal year, has been adopted).

Statute: Arizona Revised Statutes, Section 10-2300

TAXES:

Department of Revenue
Corporate Section
P.O. Box 29079
Phoenix, AZ 85038
602-255-3381
800-352-4090 (in-state only)
www.revenue.state.az.us

Automatic exemption: No

CHARITABLE SOLICITATION:

Secretary of State
Charitable Organization
1700 West Washington
7th Floor
Phoenix, AZ 85007
800-458-5842
www.azsos.gov/business_services/charities

Statute: Arizona Revised Statutes, Sections 44-1522, 44-6551 et seq.

Exemption: First $25,000 or 10 or less donors

Annual filing: Yes

Accept URS: No

Arkansas

INCORPORATION:
Secretary of State
Business and Commercial Services Division
Suite 250 of the Victory Building
1401 West Capitol Avenue
Little Rock, AR 72201
501-682-3409
888-233-0325
www.sosweb.state.ar.us/corp_ucc_business.html

What must be filed:
Complete both copies of the fill-in-the-blanks Articles and file them with the Secretary of State. Make sure that the Articles are signed by all incorporators.

Name requirements:
The corporate name may not contain a word or phrase that indicates that it is organized for a purpose other than one or more of the purposes contained in your Articles of Incorporation. It has to contain "corporation," "incorporated," "company," or an abbreviation. Note: Name may not end in "company" if preceded by "and."

Directors requirements:
Your corporation must have at least three directors. The directors don't have to be residents of Arkansas.

Articles requirements:
The minimum requirements for the Articles are as follows:
- the name of the corporation
- the determination whether the corporation shall be a public-benefit, a mutual-benefit or a religious corporation
- a statement whether or not the corporation will have members
- if applicable, provisions regarding the distribution of assets on dissolution
- the street address and the name of the corporation's initial registered office
- the address and signature of each incorporator

Filing fees:
$50, payable to the Secretary of State. For online filing, add a processing fee of $5.

Reports:
Not required.

Statute: Arkansas Code, Title 4, Sec. 28-206

TAXES:
State of Arkansas
Revenue Division
P.O. Box 8054
Little Rock, AR 72203
501-682-4775
Fax: 501-682-7114
www.state.ar.us/dfa

Automatic exemption: No

CHARITABLE SOLICITATION:
Office of the Attorney General
Consumer Protection Division
323 Center Street
Suite 200
Little Rock, AR 72201
501-682-1109
800-482-8982
www.ag.state.ar.us

Statute: Arkansas Code, Title 4, Sec. 28-406

Exemption: $25,000, provided all fundraising activities are carried out by volunteers

Annual filing: Yes

Accept URS: Yes, but supplemental form required

California

INCORPORATION:

Secretary of State
Corporations
1500 11th Street
Sacramento, CA 95814
916-657-5448
www.ss.ca.gov/business/corp/corporate.htm

Fresno Regional Office:
1315 Van Ness Avenue
Suite 203
Fresno, CA 93721
559-445-6900

Los Angeles Regional Office:
300 South Spring Street
Room 12513
Los Angeles, CA 90013
213-897-3062

San Diego Regional Office:
1350 Front Street
Suite 2060
San Diego, CA 92101
619-525-4113

San Francisco Regional Office:
455 Golden Gate Avenue
Suite 14500
San Francisco, CA 94102
415-557-8000

What must be filed:

Draft your own Articles accordingly to the applicable sample Articles provided by the state. The documents must be typed in black ink on one side of the paper only. To avoid the initial annual franchise tax of $800 complete the application form for exemption from franchise tax (form 3500), enclose all attachments called for in the instructions, and file this application together with the original and four copies of your Articles. Also enclose the $25 application filing fee, the state filing fee, and a self-addressed envelope. The Secretary of State will certify two copies without charge. Any additional copies will be certified upon request and payment of $8 per copy.

Name requirements:

The following words are not allowed in the corporation's name: "bank," "trust," or "trustee." The name shall not be the same or deceptively similar to the name or any other corporation existing in California.

Directors requirements:

You must have at least one director. The directors do not have to be residents of California.

Articles requirements:

Articles must have the following minimum contents:

- the corporate name
- the general purpose (Mutual Benefit Corporation, Public Benefit Corporation, Religious Corporation) *and* the specific purpose of the corporation
- name and California street address of the initial agent (post office box alone is not acceptable)
- signature and typed name (directly below the signature) of at least one incorporator
- if directors are stated in the Articles, each named person must acknowledge and sign the Articles
- special statements required to be included in the Articles to get the tax exemption (only where applicable—please contact the Franchise Tax Board under the address typed below)

Filing fees:

$25, for expedited processing of documents, add a special handling fee of $15. The special handling fee must be remitted by a separate check and will be retained whether documents are filed or rejected.

Reports:

You have to file an annual report within 120 days of the end of corporation's fiscal year.

Statute: California Code, Nonprofit Corporation Law, Public Benefit Corporations, Section 5122

TAXES:

California Franchise Tax Board
Tax Forms Request
P.O. Box 942840
Sacramento, CA 94240
800-852-5711
www.ftb.ca.gov

Automatic exemption: No

CHARITABLE SOLICITATION:

State of California
Office of the Attorney General
P.O. Box 903447
Sacramento, CA 94203
916-445-2021
www.ag.ca.gov/charities

Statute: California Govt Code Sec. 12580-12596; California Code of Regulations, Title 11, 300-310, 999.1-999.4; California Business and Professional Code Sec. 17510-17510.85; 22930; California Corp. Code Sec. 5223-5250

Exemption: $25,000

Annual filing: Yes

Accept URS: Yes

Colorado

INCORPORATION:

Secretary of State
Corporations Office
1700 Broadway
Suite 200
Denver, CO 80290
303-894-2200 (press 2)
Fax: 303-869-4864
www.sos.state.co.us/pubs/business/main.htm

What must be filed:

Make a copy of the fill-in-the-blanks Articles and complete both documents by typing them in black ink. File both originals and enclose the filing fee. Include a typed or machine printed self-addressed envelope.

Name requirements:

By law the corporate name may not include any word or phrase that implies a purpose not included in the Articles of Incorporation. But because the law does not require your Articles to state a certain purpose, the Secretary of State will accept any name that is not deceptively similar to any other domestic corporation already on file with the Secretary of State.

It is not necessary to use a *corporate ending* (e.g., Corporation, Co., or Incorporated).

Directors requirements:

Your company must have at least one director and one officer. They do not have to be residents of Colorado.

Articles requirements:

The minimum requirements for a Colorado nonprofit corporation are as follows:
- the corporate name
- the name and street address of the corporation's registered agent and office
- the name and address of each incorporator
- a statement whether or not the corporation will have members
- provisions regarding distribution of assets upon dissolution
- the number of directors your corporation shall have

Make sure that each incorporator listed signs the Articles.

Filing fees:

$75, payable to the Secretary of State.

Reports:

You have to file reports every two years (between January 1 and May 1).

Statute: Colorado Revised Statutes, Chapter 7–122 of the *Colorado Nonprofit Corporation Act*

TAXES:

Department of Revenue
Denver Service Center
1375 Sherman Street
Denver, CO 80261
303-238-7378
www.revenue.state.co.us

Automatic exemption: Yes

CHARITABLE SOLICITATION:

State of Colorado
Office of Secretary of State
Licensing Section
1560 Broadway
Suite 200
Denver, CO 80202
303-894-2200, x6407
www.sos.state.co.us/pubs/bingo_raffles/
charitable.htm

Statute: Colorado Revised Statutes, Title 6, Article 16

Exemption: $25,000

Annual filing: By campaign—no renewal required

Accept URS: No

Connecticut

INCORPORATION:
Secretary of State
30 Trinity Street
Hartford, CT 06106
860-509-6002
www.sots.state.ct.us

What must be filed:
Type or print your Certificate of Incorporation in black ink. File only the original together with the filing fee.

Name requirements:
Your corporation name must include the words "corporation," "incorporated," or "company," or the abbreviation "corp.," "inc.," or "co." and must be distinguishable from other company names on file with the Secretary of State.

A name reservation can be made for a $30 fee for 120 days using the application form provided by the State.

Directors requirements:
The corporation must have at least three directors. They do not have to be residents of Connecticut.

Articles requirements:
In Article 2 check the appropriate box whether your corporation shall have members and what rights they shall have. Enter the name and address of your registered agent in Article 3 and make sure the agent signs the Acceptance of appointment.

As a nonprofit, nonstock corporation the purpose of your corporation may be "to engage in any lawful act or activity for which corporations may be formed under the Connecticut Revised Non stock corporation Act" (Article 4).

Filing fees:
$465 (includes a $30 statutory franchise tax), payable to the Connecticut Secretary of State.

Reports:
The Organization and First Report must be filed within 30 days of the date on which the corporation holds its organization meeting. The filing fee $25.

Statute: Connecticut General Statutes, Nonstock Corporations, Sec. 33-427

TAXES:
Department of Revenue Services
Taxpayer Services Division
25 Sigourney Street
Hartford, CT 06106
860-297-5962
800-382-9463 (in-state only)
Fax: 860-297-5698
www.ct.gov/drs/site/default.asp

Automatic exemption: Yes

CHARITABLE SOLICITATION:
Public Charities Unit
c/o Office of the Attorney General
P.O. Box 120
Hartford, CT 06141
203-566-5836
www.ct.gov/ag/site/default.asp

Statute: Connecticut General Statutes, Sec. 21A-190A, et seq.

Exemption: Less than $50,000 annually and not paying anyone primarily to raise funds

Annual filing: Yes

Accept URS: Yes

Delaware

INCORPORATION:

State of Delaware
Department of State
Division of Corporations
P.O. Box 898
Dover, DE 19903
302-739-3073
Fax: 302-739-3812
302-739-3813 (for requests)
www.state.de.us/corp

What must be filed:

Complete the fill-in-the-blanks form Certificate of Incorporation for "nonstock corporations." Print or type your documents in black ink and submit any additional documents in the US letter size "8.5x11". File the original Certificate of Formation and one exact copy. Enclose the filing fee.

Name requirements:

Your corporate name must include one of the following words: "Association," "Company," "Corporation," "Club," "Foundation," "Fund," "Incorporated," "Institute," "Society," "Union," "Syndicate," or one of the abbreviations "Co.," "Corp.," "Inc." A name reservation can be made by calling 900-420-8042 or 900-555-2677. The name will be reserved for 30 days for a fee of $10.

Directors requirements:

Your corporation must have one or more directors. They do not have to be residents of Delaware.

Articles requirements:

Nonprofit corporations must add, "This Corporation shall be a nonprofit corporation" in the third Article.

In Article 4 you are asked to state your membership conditions but you can also leave that to be regulated by your Bylaws.

Filing fees:

$107 payable to Delaware Secretary of State.

The Division of Corporations offers expedited service for additional fees:

- Priority 1 (completed within 2 hours of receipt when received by 7:00 pm E.S.T.): $500
- same day (when received by 2:00 pm): up to $200
- Twenty-four-hour (filing will be completed the next business day): up to $100

Reports:

The annual report has to be submitted to the Division of Corporations in November/December each year. The filing for the annual report is $20.

Statute: Delaware Code Annotated, Title 8, Sec. 102

TAXES:

Department of Finance
Division of Revenue
Carvel State Office Building
820 North French Street
Wilmington, DE 19801
302-577-8205

Business Master File Bureau:
302-577-8250
www.state.de.us/revenue

Automatic exemption: No

CHARITABLE SOLICITATION:

Attorney General
Civil Division
820 North French Street
Wilmington, DE 19801
302-577-8400

Statute: There is no statute requiring registration

Exemption: No current registration requirements for solicitation of charitable contributions

Annual filing: No

Accept URS: No

District of Columbia

INCORPORATION:
Department of Consumer and Regulatory Affairs
Corporation Division
941 North Capitol Street, NE
Washington, DC 20002
202-442-4400
www.dcra.dc.gov/main.shtm or
www.dcra.dc.gov

What must be filed:
Draft your own Articles accordingly to the instructions and the sample Articles given by the State. Use plain bond paper, either U.S. letter or legal size. Submit two originally signed and notarized sets of Articles.

Name requirements:
The corporate name may not include language that implies the corporation is organized for purposes other than those stated in the Articles of Incorporation. The name may not be the same or similar to the name of a corporation registered under the law of D.C. and shall not indicate that corporation is organized under an act of Congress. Name reservations can be made for 60 days or a filing fee of $25.

Directors requirements:
The corporation must at least have three directors. They do not have to be residents of D.C.

Articles requirements:
The minimum requirements for the Articles are as follows:
- the name of the corporation
- the period of duration (this can be perpetual or a specific period)
- a specific purpose for which the corporation is organized
- a statement whether the corporation shall have members
- if your corporation shall have members, the number of classes of members and the different qualifications and rights of the members of each class
- the manner in which directors shall be elected or appointed and a statement of which class of members shall have the right to elect directors
- a provision of the regulation of the internal affairs of the corporation
- the name of the initial registered agent and the address of the initial registered office

- the number of initial directors the corporation shall have and their names and addresses
- the names and addresses of each incorporator (incorporators must be at least 21 years of age)

Filing fees:
$70, payable to the D.C. Treasurer.

Reports:
You have to file a report every two years by January 15.

Statute: D.C. Code, Title 29, Chapter 5

TAXES:
Office of Tax and Revenue
Customer Service Center
941 Capitol Street, NE
1st Floor
Washington, DC 20002
202-727-4829
www.cfo.dc.gov/otr

Automatic exemption: No

CHARITABLE SOLICITATION:
Department of Consumer and Regulatory Affairs
941 North Capital Street, NE
Washington, DC 20002
202-442-4513

Statute: D.C. Code Sec. 2-711

Exemption: Less than $1,500 annually, provided all functions in the corporation are carried out by unpaid persons

Annual filing: Yes

Accept URS: Yes, but supplemental form required

Florida

INCORPORATION:

Secretary of State
Division of Corporations
P.O. Box 6327
Tallahassee, FL 32314
800-755-5111 (general inquiries)
850-245-6052 (nonprofit articles)
www.dos.state.fl.us/doc

What must be filed:

Complete the sample Articles and file the original and one copy. Also complete the transmittal letter provided by the state and attach it to your Articles. Enclose the correct filing fee.

Name requirements:

The corporation name must include one of the words "Corporation," "Corp.," "Incorporated," or "Inc." As a nonprofit corporation you must not use the words "Company" or "Co." You can reserve a name for a fee of $35 for a period of 120 days.

Directors requirements:

There must be at least three directors who must be 18 years of age or older but not need to be residents of Florida.

Articles requirements:

The minimum requirements for the Articles are as follows:
- the name of the corporation
- the principal place of business and mailing address of the corporation
- a specific purpose for which the corporation is formed
- a statement, in which manner the directors are elected or appointed
- the name and Florida street address of your initial registered agent—make sure your registered agent signs the Articles in the space on the bottom page
- the name and signature of each incorporator

Filing fees:

$70 (includes $35 filing fee and $35 for the Designation of the Registered Agent).

For an optional $8.75 plus $1.00 per page of each page over eight, not to exceed a maximum of $52.20, you receive a Certified Copy.

Make your checks payable to the Department of State.

Reports:

The annual report must be filed on or before May 1 each year. The filing fee is $61.25.

Statute: Florida Statutes, Chapter 617

TAXES:

Florida Department of Revenue
Taxpayer Services
1379 Blountstown Highway
Tallahassee, FL 32304
850-488-6800
800-352-3671
http://sun6.dms.state.fl.us/dor

Automatic exemption: No

CHARITABLE SOLICITATION:

Florida Department of Agriculture and
Consumer Services
407 South Calhoun
Tallahassee, FL 32399
850-922-2972
www.doacs.state.fl.us/onestop/cs/solicit.html

Statute: Florida Statutes, Chapter 496

Exemption: Less than $25,000 carried out by unpaid fundraisers

Annual filing: No

Accept URS: No

Georgia

INCORPORATION:
Secretary of State
Corporations Division
2 Martin Luther King, Jr. Drive, SE
Suite 315, West Tower
Atlanta, GA 30334
404-656-2817
Fax: 404-657-2248
www.sos.state.ga.us/corporations
www.georgiacorporations.org

What must be filed:
Draft your own Articles accordingly to the guidelines given by the state. Submit the original and one exact copy. Also fill in the "Transmittal Information" form and attach it to the Articles. Enclose the filing fee.

Note that all corporations have to publish a notice of intent to incorporate in the official legal newspaper of the county in which the registered office of the corporation is located (the Clerk of Superior Court will give you advice). You must forward your notice of intent together with a $40 publication fee directly to the newspaper on the next business day after filing your Articles. A sample notice of incorporation is included in the instructions how to draft your Articles.

Name requirements:
A corporate name can and should be reserved prior to filing. A reservation can be made: by faxing a request to 404-651-7842, at the Corporations Divisions website, or by writing to the Division. Reservations are not available by phone. You will receive a name reservation number that remains in effect for 90 days.

Directors requirements:
Your corporation must have at least 3 directors. They do not have to be residents of Georgia.

Articles requirements:
The Articles must contain the following minimum:
- the name of the corporation
- a statement that the corporation is organized pursuant to the Georgia Nonprofit Corporation Code
- the name of the registered agent and the street address of its office in Georgia (a post office box address alone is not acceptable)
- the name and address of each incorporator
- a statement whether the corporation shall have members
- the mailing address of the corporation
- a signature of one of the incorporators named in the Articles

Filing fees:
$125, payable to the Secretary of State

Reports:
You have to file an annual report between January 1 and April 1.

Statute: Georgia Code Annotated, Title 14-2-120, Sec. 2702

TAXES:
Georgia Department of Revenue
Income Tax Division
1800 Century Center Boulevard, NE
Atlanta, GA 30345
404-417-2400
www.etax.dor.ga.gov

Automatic exemption: No

CHARITABLE SOLICITATION:
Secretary of State
Business Services and Regulation
2 Martin Luther King, Jr. Drive
Suite 306, West Tower
Atlanta, GA 30334
404-656-3920
www.sos.state.ga.us/securities

Statute: Georgia Code Annotated Sec. 43-17-1, et seq.

Exemption: Less than $25,000 annually

Annual filing: Yes

Accept URS: Yes, but supplemental form required

Hawaii

INCORPORATION:

Department of Commerce and Consumer Affairs
Business Registration Division
P.O. Box 40
Honolulu, HI 96810
808-586-2744 (administration)
808-586-2727 (documents registration)
Fax: 808-586-2733
www.hawaii.gov/dcca/areas/breg
www.businessregistrations.com

Residents on the neighbor islands may call the following numbers followed by 6-2727 and the # sign:
274-3141 Kauai
984-2400 Maui
974-4000 Hawaii
800-468-4644 Lanai & Molokai

What must be filed:

Complete both copies and file them with the Secretary of State. Enclose the filing fee.

Name requirements:

The corporate name may not include language that implies the corporation is organized for purposes other than those stated in the Articles of Incorporation. The name may not be the same or similar to the name of a corporation registered under the law of Hawaii, unless with written consent of the registered name holder, and with added words to distinguish the names.

Directors requirements:

The corporation must at least have three members and also at least one president, one vice president, one secretary, and one treasurer.

Articles requirements:

The Articles shall set forth the following minimum:

- the name of the corporation
- the address of the corporation's office
- the purpose for which the corporation is organized
- the names and street addresses of the initial directors
- the names and street addresses of the initial officer
- a statement whether the corporation shall have members
- the signature of each incorporator

Filing fees:

$50, payable to the "Department of Commerce and Consumer Affairs," for an extra $50 you get expedited service (filing will be done within five business days, otherwise at least 20 business days).

Reports:

You have to file an annual report between January 1 and March 31.

Statute: Hawaii Revised Statutes, Title 23, Section 415B-34

TAXES:

State of Hawaii
Department of Taxation
P.O. Box 259
Honolulu, HI 96809
808-587-4242
800-222-3229
Fax: 808-587-1488
www.state.hi.us/tax/tax.html

Automatic exemption: Yes

CHARITABLE SOLICITATION:

Department of Commerce and Consumer Affairs
P.O. Box 3469
Honolulu, HI 96801
808-586-2744

Statute: Hawaii Statutes, Chapter 467B, *Solicitation of Funds from the Public*

Exemption: No current registration requirements for solicitation of charitable contributions

Annual filing: No

Accept URS: No

Idaho

INCORPORATION:

Secretary of State
700 West Jefferson Street
P.O. Box 83720
Boise, ID 83720
208-334-2300
Fax: 208-334-2080
www.idsos.state.id.us/corp/corindex.htm

What must be filed:

Fill-in forms are provided by the state. File the original and one exact copy together with the filing fee.

Name requirements:

Your company name must contain the words "corporation," "company," "incorporated," or "limited" or an abbreviation of these words.

You can reserve a name by filing an application with the Secretary of State. If the name is available it will be reserved for a period of four months for a fee of $20.

Directors requirements:

The corporation must have at least three directors, but if the corporation is going to be a *religious* corporation, your board of directors needs only one person.

Articles requirements:

The Articles must contain the following minimum requirements:

- the name of the corporation
- the purpose for which the corporation is formed (this can be to transact any and all lawful activity for which a nonprofit corporation can be formed)
- the names and addresses of the initial directors
- the name of the initial registered agent and the address of the registered office
- the name and address of each incorporator
- a statement whether or not the corporation shall have members
- any other provision regarding the distribution of assets on dissolution

Make sure that each incorporator signs the Articles.

Filing fees:

$30, payable to the Secretary of State. If expedited service is requested, add $20 to the filing fee.

Reports:

During the first year there is no annual report needed. The first and all subsequent annual reports shall be delivered to the secretary of state each year before the end of the month during which your corporation was initially incorporated. (Idaho Statutes, Title 30, Chapter 3, Sec. 136.)

There is no fee for filing the annual report.

Statute: Idaho Statutes, Title 30, Chapter 3, *Idaho Nonprofit Corporation Act*

TAXES:

State Tax Commission
Department of Revenue and Taxation
P.O. Box 36
Boise, ID 83772
208-334-7660
800-972-7660
www.tax.idaho.gov

Automatic exemption: Yes

CHARITABLE SOLICITATION:

State of Idaho
Office of Attorney General
700 West Jefferson Street
P.O. Box 83720
Boise, ID 83720
208-334-2400

Statute: Idaho Statutes, Title 48, Chapter 10, *Charitable Solicitation Act*, and Chapter 12, *Telephone Solicitation Act*

Exemption: No current registration requirements for solicitation of charitable contributions

Annual filing: No

Accept URS: No

Illinois

INCORPORATION:

Secretary of State
Business Services Department
Springfield Office
Michael J. Howlett Building
501 South Second Street
Room 328
Springfield, IL 62756
217-782-6961
www.sos.state.il.us/departments/
    business_services/home.html

Chicago Office:
69 West Washington Street
Suite 1240
Chicago, IL 60602
312-793-3380

What must be filed:

Type or print your documents in black ink and file the original and one exact copy. Enclose the filing fee.

After you receive the certificate and your file stamped Articles from the Secretary of State, you must file them with the office of the Recorder of Deeds of the county in which your registered office is located. The recording must be within 15 days after receiving your certificate.

Name requirements:

Your corporate name may not contain words regarding any political party. It must be distinguishable from any other Illinois corporation on file with the Secretary of State. Select a name that does not indicate that your corporation is a corporation for profit.

For name availability call 217-782-9520 prior to filing. A name reservation can be made by a written request listing the name wanted and a brief description of the corporate purpose. The fee is $25.

Directors requirements:

The company must at least have three directors, who do not have to be residents or corporation members.

Articles requirements:

The purpose for which the corporation is formed (Article 4) must be a specific purpose and may not be too general or broad. A list of allowable purposes can be found in the booklet provided by the state (see page 3 of the booklet). Also in Article 4 check the appropriate box whether your corporation shall be a Condominium Association or whether your corpora-

tion shall be Cooperative Housing or Homeowner's Association.

Filing fees:

$50, payable to the Secretary of State.

Reports:

The annual report is due before the first day of the corporation's anniversary month each year. The forms will be sent to your registered agent approximately sixty (60) days before the due date.

Statute: Illinois Compiled Statutes Chapter 805, Act 105, 1992, *The General Not For Profit Corporation Act of 1986*

TAXES:

Illinois Department of Revenue
Willard Ice Building
101 West Jefferson Street
Springfield, IL 62702
217-782-3336
800-732-8866
www.state.il.us/dor

Chicago Office:
James R. Thompson Center
100 West Randolph Street
Chicago, IL 60601

Automatic exemption: Yes

CHARITABLE SOLICITATION:

Charitable Trusts and Solicitation Division
100 West Randolph
11th Floor
Chicago, IL 60601
312-814-2595
www.ag.state.il.us/charities/index.html

Statute: Illinois Compiled Statutes, Chapter 760, Act 55/1; Illinois Compiled Statutes, Chapter 225, Act 460/1

Exemption: Corporations with gross revenue less than $15,000 and unpaid fundraisers are required to register but are exempt from annual financial filing

Annual filing: Yes

Accept URS: Yes

Indiana

INCORPORATION:
Secretary of State
Business Services Division
302 West Washington Street
Room E018
Indianapolis, IN 46204
317-232-6576
Fax: 317-233-3387
www.in.gov/sos/business/corporations.html

What must be filed:
Type or print all three copies of the fill-in-the-blanks forms and file them with the Secretary of State. Enclose the filing fee.

Name requirements:
The corporate name must include one of the words "Corporation," "Incorporated," "Limited," or "Company" or any abbreviation of these words.

Directors requirements:
The corporation must have at least three directors. They do not have to be residents of Indiana.

Articles requirements:
In Article 3 check the appropriate box whether the corporation is a public benefit, a religious, or a mutual benefit corporation. Also check in Article 5 whether the corporation will have members. Make sure that the Articles are signed by each incorporator.

Filing fees:
$30, payable to the Secretary of State

Reports:
Nonprofit corporations have to file annual reports with a $10 filing fee.

Statute: Indiana Code Sec. 23-17, *Indiana Nonprofit Corporation Act of 1991*

TAXES:
Department of Revenue
100 North Senate Avenue
Indianapolis, IN 46204
317-615-2662
www.state.in.us/dor

Automatic exemption: No

CHARITABLE SOLICITATION:
Office of Indiana Attorney General
Consumer Protection Division
Indiana Government Center South
5th floor
402 West Washington Street
Indianapolis, IN 46204
317-232-6330

Statute: Indiana Code 23-7, Chapter 8

Exemption: No current registration requirements for solicitations of charitable contributions

Annual filing: No

Accept URS: No

Iowa

INCORPORATION:
Secretary of State
Corporations Division
1ˢᵗ floor, Lucas Building
321 East 12ᵗʰ Street
Des Moines, IA 50319
515-281-5204
Fax: 515-242-5953
www.sos.state.ia.us/business/nonprofcorp.html

What must be filed:
Draft your own Articles of Incorporation accordingly to the guidelines and Section 504A.29 of the *Iowa Nonprofit Corporation Act*. See "Articles Requirements" below for details. Deliver the original document and one exact copy together with the filing fee.

Name requirements:
The corporate name may not include language that implies the corporation is organized for purposes other than those stated in the Articles of Incorporation. The name may not be the same or similar to the name of a corporation registered under the law of Iowa.

Directors requirements:
Your corporation must have at least one director who does not have to be a resident of Iowa.

Articles requirements:
The Articles must include the following minimum:
- the name of the corporation and the Chapter of the Code under which incorporated
- if you want your corporation to be formed for a limited time the period of duration, skip that if it shall be perpetual
- the purpose for which the organization is organized (must be a charitable, literary, educational, or scientific purpose)
- any provisions that set forth the regulation of the internal affairs of the corporation, including provisions of the distribution of assets upon dissolution
- the name of the registered agent and the address of the initial registered office
- the number and the names and addresses of the initial directors
- if applicable, any provision limiting any of the corporate powers

- the date on which the corporate existence shall begin (not more than ninety days in the future)—you can skip this, your corporation will then exist from the date the state issues the certificate of incorporation
- the name and address of each incorporator

Make sure that the person executing the documents signs and states his or her name and capacity in which he or she signs.

Filing fees:
$20, payable to the Secretary of State.

Reports:
You have to file an annual report between January 1 and March 31.

Statute: Iowa Code Sec. 504A.29

TAXES:
Iowa Department of Revenue
Taxpayer Services
P.O. Box 10457
Des Moines, IA 50306
515-281-3114 (Des Moines or out of State)
800-367-3388 (in-state, Quad Cities, Omaha)
Fax: 515-242-6487
www.state.ia.us/tax

Automatic exemption: No

CHARITABLE SOLICITATION:
Attorney General
Consumer Protection Division
Hoover State Building
1305 East Walnut
Des Moines, IA 50319
515-281-5926

Statute: Iowa Code Chapter 13C

Exemption: No current registration requirements for solicitation of charitable contributions

Annual filing: No

Accept URS: No

Kansas

INCORPORATION:

Secretary of State
Corporation Division
1st Floor, Memorial Hall
120 SW 10th Avenue
Topeka, KS 66612
785-296-4564
www.kssos.org

What must be filed:

Complete the fill-in-the-blanks form and file the original and one exact copy. Note that the Articles of Incorporation must be notarized. Enclose the filing fee.

Name requirements:

The corporation's name must include one of the following words indicating a corporation: "Fund," "Incorporated," "Inc.," "Association," "Church," "Club," "Foundation," "Institute," or "Society." It must be different from any corporation's name already existing in Kansas.

Directors requirements:

Your corporation must have at least three directors. They do not have to be residents of Kansas.

Articles requirements:

The purpose your corporation is formed for must be stated in Article 3, a general statement that the purpose is to "engage in any lawful act or activity for which nonprofit corporations may be organized under the Kansas General Corporation Code" is sufficient. You should check with the IRS prior to filing whether your purpose must be specific one.

If you want to apply for the federal tax exempt status you must check the "No" box in Article 4 to make clear that your corporation won't issue capital stock.

Enter the names and mailing addresses of the persons serving as initial directors until the first annual meeting. Make sure the incorporator (minimum of one) signs the Articles.

Filing fees:

$20, payable to the Secretary of State.

Reports:

Your corporation must file an annual report with an annual privilege fee (ask Secretary of State for actual fee; fee right now is $20.00). The report form will be send to the registered office prior to the due date. The first report will not be required until your corporation is at least six months old. It is due the 15th day of the sixth month following the close of the corporation's fiscal year.

Statute: Kansas Statutes Annotated, Sec. 17-6002, Corporations

TAXES:

Kansas Department of Revenue
Docking State Office Building
Room 150
915 SW Harrison Street
Topeka, KS 66612
785-368-8222
Fax: 785-291-3614
www.ksrevenue.org

Automatic exemption: Yes

CHARITABLE SOLICITATION:

Secretary of State
Corporate Division
1st Floor, Memorial Hall
120 SW 10th Avenue
Topeka, KS 66612
785-296-4564
www.kssos.org/business/business_charitable.html

Statute: Kansas Statutes Annotated, Sec. 17-1760, et seq.

Exemption: $10,000

Annual filing: Yes

Accept URS: Yes

Kentucky

INCORPORATION:
Office of the Secretary of State
P.O. Box 718
Frankfort, KY 40602
502-564-3490
Fax: 502-564-5687
www.sos.ky.gov/business

Filings Branch:
Office of the Secretary of State—Filings Branch
P.O. Box 718
700 Capital Avenue
Suite 154
Frankfort, KY 40601
502-564-2848
Fax: 502-564-4075

Annual Reports Filings:
Office of the Secretary of State—Annual Reports
P.O. Box 1150
700 Capital Avenue
Suite 156
Frankfort, KY 40601
502-564-2848
Fax: 502-564-4075

Records Branch:
Office of the Secretary of State—Records Branch
P.O. Box 718
700 Capital Avenue
Suite 156
Frankfort, KY 40601
502-564-7330
Fax: 502-564-4075

What must be filed:
The Articles must be typewritten or printed and signed by an incorporator if no director has been selected. File the original and two exact copies of your Articles and enclose the correct filing fee. The Secretary of State will return two "filed" stamped copies to your registered agent's office.

Name requirements:
The corporation name must include the words "corporation" or "incorporated" or the abbreviation "Inc." You can also use the word "company" or the abbreviation "Co.," which must not be preceded by the word "and" or the abbreviation "&."

Check the name availability prior to filing by calling 502-564-2848. A name reservation can be made for a fee of $15 for a period of 120 days. You can also check name availability on the Internet.

Directors requirements:
A Kentucky nonprofit corporation must have at least three directors.

Articles requirements:
The minimum requirements for the Articles are:
- the corporate name
- the purpose or purposes for which the corporation is organized
- the name of the initial registered agent and the address of its office
- the mailing address of the corporation's principal office
- the number of the initial directors and the names and mailing addresses of these persons
- the name and mailing address of each incorporator
- any provisions for distribution of assets on dissolution or final liquidation of your corporation

Filing fees:
$8, payable to the Secretary of State.

Reports:
You have to file an annual report each June.

Statute: Kentucky Revised Statutes, Chapter 273

TAXES:
>Kentucky Revenue Cabinet
>Corporation Income Tax Section
>200 Fair Oaks Lane
>Frankfort, KY 40602
>502-564-4581
>Fax: 502-564-3875
>www.revenue.ky.gov

Automatic exemption: No

CHARITABLE SOLICITATION:
>Attorney General's Office
>Division of Consumer Protection
>1024 Capitol Center Drive
>Frankfort, KY 40601
>502-696-5389
>http://ag.ky.gov/consumer

Statute: Kentucky Revised Statutes Sec. 367.650

Exemption: None

Annual filing: Yes

Accept URS: Yes

Louisiana

INCORPORATION:

Secretary of State
Corporations Section
P.O. Box 94125
Baton Rouge, LA 70804
225-925-4704
Fax: 225-925-4726
www.sec.state.la.us/comm/corp/corp-index.htm
#index

What must be filed:

To obtain a federal tax identification number call the IRS at 901-546-3920 prior to filing your Articles.

Complete the fill-in-the-blanks form provided by the state. Make sure that your registered agent signs the affidavit on the bottom of the second page. Both Articles and affidavit have to be notarized. File only the original and enclose the filing fee.

Within 30 days after filing your Articles, a multiple original or a copy certified by the Secretary of State and a copy of the Certificate of Incorporation must be filed with the office of the recorder of mortgages in the parish where the corporation's registered office is located.

Name requirements:

The name may not be the same or similar to the name of a corporation registered under the law of Louisiana, unless the corporation has failed to do business for two years or to pay franchise taxes for five years. The name may not imply the corporation is an administrative agency and shall not include the following words and phrases: "banking," "banker," "state," "parish," "redevelopment" "corporation," "electric cooperative," "credit union," "assurance," "bank," "building and loan," "casualty," "cooperative," "deposit," "fiduciary," "guarantee," "homestead," "indemnity," "insurance," "mutual," "savings," "security," "surety," or "trust."

Directors requirements:

The corporation must have at least three directors. State the term of office of each director in Article 8.

Articles requirements:

In Article 2 check the first box if you do not want the purpose of the corporation to be limited.

If you want to apply for the federal tax-exempt status you must check "Non-stock basis" in Article 9 to make clear that your corporation does not issue stock. You then have to fill in Article 10, characterizing the qualifications which must be met to be a member of your corporation.

Filing fees:

$60, payable to the Secretary of State.

Reports:

You have to file an annual report each year on or before the anniversary date of incorporating in Louisiana. The filing fee is $25.

Statute: Louisiana Revised Statutes, Chapter 12:203

TAXES:

Department of Revenue and Taxation
P.O. Box 201
Baton Rouge, LA 70802
225-219-7318
www.rev.state.la.us

Automatic exemption: Yes

CHARITABLE SOLICITATION:

Attorney General
Consumer Protection Division
P.O. Box 94095
Baton Rouge, LA 70804
225-342-7900
www.ag.state.la.us/comsumers.aspx

Statute: Louisiana Revised Statutes 51:1901-1904

Exemption: None

Annual filing: Yes

Accept URS: Yes

Maine

INCORPORATION:

Office of the Secretary of State
Bureau of Corporation, Elections,
    and Commissions
101 State House Station
Augusta, ME 04333
207-624-7736
Fax: 207-287-5874
www.state.me.us/sos/cec/corp

What must be filed:

Type or print your Articles in black ink. Make sure all your documents are dated by month, day and year and all bear original signatures. File the original and attach the completed Acceptance of Appointment as registered agent. Make sure to enclose the correct filing fee.

Name requirements:

You can reserve a corporate name prior to filing by submitting the Application for Reservation of Name form. If available, the name will be reserved for 120 days for a fee of $5.

Directors requirements:

The corporation must have at least three directors. They do not have to be residents of Maine and there are no age restrictions.

Articles requirements:

If you do not want the purpose for which your corporation is formed to be limited just leave Article 2 blank, so that the corporation is organized for all purposes permitted under the law. Enter the number of your initial directors and of the directors to be elected on your first meeting in Article 4 and check the appropriate box in Article 5, whether or not your corporation shall have members.

Articles 6 and 7 are optional, check with the IRS prior to filing your Articles, if your corporation has to meet the requirements stated in Article 7.

Filing fees:

$20, payable to the Deputy Secretary of State.

Reports:

The annual report must be filed no later than June 1 the year following the year of incorporation. Use the Annual Report form issued by the Secretary of State.

Statute: Maine Revisted Statutes Annotated, Title 13-B

TAXES:

Maine Revenue Services
24 State House Station
Augusta, ME 04333
207-287-2076
Fax: 207-624-9694
www.maine.gov/revenue

Automatic exemption: No

CHARITABLE SOLICITATION:

Charitable Solicitations Registrar
State House Station #35
Augusta, ME 04333
207-624-8603
www.state.me.us/pfr/olr/categories/cat10.htm

Statute: 9 Maine Revised Statutes Annotated, Title 9, Sec. 5001-5016

Exemption: $10,000 or 10 or less donors

Annual filing: Yes

Accept URS: Yes

Maryland

INCORPORATION:

State Department of Assessments and Taxation
Corporate Charter Division
301 West Preston Street
Room 801
Baltimore, MD 21201
410-767-1340 (Corporate Charter Filings &
     Processings)
410-767-1350 (Corporate Charter Legal Unit)
Fax: 410-333-5873
www.dat.state.md.us/sdatweb/charter.html

What must be filed:

Your documents must be typed. File only the original and enclose the filing fee.

Name requirements:

Your corporate name must contain the words "Corporation," "Incorporated," "Limited," "Inc.," "Corp.," or "Ltd." It must be distinguishable from any other corporate name already on file with the Secretary of State.

For name availability, call 410-767-1330 prior to filing.

Directors requirements:

The corporation must have at least one director. The director does not have to be a resident of Maryland.

Articles requirements:

Characterize the purpose for which the corporation is formed with one or two sentences in Article 3 and make sure the purpose is charitable, religious, educational, or scientific.

Enter the minimum and maximum number of directors your corporation shall have and give the name and address of the initial director(s) in the space below.

Filing fees:

$50, payable to the Department of Assessments and Taxation.

Reports:

You have to file an annual report by April 15.

Statute: Annotated Code of Maryland, Corporations and Associations, Sec. 2-104

TAXES:

Comptroller of Maryland
80 Calvert Street
Annapolis, MD 21401
410-260-7980
800-MD-TAXES
www.comp.state.md.us

Automatic exemption: No

CHARITABLE SOLICITATION:

Secretary of State
Charitable Division
State House
Annapolis, MD 21401
410-974-5534
www.marylandsos.gov

Statute: Annotated Code of Maryland, Business Regulations Act, Sec. 6-101, et seq.

Exemption: $25,000

Annual filing: Yes

Accept URS: Yes

Massachusetts

INCORPORATION:
Secretary of the Commonwealth
Corporations Division
One Ashburton Place
17ᵗʰ Floor
Boston, MA 02108
617-727-9640
Fax: 617-742-4538
www.state.ma.us/sec/cor

What must be filed:
Complete the sample Articles and file the original document with the Secretary of State.

Name requirements:
Your corporate name must include the words "Limited," "Incorporated," or "Corporation," or abbreviations of these words. Religious organizations are exempt from this requirement.

For name availability call 617-727-9640. You can reserve a name prior to filing either by submitting a written application to the Secretary of State or in person. The name will be reserved for thirty (30) days for a fee of $15. The reservation can be renewed once for another $15.

Directors requirements:
The corporation must have at least 3 directors. They do not have to be residents of Massachusetts.

Articles requirements:
The purpose your corporation is formed for can be explained in simple language in Article 2, but if you want to apply for the tax-exempt status, characterize that purpose more specifically in Article 4. Check with the IRS for what requirements must be met to receive the tax-exemption.

Filing fees:
$35, payable to the Commonwealth of Massachusetts.

Reports:
The annual report is due before November 1 each year. The filing fee is $15.

Statute: Massachusetts General Laws, Chapter 180

TAXES:
Department of Revenue
Customer Service Bureau
P.O. Box 7010
Boston, MA 02204
617-887-6367
800-392-6089 (in-state only)
www.dor.state.ma.us

Automatic exemption: No

CHARITABLE SOLICITATION:
Department of the Attorney General
Division of Public Charities
One Ashburton Place
14ᵗʰ Floor
Boston, MA 02108
617-727-2200
www.ago.state.ma.us/charity.asp

Statute: Massachusetts General Laws, Chapters 12 and 68

Exemption: $5,000 or 10 or less donors

Annual filing: Yes

Accept URS: Yes

Michigan

INCORPORATION:
Michigan Department of Commerce
Corporation and Securities Bureau
Corporation Division
P.O. Box 30054
Lansing, MI 48909
517-241-6470
Fax: 517-241-0538
www.michigan.gov

What must be filed:
Complete the fill-in-the-blanks form by typing or printing legibly in black ink. File only the original document together with the correct filing fee.

Name requirements:
The corporate name may not include language that implies the corporation is organized for purposes other than those stated in the Articles of Incorporation. The name may not be the same or similar to the name of a corporation registered under the law of Michigan, unless the name holder's written consent. Name reservations can be made for 120-240 days at that Bureau of Commercial Services for a $10 fee.

Directors requirements:
Your corporation must have at least one director. He does not have to be a resident of Michigan. There are no age restrictions for the directors.

Articles requirements:
Characterize the purpose for which your corporation is formed. This purpose must be specific, a general statement is not sufficient.

Complete either Article III (2) or III (3) depending on whether or not your corporation will issue stock. If you want to apply for the federal tax-exempt status your corporation will be on a non stock basis.

Note that except for educational corporations, which must have at least three incorporators, your corporation must only have one incorporator.

Filing fees:
$20 includes a $10 organization fee payable to the State of Michigan.

Reports:
You have to file an annually report by October 1. Note that the report must include any distribution of funds to shareholders or members and the amount of loans made to those persons and representatives of your corporation (directors, officers, etc.).
(*Michigan Nonprofit Corporation Act*, 450.2 Sec. 911)

Statute: Michigan Compiled Laws, Sec. 21.197/202

TAXES:
Michigan Department of Treasury
Lansing, MI 48922
517-373-3200
www.michigan.gov/treasury

Automatic exemption: Yes

CHARITABLE SOLICITATIONS:
Department of the Attorney General
Charitable Trust Section
P.O. Box 30212
Lansing, MI 48909
517-373-1152
www.michigan.gov/ag

Statute: Michigan Compiled Laws Annotated Sec. 400.271

Exemption: $8,000, provided nobody is paid to fundraise and the financial statements of your corporation are available to the public

Annual filing: Yes

Accept URS: Yes

Minnesota

INCORPORATION:
Secretary of State
Division of Corporations
180 State Office Building
100 Rev. Dr. Martin Luther King Jr. Boulevard
St. Paul, MN 55155
651-297-5199
Fax: 651-297-5192
www.sos.state.mn.us

What must be filed:
Print or type your document(s) legibly in black ink. File only the original.

Name requirements:
Corporate name has to be distinguishable from names of other corporations under the law of Minnesota. Nonprofit corporations can use words indicating that they are incorporated (e.g., "Incorporated," "Corp.," "Corporation," or "Company") but they are not required to use these words.

Directors requirements:
The corporation must have at least three directors. They do not have to be residents of Minnesota.

Articles requirements:
Check the "Nonprofit Corporation" box at the top of your Articles. Enter the name of your initial registered agent and the address of its registered office in Article 2. Make sure that each incorporator (minimum of one) signs the Articles.

Filing fees:
$70, payable to the Secretary of State.

Reports:
The state provides a form that must be filed during the year.

Statute: Minnesota Statutes Annotated Sec. 317A.111

TAXES:
Minnesota Department of Revenue
Franchise Tax for Nonprofit Organizations
Mail Station 3350
St. Paul, MN 55146
612-296-0555
www.taxes.state.mn.us

Automatic exemption: No

CHARITABLE SOLICITATION:
Office of Attorney General
Charities Division
Suite 1200, NCL Tower
445 Minnesota Street
St. Paul, MN 55101
612-296-6172
www.ag.state.mn.us/charities

Statute: Minnesota Statutes, Chapter 309

Exemption: $25,000 annually, provided nobody is paid to fundraise

Annual filing: Yes

Accept URS: Yes

Mississippi

INCORPORATION:

Secretary of State
Corporations Division
P.O. Box 136
Jackson, MS 39205
601-359-1633
800-256-3494
Fax: 601-359-1607
www.sos.state.ms.us/busserv/corp/
     corporations.asp

What must be filed:

Complete the fill-in-the-blanks form exactly as described in the instructions. File only the original and enclose the filing fee. Attach the completed statement that your corporation is organized only for the purposes that will be recognized for the tax exemption.

Name requirements:

Nonprofit corporation names do not have to include words indicating their corporation status, but they may include such words (e.g., "Corporation," "Incorporated," "Inc.," or "Corp."). A name reservation can be made for a fee of $25.

Directors requirements:

The number of directors is not specified in the statutes. You can fix the number of directors in the corporation's Articles or bylaws. The directors do not have to be residents of Mississippi.

Articles requirements:

In Article 4 nonprofit corporations can determine the period of duration, enter either a certain number of years or check "perpetual."

Give the name and address of each incorporator in Article 7.

Filing fees:

$75, payable to the Secretary of State.

Reports:

There is no duty to file an annual report. Rather the secretary of state requests an information report.

Statute: Mississippi Code Annotated Sec. 79-11-137

TAXES:

Mississippi State Tax Commission
P.O. Box 1033
Jackson, MS 39125
601-923-7000
www.mstc.state.ms.us

Automatic exemption: Yes

CHARITABLE SOLICITATION:

Secretary of State
Charities Registration
P.O. Box 136
Jackson, MS 39215
601-359-1317
www.sos.state.ms.us/regenf/charities/charities.asp

Statute: Mississippi Code Annotated Sec. 79-11-501, et seq.

Exemption: $4000, provided no one is paid to fundraise

Annual filing: Yes

Accept URS: Yes, but supplemental form required

Missouri

INCORPORATION:

Secretary of State
Corporation Division
P.O. Box 778
Jefferson City, MO 65102
573-751-4153
866-223-6535
www.sos.mo.gov/business/corporations

Kansas City Branch Office:
Kansas City State Office Building
615 East 13th Street
Fifth Floor
Room 513
Kansas City, MO 64106
816-889-2925

Springfield Branch Office:
Springfield State Office Building
149 Park Central Square
Room 624
Springfield, MO 65806
417-895-6330

St. Louis Branch Office:
Wainwright State Office Building
111 North Seventh Street
Room 234
St. Louis, MO 63101
314-340-7490

What must be filed:

Complete the fill-in-the-blanks forms and file your Articles in duplicate, make sure both documents are originally signed. Enclose the filing fee.

Name requirements:

The corporate name must be distinguishable from any other company or corporation name already on record with the Secretary of State.

Directors requirements:

The corporation must have at least one president and/or chairman, one secretary, and one treasurer.

Articles requirements:

If you want to apply for the tax exempt status, make sure to meet the special requirements listed in the separate instructions. These requirements are as follows:

- the purpose for which the corporation is formed (Article 8) must be a charitable, educational, religious, or scientific one (to meet the state's requirements you also have to indicate exactly what your corporation is doing)
- the net income of the corporation may not distributed to the member, directors, or other private persons except for reasonable compensation for services rendered
- the corporation may not take part in any political or legislative activities
- upon the dissolution of the corporation the remaining assets must be distributed either for the corporation's purposes or to any other similar corporation qualified as exempt organizations

Filing fees:

$25, payable to the Director of Revenue.

Reports:

The annual report, listing the officers and directors of the corporation, is due by August 31st each year but not in the first year of existence. The corporation will not remain in good standing if the report is not filed by November 30th.

Statute:

Missouri Revised Statutes, Chapter 347

TAXES:

Corporation Income Tax
P.O. Box 700
Jefferson City, MO 65105
573-751-4541
800-877-6881 (forms)
www.dor.mo.gov

Automatic exemption: Yes

CHARITABLE SOLICITATION:

Attorney General
Supreme Court Building
P.O. Box 899
Jefferson City, MO 65102
314-751-8769
www.ago.mo.gov

Statute: Missouri Revised Statutes, Sec. 407.450, et seq.

Exemption: None

Annual filing: Yes

Accept URS: Yes

Montana

INCORPORATION:
Secretary of State
Business Services Bureau
P.O. Box 202801
Helena, MT 59620
406-444-3665
Fax: 406-444-3976
www.sos.mt.gov/bsb

What must be filed:
First you have to check if the chosen name of your corporation is available. For this information you have to call the office of the Secretary of State. Then file the fill-in-the-blanks Articles and make a copy of the completed Articles. Mail both documents to the Secretary of State and enclose the filing fee.

Name requirements:
The name may not include language that implies the corporation is created for purposes other than stated in the Articles. It may not be the same or deceptively similar to the name of a corporation under the law of Montana. The name may not be fictitious.

Directors requirements:
The corporation must have at least three directors. They do not have to be residents of Montana.

Articles requirements:
Your Articles have to include at least following contents:
- corporate name
- name and address of the registered agent and office in Montana
- name and address of each incorporator
- the specific purpose of the corporation (because the Internal Revenue Service requires specific language in order to qualify for nonprofit tax status it is advised that you contact the IRS)
- a statement whether the corporation will have members
- distribution of assets in the case of dissolution

Filing fees:
$20, payable to the Secretary of State. Add an additional $20 for priority filing.

Reports:
You have to file an annual report to April 15.

Statute: Montana Revised Statutes Sec. 35-2-202

TAXES:
Department of Revenue
P.O. Box 5805
Helena, MT 59604
406-444-6900
Fax: 406-444-1505 (income taxes)
Fax: 406-444-0629 (business and misc. taxes)
www.state.mt.us/revenue/css/default.asp

Automatic exemption: No

CHARITABLE SOLICITATION:
Secretary of State
Room 225
Capitol Station
Helena, MT 59620
406-444-3665

Statute: Montana Revised Statutes Sec. 35-2-118

Exemption: No current registration requirements for solicitation of charitable contributions

Annual filing: No

Accept URS: No

Nebraska

INCORPORATION:
Secretary of State
Corporations Division
P.O. Box 94608
Lincoln, NE 68509
402-471-4079
Fax: 402-471-3666
www.sos.state.ne.us/business/corp_serv

What must be filed:
You have to draw your own Articles. Follow the instructions given by the state. The document must be executed by an incorporator. The executing incorporator has to state her or his name and capacity ("incorporator") beneath or opposite the signature. Send the original and one copy to the secretary of state for filing. Make sure that you enclose the correct filing fee.

Name requirements:
The corporate name may not contain a word or a phrase that indicates that the corporation is organized for other than or more of the purposes contained in the Articles of incorporation. The name may not be the same or deceptively similar to other registered corporations or reserved names.

Directors requirements:
The corporation must have at least two directors. They do not have to be residents of Nebraska.

Articles requirements:
Articles have to include the following basic contents:
- the corporate name
- a statement about the general purpose of the corporation (public benefit corporation, mutual-benefit corporation or religious corporation)
- street address (post office box is not acceptable) of corporation's registered office and the name of its initial registered agent at that office
- name and street address of each incorporator
- a statement whether or not the corporation will have members
- provisions not consistent with the law regarding the distribution of assets on dissolution

Filing fees:
$30 plus $5 per page recording fee, payable to the Secretary of State.

Reports:
You have to file an annual report to January 1.

Statute: Nebraska Revised Statutes Chapter 21-1905 et seq.

TAXES:
Department of Revenue
P.O. Box 94818
Lincoln, NE 68509
402-471-5729
800-742-7474 (in-state and Iowa only)
Fax: 402-471-5608
www.revenue.state.ne.us

Automatic exemption: Yes

CHARITABLE SOLICITATION:
Secretary of State
2300 State Capitol
Lincoln, NE 68509
402-471-2554

Statute: Statutes 28-1440–1446 (unenforceable by a 1996 court decision—check the current status with the Secretary of State), 28-1447–1449

Exemption: No current registration requirements

Annual filing: No

Accept URS: Yes

Nevada

INCORPORATION:
Secretary of State
Annex Office
202 North Carson Street
Carson City, NV 89701
775-684-5708
Fax: 775-684-5725
www.sos.state.nv.us/comm_rec

Customer Service:
101 North Carson Street
Carson City, NV 89701
775-684-5708
Fax: 775-684-5724

Commercial Recordings Main Office:
202 North Carson Street
Carson City, NV 89701
775-684-5708
Fax: 775-684-5725

New Filings Division:
206 North Carson Street
Carson City, NV 89706
775-684-5708
Fax: 775-684-7138 (Expedite Requests Only)

What must be filed:
Type or print your Articles in black ink only. File the original and as many copies as you want to be certified and returned to you. Note that you must at least keep one certified copy in the office of your resident agent. Make sure that each incorporator's signature is notarized.

Name requirements:
The corporate name may not appear to be that of a natural person and may not contain a given name or initials unless it is accompanied by one of the words "Corporation," "Corp.," "Incorporated," "Inc.," "Limited," "Ltd.," "Company," or "Co." The name may not be the same or deceptively similar to the name of any other corporation presently on file in Nevada.

For name availability check with the Secretary of State prior to filing by calling 702-687-5203. You can make a name reservation either by email, fax, mail, or in person. Check the name reservation information provided by the state.

Directors requirements:
Choose in Article 4 whether the Governing Board shall be styled as directors or trustees. The Governing Board must at least have one director or trustee. It also needs a president, secretary, and treasurer.

Articles requirements:
Enter the name and address of the initial resident agent in Article 2 and make sure that agent signs the certificate of acceptance on the bottom of the page.

To characterize the purpose for which the corporation is formed in accordance to the IRS requirements check with the IRS prior to filing.

Give the names and addresses of the initial Governing Board in Article 4. Do not forget that each incorporator's signature must be notarized.

Filing fees:
$45; expedited filing service, which allows 24-hour filing, offered for an additional fee of $100.

Reports:
The fee for the corporation's annual report (annual list of officers and directors) is $15.

Statute: Nevada Revised Statutes Chapter 82

TAXES:
Department of Taxation
1550 East College Parkway
Suite 115
Carson City, NV 89706
775-684-2000
Fax: 775-684-2020
www.tax.state.nv.us

Automatic exemption: Yes (state corporate income tax)

CHARITABLE SOLICITATION:
Secretary of State
Capitol Complex
Carson City, NV 89710
702-687-5203

Statute: Nevada Revised Statutes Chapter 598 and Chapter 692

Exemption: No current registration requirements for solicitation of charitable contributions

Annual filing: No

Accept URS: No

New Hampshire

INCORPORATION:
> Department of State
> Corporate Division
> 107 North Main Street
> Concord, NH 03301
> 603-271-3246
> Fax: 603-271-3247
> www.sos.nh.gov/corporate

What must be filed:
> Print or type your documents in black ink and leave one-inch margins on both sides.
> File the original and one exact copy. Both documents must bear original signatures. Note that your Articles of Agreement must be filed with the clerk of the city or town of the principal place of business prior to filing with the Secretary of State. Enclose the filing fee.

Name requirements:
> Your corporate name may not be the same or deceptively similar to an existing corporation name. For name availability call 603-271-3246 prior to filing.

Directors requirements:
> Note that you need five or more incorporators to form a nonprofit corporation in New Hampshire but only one or more directors.

Articles requirements:
> The most important requirement for forming your nonprofit corporation is that you need five or more incorporators.
> The legal purposes your corporation may be formed for are listed in Chapter 292:1 of the New Hampshire Revised Statutes.
> In Article 7 you have the opportunity to make provisions eliminating or limiting the personal liability of a director or officer of your corporation.

Filing fees:
> The filing fee for the filing with the city or town clerk is $5, the fee for filing with the Secretary of State is $25.

Reports:
> The corporation must file the first report, called "return," in the year 2005 (regardless of the date of incorporation) and every five years thereafter. The fee for the return is $25.

Statute: New Hampshire Revised Statutes Annotated Chapter 292

TAXES:
> Department of Revenue Administration
> 45 Chenell Drive
> Concord, NH 03301
> 603-271-2191
> Fax: 603-271-6121
> www.nh.gov/revenue

Automatic exemption: Yes

CHARITABLE SOLICITATION:
> The Attorney General
> Registrar of Charitable Trusts
> State House Annex
> 33 Capitol Street
> Concord, NH 03301
> 603-271-3591
> www.doj.nh.gov/charitable

Statute: Revised Statutes Annotated Sec. 7:19

Exemption: None

Annual filing: Yes

Accept URS: Yes

New Jersey

INCORPORATION:
New Jersey Division of Revenue
Corporate Filing Unit
P.O. Box 308
Trenton, NJ 08625
609-292-9292
Fax: 609-984-6849
www.state.nj.us/njbgs

What must be filed:
Type your documents in black ink. File the original and two exact copies. Enclose a self-addressed stamped envelope to receive a filed copy and the correct filing fee.

Name requirements:
Your corporate name must include the words "A New Jersey Nonprofit Corporation," "Corporation," "Incorporated," "Inc.," or "Corp."

For name availability call 609-292-9292 prior to filing, a payment for name reservation can be made by credit card.

Directors requirements:
The first board of directors (trustees) must have at least three members. They do not have to be residents of New Jersey.

Articles requirements:
To obtain the tax exempt status after filing your Articles make sure the purpose for which your corporation is organized (Article 2) will meet the IRS requirements for tax exemption.

You can leave most of the regulation for the corporations inner affairs to your bylaws if you do not want these affairs to be regulated by the Certificate of Incorporation.

Filing fees:
$100, payable to the Department of State. New Jersey offers an expedited service (filing complete within 8.5 hours) for an additional fee of $10. The expedited service request must be delivered either in person or by messenger service (FedEx or UPS—not U.S. Postal Overnight).

Reports:
The annual report form will be mailed to the registered agents office prior to the anniversary date of your corporation.

Statute: New Jersey Statutes Sec. 15A:2-8

TAXES:
New Jersey Division of Taxation
P.O. Box 628
Trenton, NJ 08646
609-292-1730(Business/Tax Registration)
609-292-9292 (Business Services)
www.state.nj.us/treasury/revenue

Automatic exemption: No

CHARITABLE SOLICITATION:
NJ Division of Consumer Affairs
Charities Registration & Investigation
P.O. Box 45021
Newark, NJ 07101
973-504-6215
www.state.nj.us/lps/ca

Statute: New Jersey Statutes Sec. 45:17A, et seq.

Exemption: None

Annual filing: Yes

Accept URS: Yes

New Mexico

INCORPORATION:

Public Regulation Commission
Corporations Bureau
P.O. Box 1269
Santa Fe, NM 87504
505-827-4502
505-827-4508
800-947-4722 (in-state only)
Fax: 505-827-4387
www.nmprc.state.nm.us/corporations/
    corpshome.htm

What must be filed:

Type or print your Articles legibly in black ink. File duplicate originals and attach the completed, signed and notarized affidavit of acceptance of your registered agent. Enclose the correct filing fee.

Name requirements:

The corporate name must not be the same or deceptively similar to any other company name already existing in New Mexico.

You can check for name availability by calling the Secretary of State at 505-827-4511.

Directors requirements:

The corporation must have at least three directors. The directors do not have to be residents of New Mexico.

Articles requirements:

The minimum requirements for forming the corporation are as follows:

- the name of the corporation
- the period of its duration, which may be perpetual
- a definition of the purpose for which the corporation is formed
- provisions regulating the internal affairs of the corporation including provisions for distributing remaining assets upon the dissolution of the corporation
- the name of its initial agent and the address of the agent's office
- the number of persons serving as the initial directors and the names and addresses of these directors
- the name and address of each incorporator

Filing fees:

$25, payable to the State Corporation Division. Only checks or cashier's checks are accepted. Certified copies are $10 each, if requested.

Reports:

You must file an annual corporate report due the 15th day of the 5th month after the end of the fiscal year of the corporation. The first report is due within 30 days from date of incorporation in New Mexico.

Statute: New Mexico Statutes Annotated Chapter 53-8-31

TAXES:

Taxation and Revenue Department
P.O. Box 630
Santa Fe, NM 87504
505-827-0700
Fax: 505-827-0469
www.state.nm.us/tax

Automatic exemption: Yes

CHARITABLE SOLICITATION:

Registrar of Charitable Organizations
Office of Attorney General
111 Lomas Boulevard NW
Suite 300
Albuquerque, NM 87102
505-222-9092
www.ago.state.nm.us

Statute: New Mexico Statutes Annotated, 22:57-22-1, et seq.

Exemption: less than $2,500

Annual filing: Yes

Accept URS: Yes

New York

INCORPORATION:

Department of State
Division of Corporations, State Records, and
Uniform Commercial Code
41 State Street
Albany, NY 12231
518-473-2492
Fax: 518-474-1418
www.dos.state.ny.us/corp/corpwww.html

What must be filed:

If you draft your own Articles of Incorporation (not using the forms) make sure that your documents contain a separate page which sets forth the title of the document being submitted and the name and address of the person to which the receipt for filing shall be mailed. Enclose the filing fee.

Name requirements:

Unless corporation is formed for religious purposes, the corporate name must contain the words "corporation," "incorporated," "limited," or an abbreviation of these words. A name reservation can be made for a fee of $10.

Directors requirements:

The corporation must have at least three directors. They do not have to be residents of New York.

Articles requirements:

The Certificate of Incorporation must set forth the following minimum:
- the name of the corporation
- a statement that the corporation is formed pursuant to subparagraph (a)(5) of Section 102 of the Not-For-Profit Corporation Law, the type of corporation it shall be under section 201 (Type A-D), and the purpose for which the corporation is formed
- the county where the corporate office is to be located
- the name and address of each director, if your corporation is an A, B, or C type corporation
- the duration of the corporation, if not perpetual
- a designation of the Secretary of State as agent of the corporation upon whom process may be served and the P.O. address to which the secretary of state shall mail a copy on any process against it served upon him or her
- if applicable, the name of the registered agent and the address of its initial registered office and a statement that he or she is the agent upon whom process against the corporation may be served
- any provision for the regulation of the internal affairs of the corporation that is not inconsistent with the law (e.g., types or classes of membership, distribution of assets upon dissolution, etc.)

Filing fees:

$85, payable to the Secretary of State. New York offers an expedited service (filing within 24 hours of receipt) for an additional $25—make sure to print "Attention: Expedited Handling" on the envelope.

Reports:

You have to file a report by request of the Secretary of State.

Statute: New York Not-For-Profit Corporation Law, Sec. 402

TAXES:

State Department of Taxation and Finance
Taxpayer Assistance Center
W. A. Harriman Campus
Albany, NY 12227
800-972-1233
www.tax.state.ny.us/sbc

Automatic exemption: No

CHARITABLE SOLICITATION:

Office of the Attorney General
Charities Bureau
120 Broadway
3rd Floor
New York, NY 10271
212-416-8430
www.oag.state.ny.us/charities/charities.html

Statute: New York Executive Law Art. 7-A

Exemption: 25,000 and unpaid fundraising

Annual filing: Yes

Accept URS: Yes

North Carolina

INCORPORATION:
Secretary of State
Corporations Division
P.O. Box 29622
Raleigh, NC 27626
919-807-2225
Fax: 919-807-2039
www.secretary.state.nc.us/corporations

What must be filed:
Draft your Articles accordingly to the sample and the instructions given in the booklet. File the original and one exact copy together with the filing fee.

After filing the copy will be returned "file-stamped" to the incorporator(s).

Name requirements:
The booklet contains a comprehensive chapter about how to select and determine a corporate name. Your corporate name must be distinguishable from any other corporate name already on record with the Secretary of State. You can call or write to the Secretary of State prior to filing whether the name you want to use is available. A name reservation can be made for a fee of $10.

Directors requirements:
The corporation is required to have at least one director. He or she does not to be a resident of North Carolina.

Articles requirements:
The Articles of Incorporation require the following minimum:
- the corporate name
- a statement, whether the corporation shall be a "charitable or religious corporation" pursuant to the North Carolina. General Statutes Sec. 55A-2-02 (a)(2)
- the name of the initial registered agent and the street address of its initial registered office (if mailing address is different, give the mailing address)
- the name and address of each incorporator (at least one incorporator required)
- a statement whether the corporation shall have members
- provisions regarding the distribution of assets upon the dissolution of the corporation
- the street address (and, if different, the mailing address) and county of the principal office
- the signature and capacity of each incorporator

Filing fees:
$60, payable to the Secretary of State. There is an expedited service available for:
- an additional $ 200 for filing on the same day (documents must be received by 12:00 noon)
- an additional $ 100 for filing within 24 hours

Reports:
An annual report is not required.

Statute: North Carolina General Statutes, Chapter 55A

TAXES:
Department of Revenue
P.O. Box 25000
Raleigh, NC 27640
877-252-3052
www.dor.state.nc.us

Automatic exemption: No

CHARITABLE SOLICITATION:
State of North Carolina
Department of the Secretary of State
Solicitation Licensing Section
2 South Salisbury Street
Raleigh, NC 27601
919-807-2214
www.sosnc.com

Statute: North Carolina General Statutes, Chapter 131F

Exemption: Less than $25,000 if nobody is paid to fundraise

Annual filing: Yes

Accept URS: No

North Dakota

INCORPORATION:
Secretary of State
Capitol Building
600 East Boulevard Avenue Department 108
1ˢᵗ Floor
Bismarck, ND 58505
701-328-4284
800-352-0867 x8-4284
Fax: 701-328-2992
www.nd.gov/sos/nonprofit/registration/
    corporation

What must be filed:
Complete the Articles and file in duplicate. Attach the signed consent to serve and enclose the filing fee for the Articles and for the consent.

Name requirements:
Your corporate name must be distinguishable from any other corporate name already on file with the Secretary of State. The name must not include such words as "bank," "banker," or "banking."

Directors requirements:
The corporation must at least have three directors. They do not have to be residents of North Dakota. Your corporation must have at least two officers: a president and a secretary.

Articles requirements:
The Articles require the following minimum:
- the name of the corporation
- if not perpetual, the duration of its existence
- a specific characterization of the purpose for which the corporation is formed
- provisions for the distribution of assets upon the dissolution or final liquidation of the corporation
- the name of the initial registered agent and the address of the agent's registered office
- the number of your initial directors and their names and addresses

Filing fees:
$40 for filing the Articles, another $10 for filing the consent, both fees have to be paid.

Reports:
You must file an annual report by February 1 each year. The first report is due in the year following the starting year of your corporation.

Statute: North Dakota Century Code Chapter 10-33

TAXES:
Office of State Tax Commissioner
600 East Boulevard Avenue
Department 127
Bismarck, ND 58505
701-328-2770
800-638-2901
Fax: 701-328-3700
www.nd.gov/tax

Automatic exemption: Yes

CHARITABLE SOLICITATION:
Secretary of State
State of North Dakota
600 East Boulevard Avenue
Bismarck, ND 58505
701-328-3665
800-352-0867 x83665
www.nd.gov/sos/nonprofit/registration

Statute: North Dakota Century Code Chapter 50-22

Exemption: None

Annual filing: Yes

Accept URS: Yes, but supplemental form required

Ohio

INCORPORATION:

Secretary of State
Corporations Division
180 East Broad Street
16th Floor
Columbus, OH 43215
614-466-3910
877-767-3453
www.sos.state.oh.us/sos/businessservices/
     nonprof.aspx

What must be filed:

Complete the fill-in-the-blanks Articles and file them with the Secretary of State. Make sure that the Articles are signed by the incorporators and their names are printed or typed beneath their signatures. Enclose the filing fee. The trustees do not have to sign the Articles.

Name requirements:

The name of the corporation is not required to have an corporate ending (e.g., "Inc.," "Corp."). It may not be the same or deceptively similar to another corporation under the law of Ohio.

Directors requirements:

The corporation must have not less than three directors. They do not have to be residents of Ohio.

Articles requirements:

The basic requirements are as follows:
- the corporate name
- the names and addresses of the initial trustees (not fewer than three natural persons)
- name and address of a statutory agent
- the specific purpose of the corporation (a general purpose clause will not be accepted)

Filing fee:

$125, payable to the Secretary of State.

Reports:

You have to file an statement of continued existence each five years. You will get a written notice and the necessary forms from the Secretary of State.

Statute: Ohio Revised Code, Chapter 1702.04

TAXES:

Business Tax Division
4485 Northland Ridge Boulevard
Columbus, OH 43229
614-387-0232 (General Information)
888-405-4039 (Business Taxpayer Assistance)
Fax: 614-387-1851
www.tax.ohio.gov

Automatic exemption: Yes

CHARITABLE SOLICITATION:

Ohio Attorney General
Charitable Foundation Section
101 East Town Street
4th Floor
Columbus, OH 43215
614-466-3180
www.ag.state.oh.us

Statute: Ohio Revised Code, Chapter 1716

Exemption: $25,000, provided the corporation does not compensate any person primarily to solicit

Annual filing: Yes

Accept URS: Yes

Oklahoma

INCORPORATION:
Secretary of State
Corporation Division
2300 North Lincoln Boulevard
Room 101
State Capitol Building
Oklahoma City, OK 73105
405-521-3912
Fax: 405-521-3771
www.sos.state.ok.us/business/business_filing.htm

What must be filed:
Type or print your documents clearly and file the original in duplicate. Enclose the filing fee.

Name requirements:
Your corporate name must contain one of the following words or abbreviations: "association," "company," "corporation," "club," "foundation," "fund," "incorporated," "institute," "society," "union," "syndicate," "limited," "co.," "corp.," "inc.," or "ltd."

For name availability check with the Corporate Filing Division at 405-522-4560 prior to filing. A corporate name can be reserved by filing a name reservation application with a fee of $10 for a period of sixty days.

Directors requirements:
The corporation must at least have one director or trustee. He or she does not have to be resident of Oklahoma. There needs to be at least three incorporators.

Articles requirements:
The basic requirements are as follows:
- the corporate name
- the name of the initial registered agent and the address of its initial registered office
- if the corporation is a church, the street address of its location
- if not perpetual, the duration of your corporation
- the specific purpose for which the corporation is formed
- the number, names, and mailing addresses of the initial directors
- the names and mailing address of each incorporator

Make sure that each incorporator signs the Articles.

Filing fees:
$25, payable to the Secretary of State.

Reports:
You have to file an annual report by March 31.

Statute: Oklahoma Statutes, Title 18, *Oklahoma General Corporation Act*

TAXES:
Oklahoma Tax Commission
2501 Lincoln Boulevard
Oklahoma City, OK 73194
405-521-3160 (Taxpayer Assistance)
405-521-3126 (Corporate Income Tax)
www.oktax.state.ok.us

Automatic exemption: Yes

CHARITABLE SOLICITATION:
Office of the Secretary of State
2300 North Lincoln
#101
Oklahoma City, OK 73105
405-521-3049
www.sos.state.ok.us/forms/forms.htm#charity

Statute: Oklahoma Statutes Title 18:552, et seq.

Exemption: Less than $10,000

Annual filing: Yes

Accept URS: Yes

Oregon

INCORPORATION:
Secretary of State
Corporation Division
255 Capitol Street, NE
Suite 151
Salem, OR 97310
503-986-2200
Fax: 503-378-4381
www.sos.state.or.us/corporation

What must be filed:
Type or print the Articles in black ink. If you file your documents by mail, attach one exact copy of the original. Enclose the filing fee.

Name requirements:
The corporate name must contain the words "corporation," "incorporated," "company," "limited," or an abbreviation of these words. The name must be distinguishable from other active names on the Business Records.

For name availability call 503-986-2200. For a name reservation send an application and a $10 fee to the filing office. If the name is available, it will be reserved for 120 days.

Directors requirements:
A certain number of directors is not required, but you have to fix the number of initial directors in the Articles and the number of subsequent directors in the bylaws.

Articles requirements:
The basic requirements are as follows:

- corporate name
- name and address of registered agent (the address must be an Oregon street address and identical with the agent's business office, post office boxes are not acceptable)
- additional the agent's mailing address
- corporation's address for mailing notices
- type of corporation (public benefit, mutual benefit, religious)
- a statement whether the corporation will have members or not
- a statement concerning the distribution of assets upon dissolution
- names and addresses of all incorporators

Make sure that each incorporator signs the document and print or typewrite the names beneath the signatures.

Filing fees:
$50 for filing the Articles, payable to the "Corporation Division." Fees can be paid by check or by Visa or Mastercard.

Reports:
The annual report must be delivered to the secretary of state on the anniversary date of your corporation. The annual report form is sent to the registered agent forty-five days prior to the due date. The annual fee is $10.

Statute: Oregon Revised Statutes, Chapter 65 *Oregon Business Corporation Act*

TAXES:
Department of Revenue
955 Center Street, NE
Salem, OR 97301
503-378-4988
800-356-4222 (in-state only)
Fax: 503-945-8738
www.oregon.gov/dor

Automatic exemption: Yes

CHARITABLE SOLICITATION:
Oregon, Department of Justice
Charitable Activities Section
1515 SW 5th Avenue
Suite 410
Portland, OR 97201
503-229-5725
www.doj.state.or.us/charigroup

Statute: Oregon Revised Statutes Sec. 128.610–129

Exemption: None

Annual filing: Yes

Accept URS: Yes

Pennsylvania

INCORPORATION:

Department of State
Corporation Bureau
206 North Office Building
Harrisburg, PA 17120
717-787-1057
888-659-9962
www.dos.state.pa.us/corps

What must be filed:

Print or type your documents in black or blue-black ink. File the original of your Articles of Incorporation, attach a cover letter and enclose the following:

- one copy of the completed docketing statement (form DSCB: 15-134A)—this form is provided by the state
- if applicable, copies of the Consent to Appropriation of Name or, copies of the Consent to Use of Similar Name
- the filing fee

Also include either a self-addressed, stamped postcard with the filing information noted or a self-addressed, stamped envelope with a copy of the filing document to receive confirmation of the file date prior to receiving the microfilmed original.

Name requirements:

The corporate name must include the words "incorporated," "corporation," "company," "limited," "fund," "association," "syndicate," or an abbreviation of these words.

Name availability can be checked either by a written request or by phone at 717-787-1057. The fee for an availability of three names is $12.

A name reservation can only be made by a written request together with a $52 fee. The reservation is good for 120 days. You will get a confirmation of your reservation by mail.

Directors requirements:

If you do not specify the number of directors in your bylaws, the minimum number is three, otherwise one.

Articles requirements:

If you want to apply for the federal tax exemption, check with the IRS prior to filing your Articles to make sure your corporation meets the special purpose required to qualify for the tax exemption (purpose must be given in Article 3).

Give the name and address of each incorporator in Article 8 (minimum of one incorporator).

Filing fees:

$125, payable to the Department of State.

Reports:

An annual report must only be filed if there is any change of the corporation's officers. If your corporation must file such a report, there is no filing fee.

Statute: Pennsylvania Consolidated Statutes Title 15

TAXES:

Department of Revenue
Bureau of Corporation Taxes
P.O. Box 8911
Harrisburg, PA 17127
717-787-1064
www.revenue.state.pa.us

Automatic exemption: No

CHARITABLE SOLICITATION:

Department of State
Bureau of Charitable Organizations
P.O. Box 8723
Harrisburg, PA 17120
717-783-1720
www.dos.state.pa.us/char

Statute: Pennsylvania Consolidated States Secs. 10-621.1, et seq.

Exemption: Less than $25,000 annually, provided nobody is paid to fundraise

Annual filing: Yes

Accept URS: Yes

Rhode Island

INCORPORATION:

Office of the Secretary of State
Corporations Division
100 North Main Street
1st Floor
Providence, RI 02903
401-222-3040
Fax: 401-222-1309
www.corps.state.ri.us/corporations.htm

What must be filed:

Complete and sign the original and the duplicate Articles. Enclose the filing fee.

When the Articles are properly completed, a Certificate of Incorporation, together with the file stamped original will be returned to you.

Name requirements:

The name may not be the same or deceptively similar to any other entity name already on file with the Corporations Division.

For name availability check prior to filing by calling the Corporations Division at 717-783-6035.

Directors requirements:

The corporation must have at least three directors. They do not have to be residents of Rhode Island.

Articles requirements:

The minimum requirements are as follows:

- the corporate name
- if not perpetual, the duration of the corporation
- the specific purpose your corporation is formed for (if you want to apply for the federal tax exemption, check with the IRS prior to filing if your corporation must meet specific requirements)
- any provisions for regulating the corporation's internal affairs
- the name of the initial registered agent and the address of its initial registered office
- the number of directors and their names and addresses
- the name and address of each incorporator

Make sure that each incorporator signs the Articles.

Filing fees:

$35, payable to the Secretary of State.

Reports:

An annual report must be filed each calendar year in the month of June beginning the year following the year of incorporation.

Statute: General Laws Rhode Island Chapter 7-6-34

TAXES:

Rhode Island Division of Taxation
One Capitol Hill
Providence, RI 02908
401-222-1120
www.tax.state.ri.us

Automatic exemption: Yes

CHARITABLE SOLICITATION:

State of Rhode Island
Department of Business Regulation
Charitable Organizations Section
233 Richmond Street
Suite 232
Providence, RI 02903
401-222-1754
www.dbr.state.ri.us

Statute: Rhode Island General Laws Title 5, Chapter 53

Exemption: $25,000 with no paid fundraisers

Annual filing: Yes

Accept URS: Yes

South Carolina

INCORPORATION:

Secretary of State
P.O. Box 11350
Columbia, SC 29211
803-734-2158
www.scsos.com/corporations.htm

What must be filed:

File the completed original and either a duplicate original or a conformed copy. Enclose the filing fee.

Name requirements:

The corporate name must include the words "corporation," "incorporated," "company," "limited," or an abbreviation of these words. It must be distinguishable from any other business name already on file with the Secretary of State.

A name can be reserved for 120 days for a fee of $25.

Directors requirements:

Your corporation must have at least one director. He or she does not have to be a resident of South Carolina.

Articles requirements:

In Article 3 check the appropriate box whether the corporation is a public benefit, religious, or mutual benefit corporation. If you want to apply for the federal tax exemption and your corporation is either a public benefit or religious corporation, check the "a" box in Article 6 to make sure that upon dissolution of the corporation, the assets will be distributed accordingly to the tax exempt purposes. If you form a mutual benefit corporation check one of the two dissolution statements in Article 7.

Each incorporator (minimum of one) must sign the Articles.

Filing fees:

$25, payable to the Secretary of State.

Reports:

You have to file an annual report by the 15th day of the 3rd month after the end of the corporation's fiscal year.

Statute: South Carolina Code Annotated Chapter 33-44

TAXES:

South Carolina Tax Commission
P.O. Box 125
Columbia, SC 29214
803-898-5000
Fax: 803-898-5822
www.sctax.org

Automatic exemption: Yes

CHARITABLE SOLICITATION:

Secretary of State
Public Charities Division
P.O. Box 11350
Columbia, SC 29211
803-734-1790
www.scsos.com/charities.htm

Statute: South Carolina Code Annotated 33-56-10

Exemption: $5,000

Annual filing: Yes

Accept URS: Yes

South Dakota

INCORPORATION:

Secretary of State
Capitol Building
500 East Capitol Avenue
Suite 204
Pierre, SD 57501
605-773-4845
Fax: 605-773-4550
www.sdsos.gov/busineservices/corporations.shtm

What must be filed:

Type the Articles and file the original document and one exact copy. Make sure that the consent of appointment is signed by the registered agent and that the Articles are notarized. Enclose the filing fee.

Name requirements:

The corporate name may not be the same or deceptively similar to the name of any other corporation registered in the State of South Dakota.

For name availability check with the Secretary of State at 605-773-4845. A name can be reserved for a period of 120 days for a fee of $15.

Directors requirements:

The board of directors must have at least three members. The directors do not have to be residents of South Dakota.

Articles requirements:

The Articles must contain the following minimum:
- the name of the corporation
- if not perpetual, the period of existence
- the purpose for which the corporation is formed—this clause must contain sufficient information to determine the type of purpose (types of purposes are given in Section 47-22-4 of the statutes)
- a statement whether the corporation shall have members and if so, provisions regulating the class of members and their rights
- regulations concerning the method of election of the directors
- any provisions regulating the internal affairs of the corporation
- the street address of your initial registered office and the name or your initial registered agent
- the number of directors and their names and addresses

- the names and addresses of the incorporators (minimum of three)
- the signature of each incorporator

Filing fees:

$20, payable to the Secretary of State

Reports:

A report containing the basic information about your corporation has to be filed every three years by the first day of the second month following the anniversary month of the corporation. The Secretary of State will provide forms for filing this report prior to the due date. The filing fee for the report is $10.

Statute: South Dakota Codified Laws Chapter 47

TAXES:

Department of Revenue and Regulation
445 East Capitol Avenue
Pierre, SD 57501
605-773-6729
800-TAX-9188
Fax: 605-773-5129
www.state.sd.us/drr2/revenue.html

Automatic exemption: Yes

CHARITABLE SOLICITATION:

Attorney General
State Capitol
500 East Capitol
Pierre, SD 57501
605-773-4400

Statute: South Dakota Codified Laws, Title 37, Chapter 30 (regulates only solicitation of charitable contributions by telephone)

Exemption: No current registration requirements

Annual filing: No

Accept URS: No

Tennessee

INCORPORATION:

Secretary of State
Division of Business Services
6th Floor
William R. Snodgrass Tower
312 Eighth Avenue North
Nashville, TN 37243
615-741-2286
Fax: 615-532-9870
www.tennessee.gov/sos/bus_svc/corporations.htm

What must be filed:

Type or print the Articles in black ink using either the fill-in-the-blanks form or, if drafting your own documents, using legal or letter size paper. The documents must be executed either by an incorporator, by the chair of the board of directors, or by a trustee. File only the original document(s) together with the filing fee.

Name requirements:

The corporate name must be distinguishable from any other name on file with the Division of Business Services, the filing guide provides sufficient information, whether or not names are distinguishable from others. It may not contain language implying that the corporation transacts business for which authorization is required or that the corporation is organized as a fraternal, veterans, service, religious, charitable, or professional organization.

For name availability call 615-741-2286 or use the database at the website prior to filing. A name reservation can be made by filing an application with the Division of Business Services together with a $20 fee.

Directors requirements:

The corporation must have at least one director. They do not have to be residents of Tennessee.

Articles requirements:

The charter must contain the following minimum:
- the corporate name
- a statement whether the corporation is a public or mutual benefit corporation or whether it is a religious corporation
- the address of the initial registered office and the name of the initial registered agent
- the name and address of each incorporator

- the street address of the principal office (may be the same as the address of the registered agent)
- a statement that the corporation is not for profit
- a statement that there will be no members
- provisions regarding the distribution of assets upon the dissolution of the corporation

Filing fees:

$100, payable to the Division of Business Services.

Reports:

The annual report must be filed on or before the first day of the fourth month following the close of the corporation's fiscal year. The report form will be sent to the registered office one month prior to the end of the corporation's fiscal year. The fee for the annual report is $20.

Statute: Tennessee Code Annotated Section 48-52

TAXES:

Tennessee Department of Revenue
Andrew Jackson Office Building
500 Deaderick Street
Nashville, TN 37242
615-253-0600
www.state.tn.us/revenue

Automatic exemption: Yes

CHARITABLE SOLICITATION:

Department of State
Division of Charitable Solicitations
312 8th Avenue North
8th Floor
William Snodgrass Tower
Nashville, TN 37243
615-741-2555
www.state.tn.us/sos/charity/index.htm

Statute: Tennessee Code Ann. Sec. 48-101-501, et seq.

Exemption: $30,000

Annual filing: Yes

Accept URS: Yes, but supplemental form required

Texas

INCORPORATION:
Secretary of State
Corporations Section
P.O. Box 13697
Austin, TX 78711
512-463-5555
Fax: 512-463-5709
www.sos.state.tx.us/corp/nonprofit_org.shtml

What must be filed:
Draft your own Articles accordingly to the instructions provided by the state or fill out the form provided. File two copies of these together with the filing fee. The filing office will return one filed stamped copy.

Name requirements:
The corporate name may include words like "corporation," "incorporated," or "company," but it is not mandatory.

For name availability call 512-463-5555 prior to filing. A name reservation can be made for a fee of $25 for a period of 120 days.

Directors requirements:
The corporation may not have less than three directors. They do not have to be residents of Texas.

Articles requirements:
The minimum contents of your Articles are as follows:
- the name of the corporation
- the period of duration, which may be perpetual
- a statement that the corporation is not for profit
- the specific purpose for which the corporation is formed (check with the IRS prior to filing what requirements your corporation has to meet to qualify for the federal tax exemption)
- the name of the registered agent and the address of the registered office.
- a statement whether corporation shall have members
- if the management of the corporation shall be vested in the members, a statement to that effect
- the number of the initial board of directors and the names and addresses of your directors
- the name and street address of each incorporator
- provisions regarding the distribution of assets upon the dissolution of the corporation

Make sure that each incorporator signs the Articles.

Filing fees:
$25, payable to the Secretary of State.

Reports:
You have to file a report upon request from the Secretary of State (once every four years). The Secretary of State will send notice and the necessary forms before the report is due.

Statute: Texas Nonprofit Corporation Act, Article 1396-3.02

TAXES:
Comptroller of Public Accounts
111 West Sixth Street
Austin, TX 78768
512-463-4600
800-252-5555
www.window.state.tx.us

Automatic exemption: No

CHARITABLE SOLICITATION:
Attorney General
Charitable Trust Section
P.O. Box 12548
Austin, TX 78711
512-463-2018

Statute: Texas does not have a general statute, but certain cities have special requirements for solicitation of charitable contributions.

Exemption: No current state registration requirements for solicitation of charitable contribution

Annual filing: No

Accept URS: No

Utah

INCORPORATION:

Department of Commerce
Division of Corporations and Commercial Code
P.O. Box 146705
Salt Lake City, UT 84114
801-530-4849
877-526-3994 (in-state only)
www.commerce.utah.gov/cor

What must be filed:

File one original and one exact copy of your self-drafted Articles. At least one document must bear the original signature. You can deliver the documents personally, by mail, or even by fax. If you choose to fax your documents, make sure to include the number of your Visa/Mastercard and the expiration date.

Name requirements:

There are no special name requirements for your corporate name, although the name may contain the words "corporation" or "incorporated." The corporate name must be distinguishable from any other corporate name already on file with the Secretary of State.

Directors requirements:

The corporation must at least have three trustees. They do not have to be residents of Utah or member of the corporation.

Articles requirements:

The minimum of what the Articles must contain is:
- the corporate name
- the term of the corporation's existence
- the purpose or purposes for which your corporation is formed—this must include the statement that it is organized as a nonprofit corporation
- the address of the corporation's principal office
- a statement whether or not the corporation shall have members
- the number of initial trustees your corporation shall have and their names and addresses
- the name and street address of each incorporator (at least one)
- the name of the corporation's initial registered agent and the street address of the registered office
- the signature of each incorporator

The Articles also must include a statement by your registered agent that he or she acknowledges his or her acceptance as registered agent.

Filing fees:

$20, payable to the Secretary of State.

Reports:

The annual report must be filed in the month of the anniversary date the corporation was created. The Division of Corporations sends an annual report notice and a reporting form to the registered agent prior to the filing date.

Statute: Utah Code Annotated, Section 16-6-46 *Corporation Laws*

TAXES:

Utah State Tax Commission
210 North 1950 West
Salt Lake City, UT 84134
801-297-2200
800-662-4335
www.tax.utah.gov

Automatic exemption: No

CHARITABLE SOLICITATION:

Department of Commerce
Division of Consumer Protection
160 East 300 South
P.O. Box 146704
Salt Lake City, UT 84114
www.commerce.utah.gov/dcp/registration

Statute: Utah Code Annotated, Title 13, Chapter 22, Sec. 1-22

Exemption: None

Annual filing: Yes

Accept URS: Yes, but supplemental form required

Vermont

INCORPORATION:
Office of the Secretary of State
Corporations Division
Heritage One Building
81 River Street
Drawer 09
Montpelier, VT 05609
802-828-2386
Fax: 802-828-2853
www.sec.state.vt.us/corps/corpindex.htm

What must be filed:
Complete the fill-in-the-blanks form by typewriting or printing. File the original and one exact copy. Enclose the filing fee.

Name requirements:
The corporate name must end with the words "corporation," "incorporated," "company," "limited," or "cooperative" (if applicable).

A name can be reserved for 120 days for a fee of $20.

Directors requirements:
The corporation must have at least three directors, if you form a marketing cooperative, it must have at least five directors.

Articles requirements:
The minimum requirements are as follows:
- the corporate name
- the name of the registered agent
- the street address of the registered office
- if not perpetual, the period of duration
- a statement, whether the corporation shall be a public benefit, mutual benefit, nonprofit corporation, or a cooperative
- the names and addresses of your initial directors
- if applicable, the names and addresses of your members
- the specific purpose for which your corporation is formed
- provisions regarding the distribution of assets upon the dissolution of the corporation
- signatures and addresses of each incorporator

Filing fees:
$75, payable to the Vermont Secretary of State.

Reports:
Nonprofit corporations must file biennial reports. The Secretary of State will send notice before the report is due. The report is due every two years.

Statute: Vermont Statutes Annotated, Title 11, *Nonprofit Corporations*

TAXES:
Department of Taxes
Agency of Administration
Pavilion Office Building
109 State Street
Montpelier, VT 05601
802-828-2551
www.state.vt.us/tax

Automatic exemption: No

CHARITABLE SOLICITATION:
Attorney General
Pavilion Office Building
Montpelier, VT 05602
802-828-3171

Statute: Vermont Statutes Annotated, Chapter 63, Title 9, Sections 2471, et seq.

Exemption: Only the paid solicitor needs to register—otherwise, there are no current requirements for solicitation

Annual filing: No

Accept URS: No

Virginia

INCORPORATION:

State Corporation Commission
P.O. Box 1197
Richmond, VA 23218
804-371-9733
866-722-2551 (in-state only)
Fax: 804-371-9133
www.scc.virginia.gov

What must be filed:

For forming a nonprofit corporation take form SCC 819 (nonstock corporation). Type or write your Articles in black ink. Complete and file only the original form and enclose the filing fee.

Name requirements:

There are no special requirements for your corporate name but it must not be the same or deceptively similar to any other corporate name existing in Virginia.

Directors requirements:

If you want the corporation to have initial directors, the minimum number is one. Each initial director has to be named in the Articles.

Articles requirements:

The minimum requirements for filing the Articles are as follows:

- the corporate name
- a statement whether or not your corporation shall have members and if so, provisions designating the classes of members and their rights
- a statement of the manner in which directors shall be elected or appointed
- the name of the initial registered agent and its status
- the address of your registered office
- optional provisions regarding the purpose for which the corporation is formed (to meet the special requirements for obtaining the federal tax exempt status, check with the IRS prior to filing the Articles for which requirements have to be met)
- if the corporation shall have initial directors, state the number of directors and their names and addresses
- the signature and printed name of each incorporator

Filing fees:

$81 payable to the State Corporation Commission (pay by check or similar payment method, no cash accepted).

Reports:

The annual report must be filed between January 1 and April 1 with a small registration fee. The Secretary of State will send a report form prior to the due date.

Statute: Virginia Code Annotated Title 13.1 Chapter 10

TAXES:

Department of Taxation
Office of Customer Services
P.O. Box 1115
Richmond, VA 23218
804-367-8037
www.tax.virginia.gov

Automatic exemption: Yes

CHARITABLE SOLICITATION:

Virginia Department of Agriculture and
Consumer Affairs
P.O. Box 1163
Richmond, VA 23209
804-786-1343
www.vdacs.virginia.gov/consumers

Statute: Virginia Code Annotated Secs. 57-48 to 57-69

Exemption: $5,000, provided all corporation's activities are carried out by volunteers

Annual filing: Yes

Accept URS: Yes

Washington

INCORPORATION:

Secretary of State
Corporations Division
P.O. Box 40234
Olympia, WA 98504
360-753-7115
www.secstate.wa.gov/corps

What must be filed:

Type or print the document in black ink. Submit the original and one copy together with the filing fee. An expedited service (filing within 24 hours) is available for an extra $20 fee. If you want the expedited service write "expedited" in bold letters on outside of envelope.

Name requirements:

The corporate name may not contain words like "corporation," "incorporated," "limited," or abbreviations "corp.," "inc.," or "ltd.;" but it may contain designations such as "Association," "Services," or "Committee."

For a fee of $20 you can reserve a corporate name for a period of 180 days.

Directors requirements:

The corporation must have one or more directors. He or she does not have to be resident of Washington.

Articles requirements:

At a minimum, the Articles must contain the following:
- the name of the corporation
- if wanted, a specific effective date of incorporation
- the term of existence
- the purpose for which the corporation is formed
- provisions regulating the distribution of assets upon dissolution of the corporation
- the name and street address of the initial registered agent and a signature by this agent, acknowledging acceptance
- the name and address of each initial director
- the name and address of each incorporator
- the signature of each incorporator

Filing fees:

$30, payable to the Secretary of State, add $20 for expedited service.

Reports:

The annual report has to be filed between January 1 and March 1 each year. The fee is $10. The report form is provided by the Secretary of State.

Statute: Washington Revised Code Chapter 24.03

TAXES:

State Department of Revenue
Taxpayer Services Division
P.O. Box 47478
Olympia, WA 98504
800-647-7706
www.dor.wa.gov

Automatic exemption: Yes

CHARITABLE SOLICITATION:

Office of the Secretary of State
Charities Division
505 East Union Avenue
2nd Floor
P.O. Box 40234
Olympia, WA 98504
360-753-0863
800-332-4483 (toll-free in WA only)
www.secstate.wa.gov/charities

Statute: Washington Revised Code Chapter 19.09, et seq.

Exemption: Less than $25,000, provided all corporation's activities are carried out by unpaid persons

Annual filing: Yes

Accept URS: Yes, but supplemental form required

West Virginia

INCORPORATION:
Secretary of State
Business Division
Building 1
Suite 157-K
1900 Kanawha Boulevard East
Charleston, WV 25305
304-558-8381
Fax: 304-558-0900
www.wvsos.com/common/startbusiness.htm

What must be filed:
Complete the Articles and file both originals. Make sure that the incorporator(s) file both documents and that the documents are notarized. Enclose the filing fee.

Name requirements:
Your corporate name must include the words "corporation," "company," "limited," "incorporated," or an abbreviation of these words. The name may not contain any word or phrase that implies that it is organized for any purposes other than those contained in the Articles of Incorporation.

Name availability can be checked by calling the Secretary of State at the phone number given above. A name reservation can be made by a written application accompanied by a $15 fee. The reservation is good for 120 days.

Directors requirements:
The corporation must have at least one director. The director does not have to be a resident of West Virginia or a member of the corporation. The corporation needs to have two officers—a president and a secretary.

Articles requirements:
The fill-in-the-blanks form provided by the State is both for stock and non-stock (nonprofit) corporations. Check the "nonprofit" box in Article 5 to denote your corporation structure. Then state the purpose your corporation is formed for in Article 7 and check the appropriate box whether provisions regulating the internal affairs of the corporation shall be set forth in the bylaws or are attached to the Articles. Give the names and street addresses of the incorporators in Article 10 and the names and number of initial directors in Article 11.

Name at least one person who shall have signature authority on documents filed with the Secretary of State (annual report). The incorporators must sign the Articles. Make sure that the signatures are notarized.

Filing fees:
The registration fee for nonprofit corporations is $25. An additional "Attorney-in-fact fee," which depends on the month your Articles will be received by the Secretary of State, is also required. Check the fee schedule to find out about the correct additional fee.

Reports:
Your first annual report must be filed between January 1 and March 31 of the first calendar year succeeding the date of incorporation. Thereafter, the reports are due between January 1 and March 31 each year.

Statute: West Virginia Code Section 31-1-27

TAXES:
West Virginia Tax Department
Taxpayer Service Division
P.O. Drawer 3784
Charleston, WV 25337
304-558-3333
800-982-8297
304-344-2068 (to order forms)
800-422-2075 (in-state to order forms)
Fax: 304-558-2501
www.state.wv.us/taxrev

Automatic exemption: Yes

CHARITABLE SOLICITATION:
Secretary of State
Room 157K, 1900
Kanawha Building East
P.O. Box 1789
Charleston, WV 25305
304-558-6000
www.wvsos.com/charity

Statute: West Virginia Code, Chapter 29, Art. 19

Exemption: Following organizations provided they do not employ a professional fundraiser and do not receive contributions in excess of $10,000 during a calender year:
- local youth athletic organizations
- community civic or service clubs
- fraternal organizations and labor unions
- local posts, camps, chapters, or similarly desig-nated elements or county units of such elements of bona fide veteran's organizations or auxiliaries that issue charters to such local elements throughout the state
- bona fide organizations of volunteer firemen, ambulance, rescue squads, or auxiliaries

Annual filing: Yes

Accept URS: Yes, but supplemental form required

Wisconsin

INCORPORATION:
Department of Financial Institutions
Division of Corporate & Consumer Services
P.O. Box 7846
Madison, WI 53707
608-261-7577
Fax: 608-267-6813
www.wdfi.org/corporations

What must be filed:
Complete the fill-in-the-blanks forms and send the original and one copy to the Department of Financial Institutions. Enclose the filing fee. For expedited service (filing procedure will be completed the next business day), mark your documents "For Expedited Service" and provide an extra $25 for each item. Indicate on the back side of your Articles where the acknowledgement copy of the filed document should be sent.

Name requirements:
The corporate name must include the words "Corporation," "Incorporated," "Limited," or the abbreviation of one of those words.

For name availability, call the filing office prior to filing. A name can be reserved either by calling 608-261-9555 or by a written application. The application must include the name and address of the applicant and the name to be reserved. If the name is available, it will be reserved for 120 days. The reservation fee is $15 for the written application, $30 for the telephone application.

If your first choice is not available, you can provide a second choice name on the reverse side of your Articles.

Directors requirements:
The corporation must have at least three directors. They do not have to be residents of Wisconsin.

Articles requirements:
The minimum requirements are as follows:
- corporate name
- the phrase: "The corporation is organized under Chapter 181 of the Wisconsin Statutes"
- name and address of the registered agent (street address of the agent's office is required,

post office box address may be part of the address, but is sufficient alone)
- mailing address of the corporation's principal office (it may be located outside of Wisconsin)
- a statement whether the corporation will have members or not
- name, address, and signature of each incorporator
- name of the person who drafted the document (printed, typewritten or stamped in a legible manner)

Filing fees:
$35 filing fee payable to the Department of Financial Institutions, $16 standard recording fee payable to Register of Deeds (if you append additional pages to the form you have to pay $2 more recording fee for each additional page).

Reports:
You have to file an annual report within the calendar quarter of the anniversary of incorporation. The forms are distributed automatically to the corporation.

Statute: Wisconsin Statutes, Chapter 181

TAXES:
Division of Income, Sales and Excise Tax
P.O. Box 8933 Mail Stop 6-40
Madison, WI 53708
608-266-2772
Fax: 608-261-6240
www.dor.state.wi.us

Automatic exemption: Yes

CHARITABLE SOLICITATION:
Department of Regulation and Licensing
Charitable Organizations
P.O. Box 8935
Madison, WI 53708
608-266-5511 x441
http://drl.wi.gov/prof/char/cred.htm

Statute: Wisconsin Statutes, Chapter 440, Subchapter 3

Exemption: $5,000

Annual filing: Yes

Accept URS: Yes

Wyoming

INCORPORATION:
>Secretary of State
>Corporations Division
>State Capitol Building
>Room 110
>200 West 24th Street
>Cheyenne, WY 82002
>307-777-7311
>Fax: 307-777-5339
>http://soswy.state.wy.us/corporat/np.htm

What must be filed:
>Complete the forms and file the original and one exact copy. The Articles must be accompanied by the written consent to appointment executed by the registered agent. Enclose the filing fee.

Name requirements:
>There are no special name requirements although your name may contain words like "corporation," "incorporated," or "company." It must be distinguishable from any other corporate name already on file and may not contain language that implies the corporation was organized for other purposes than those stated in the Articles. A name can be reserved for a fee of $10.

Directors requirements:
>The corporation must have at least three directors. They do not have to be residents of Wyoming.

Articles requirements:
>The Articles must contain the following minimum:
>- the corporate name
>- a statement whether the corporation is a religious, a public benefit or a mutual benefit corporation
>- the street address of your corporation's initial registered office and the name of the registered agent
>- the name and address of each incorporator
>- a statement whether your corporation shall have members
>- provisions regarding the distribution of assets upon the dissolution of the corporation
>- the date and signature of each incorporator
>
>Do not forget to let your registered agent sign the "Consent to Appointment."

Filing fees:
>$25, payable to the Secretary of State.

Reports:
>The annual report must be filed on the first day of the registration anniversary month. The Secretary of State will send out forms two months prior to the due date. The fee is $25.

Statute: Wyoming Statute, Section 17-6-102

TAXES:
>Department of Revenue
>Herschler Building
>122 West 25th Street
>Cheyenne, WY 82002
>307-777-7961
>http://revenue.state.wy.us

Automatic exemption: Yes

CHARITABLE SOLICITATION:
>Secretary of State
>Capitol Building
>200 West 24th Street
>Cheyenne, WY 82002
>307-777-7378

Statute: Wyoming Statutes Sec. 17-19-1501

Exemptions: No current registration requirements for solicitation of charitable contributions

Annual filing: No

Accept URS: No

Appendix C:
Nonprofit Corporate Forms

This appendix contains the blank forms that can be used to form a nonprofit corporation. Be sure to read the text of this book and each form before using it. If a form does not fit your situation, you may want to change it or consult an attorney. If you do not understand any of the forms, consult an attorney.

LETTER TO SECRETARY OF STATE

_____

(date)

_____

_____

_____

_____

Dear Sir or Madam:

Please send me any and all forms, instructions, and statutes that are available without charge for forming a **domestic nonprofit corporation**.

Thank you,

This page intentionally left blank.

LETTER TO DEPARTMENT OF REVENUE

_____
(date)

_____

_____

_____

_____

Dear Sir or Madam:

Please send me any and all forms, instructions, statutes, and other information necessary for registering and obtaining a tax exemption for a **domestic nonprofit corporation**.

Thank you,

This page intentionally left blank.

LETTER TO CHARITABLE SOLICITATION DEPARTMENT

_____
(date)

_____

_____

_____

_____

Dear Sir or Madam:

Please send me any and all forms, instructions, statutes, and other information on registration for charitable solicitation in this state for a **domestic nonprofit** corporation.

Thank you,

This page intentionally left blank.

ARTICLES OF INCORPORATION

OF

_____

A NONPROFIT CORPORATION

Articles of Incorporation of the undersigned, a majority of whom are citizens of the United States, desiring to form a Nonprofit Corporation under the Nonprofit Corporation Law of _____, do hereby certify:

Article 1: The name of the corporation shall be:

Article 2: The Place in this state where the principal office of the Corporation is to be initially located is the City of _____, _____ County.

Article 3: Said corporation is organized exclusively for charitable, religious, educational, and scientific purposes, including, for such purposes, the making of distributions to organizations that qualify as exempt organizations under Section 501(c)(3) of the Internal Revenue Code, or the corresponding section of any future tax code. The specific purpose of the corporation is to _____

_____

_____

_____.

Article 4: The corporation shall have _____ directors. The initial directors' name(s) and address(es) is/are:

Article 5: No part of the net earnings of the corporation shall inure to the benefit of or be distributable to its members, trustees, officers, or other private persons, except that the corporation shall be authorized and empowered to pay reasonable compensation for services rendered and to make payments and distributions in furtherance of the purposes set forth in Article 3 hereof. No substantial part of the activities of the corporation shall be the carrying on of propaganda, or otherwise attempting to influence legislation, and the corporation shall not participate in, or intervene in (including the publishing or distribution of statements), any political campaign on behalf of or in opposition to any candidate for public office. Notwithstanding any other provision of these articles, this corporation shall not, except to an insubstantial degree, engage in any activities or exercise any powers that are not in furtherance of the purposes of the corporation.

Article 6: Upon the dissolution of the corporation, assets shall be distributed for one or more exempt purposes within the meaning of Section 501(c)(3) of the Internal Revenue Code, or the corresponding section of any future federal tax code, or shall be distributed to the federal government, or to a state or local government, for a public purpose. Any such assets not so disposed shall be disposed of by a Court of Competent Jurisdiction of the county in which the principal office of the corporation is then located, exclusively for such purposes or to such organizations, as said Court shall determine, which are operated exclusively for such purposes.

172

Article 7: The registered agent and registered office of this corporation are:

Article 8: The corporation ☐ shall ☐ shall not have members. The classes, qualifications, rights and obligations of the members of the corporation (if any) are spelled out in the Bylaws of the corporation.

Article 9: The period of duration of the corporation is perpetual.

Article 10: Names and addresses of Incorporators:

Article 11:

In witness whereof, we have hereunto subscribed our names this _____ day of _____, 20_____.

_____   _____
Incorporator   Incorporator

_____   _____
Incorporator   Incorporator

The undersigned, being the registered (or statutory) agent listed in these Articles of Incorporation, hereby accepts the position as such and agrees to act in such capacity. The undersigned further represents that he or she is familiar with the obligations of the position and agrees to comply with them.

_____
Registered Agent

ADDENDUM TO ARTICLES OF INCORPORATION

OF

_____

A NONPROFIT CORPORATION

This Addendum to Articles of Incorporation of the above-named corporation is hereby made a part of said Articles of Incorporation as follows:

Article ___: The Place in this state where the principal office of the Corporation is to be initially located is the City of _____, _____ County.

Article ___: Said corporation is organized exclusively for charitable, religious, educational, and scientific purposes, including, for such purposes, the making of distributions to organizations that qualify as exempt organizations under Section 501(c)(3) of the Internal Revenue Code, or the corresponding section of any future tax code.

Article ___: No part of the net earnings of the corporation shall inure to the benefit of or be distributable to its members, trustees, officers, or other private persons, except that the corporation shall be authorized and empowered to pay reasonable compensation for services rendered and to make payments and distributions in furtherance of the purposes set forth in Article___ of the Articles of the Incorporation. No substantial part of the activities of the corporation shall be the carrying on of propaganda, or otherwise attempting to influence legislation, and the corporation shall not participate in, or intervene in (including the publishing or distribution of statements), any political campaign on behalf of or in opposition to any candidate for public office. Notwithstanding any other provision of these articles, this corporation shall not, except to an insubstantial degree, engage in any activities or exercise any powers that are not in furtherance of the purposes of the corporation.

Article ___: Upon the dissolution of the corporation, assets shall be distributed for one or more exempt purposes within the meaning of Section 501(c)(3) of the Internal Revenue Code, or the corresponding section of any future federal tax code, or shall be distributed to the federal government, or to a state or local government, for a public purpose. Any such assets not so disposed shall be disposed of by a Court of Competent Jurisdiction of the county in which the principal office of the corporation is then located, exclusively for such purposes or to such organizations, as said Court shall determine, which are operated exclusively for such purposes.

In witness whereof, we have hereunto subscribed our names this _____ day of _____, 20_____.

_____

Incorporator

_____

Incorporator

_____

Incorporator

_____

Incorporator

This page intentionally left blank.

BYLAWS OF

_____

NONPROFIT CORPORATION

ARTICLE I - OFFICES

The principal office of the Corporation shall be located in the City of _____
and the State of _____. The Corporation may also maintain offices at such other places as the
Board of Directors may, from time to time, determine.

ARTICLE II - PURPOSE

Section 1- Purpose. Said corporation is organized exclusively for charitable, religious, educational, and scientific purposes, including, for such purposes, the making of distributions to organizations that qualify as exempt organizations under Section 501(c)(3) of the Internal Revenue Code, or the corresponding section of any future tax code. The specific purpose of the corporation is to_____

_____

_____

_____

Section 2 - No private inurement. No part of the net earnings of the corporation shall inure to the benefit of or be distributable to its members, trustees, officers, or other private persons, except that the corporation shall be authorized and empowered to pay reasonable compensation for services rendered and to make payments and distributions in furtherance of the purposes set forth in Section 1 hereof.

Section 3 - No lobbying. No substantial part of the activities of the corporation shall be the carrying on of propaganda, or otherwise attempting to influence legislation, and the corporation shall not participate in, or intervene in (including the publishing or distribution of statements) any political campaign on behalf of or in opposition to any candidate for public office. Notwithstanding any other provision of these articles, this corporation shall not, except to an insubstantial degree, engage in any activities or exercise any powers that are not in furtherance of the purposes of the corporation.

Section 4 - Dissolution. Upon the dissolution of the corporation, assets shall be distributed for one or more exempt purposes within the meaning of Section 501(c)(3) of the Internal Revenue Code, or the corresponding section of any future federal tax code, or shall be distributed to the federal government, or to a state or local government, for a public purpose. Any such assets not so disposed shall be disposed of by a Court of Competent Jurisdiction of the county in which the principal office of the corporation is then located, exclusively for such purposes or to such organizations, as said Court shall determine, which are operated exclusively for such purposes.

Section 5 - Private Foundation. In the event that the Corporation fails to qualify as a public charity under federal tax law and is considered a private foundation, the corporation shall comply with the following: a) It will distribute its income for each tax year at such time and in such manner so that it will not become subject to the tax on undistributed taxable income imposed by section 4942 of the Internal Revenue Code, or corresponding provisions of any later federal tax laws; b) It will not engage in any act of self-dealing as defined in section 4941(d) of the Internal Revenue Code, or corresponding provisions of any later federal tax laws; c) It will not retain any excess business holdings as defined in section 4943(c) of the Internal Revenue Code, or corresponding provisions of any later federal tax laws; d) It will not make any investments in a manner that would subject it to tax under section 4944 of the Internal Revenue Code, or corresponding provisions of any later federal tax laws; and e) It will not make any taxable expenditures as defined in section 4945(d) of the Internal Revenue Code, or corresponding provisions of any later federal tax laws.

ARTICLE III - MEMBERS

Section 1 - Members. The corporation □shall □shall not have members.

Section 2 - Membership Provisions. If the corporation has members, the terms and conditions of membership shall be set out in an Addendum to these Bylaws.

ARTICLE IV - BOARD OF DIRECTORS

Section 1 - Number, Election, and Term of Office. The number of the directors of the Corporation shall be _____. This number may be increased or decreased by the amendment of these bylaws by the Board but shall in no case be less than _____ director(s). The Board of Directors shall be elected each year. If this corporation has no members then the Board shall be elected by a majority of the votes of the then current Board. If the corporation has members then the Board shall be elected by the members at their annual meeting. Each director shall hold office until the next annual meeting, and until his successor is elected and qualified, or until his prior death, resignation, or removal.

Section 2 - Vacancies. Any vacancy in the Board shall be filled for the unexpired portion of the term by a majority vote of the remaining directors at any regular meeting or special meeting of the Board called for that purpose.

Section 3 - Duties and Powers. The Board shall be responsible for the control and management of the affairs, property, and interests of the Corporation and may exercise all powers of the Corporation, except as limited by statute.

Section 4 - Annual Meetings. An annual meeting of the Board shall be held on the _____ day of _____ each year unless rescheduled by the Board. The Board may from time to time provide by resolution for the holding of other meetings of the Board, and may fix the time and place thereof.

Section 5 - Special Meetings. Special meetings of the Board shall be held whenever called by the President or by one of the directors, at such time and place as may be specified in the respective notice or waivers of notice thereof.

Section 6 - Notice and Waiver. Notice of any special meeting shall be given at least five days prior thereto by written notice delivered personally, by mail or by facsimile to each Director at his address. If mailed, such notice shall be deemed to be delivered when deposited in the United States Mail with postage prepaid. Any Director may waive notice of any meeting, either before, at, or after such meeting, by signing a waiver of notice. The attendance of a Director at a meeting shall constitute a waiver of notice of such meeting and a waiver of any and all objections to the place of such meeting, or the manner in which it has been called or convened, except when a Director states at the beginning of the meeting any objection to the transaction of business because the meeting is not lawfully called or convened.

Section 7 - Chairman. The Board may, at its discretion, elect a Chairman. At all meetings of the Board, the Chairman of the Board, if any and if present, shall preside. If there is no Chairman, or he or she is absent, then the President shall preside, and in his absence, a Chairman chosen by the directors shall preside.

Section 8 - Quorum and Adjournments. At all meetings of the Board, the presence of a majority of the entire Board shall be necessary and sufficient to constitute a quorum for the transaction of business, except as otherwise provided by law, by the Articles of Incorporation, or by these bylaws. A majority of the directors present at the time and place of any regular or special meeting, although less than a quorum, may adjourn the same from time to time without notice, until a quorum shall be present.

Section 9 - Board Action. At all meetings of the Board, each director present shall have one vote. Except as otherwise provided by Statute, the action of a majority of the directors present at any meeting at which a quorum is present shall be the act of the Board. Any action authorized, in writing, by all of the Directors entitled to vote thereon and filed with the minutes of the Corporation shall be the act of the Board with the same force and effect as if the same had been passed by unanimous vote at a duly called meeting of the Board. Any action taken by the Board may be taken without a meeting if agreed to in writing by all members before or after the action is taken and if a record of such action is filed in the minute book.

Section 10 - Telephone Meetings. Directors may participate in meetings of the Board through use of a telephone if such can be arranged so that all Board members can hear all other members. The use of a telephone for participation shall constitute presence in person.

Section 11 - Resignation and Removal. Any director may resign at any time by giving written notice to another Board member, the President, or the Secretary of the Corporation. Unless otherwise specified in such written notice, such resignation shall take effect upon receipt thereof by the Board or by such officer, and the acceptance of such resignation shall not be necessary to make it effective. Any director may be removed for cause by action of the Board.

Section 12 - Compensation. No stated salary shall be paid to directors, as such for their services, but by resolution of the Board a fixed sum and/or expenses of attendance, if any, may be allowed for attendance at each regular or special meeting of the Board. Nothing herein contained shall be construed to preclude any director from serving the Corporation in any other capacity and receiving compensation therefor.

Section 13 - Liability. No director shall be liable for any debt, obligation or liability of the corporation.

ARTICLE V - OFFICERS

Section 1 - Number, Qualification, Election, and Term. The officers of the Corporation shall consist of a President, a Secretary, a Treasurer, and such other officers, as the Board may from time to time deem advisable. Any officer may be, but is not required to be, a director of the Corporation. The officers of the Corporation shall be elected by the Board at the regular annual meeting of the Board. Each officer shall hold office until the annual meeting of the Board next succeeding his election, and until his successor shall have been elected and qualified, or until his death, resignation or removal.

Section 2 - Resignation and Removal. Any officer may resign at any time by giving written notice of such resignation to the President or the Secretary of the Corporation or to a member of the Board. Unless otherwise specified in such written notice, such resignation shall take effect upon receipt thereof by the Board member or by such officer, and the acceptance of such resignation shall not be necessary to make it effective. Any officer may be removed, either with or without cause, and a successor elected by a majority vote of the Board at any time.

Section 3 - Vacancies. A vacancy in any office may, at any time, be filled for the unexpired portion of the term by a majority vote of the Board.

Section 4 - Duties of Officers. Officers of the Corporation shall, unless otherwise provided by the Board, each have such powers and duties as generally pertain to their respective offices as well as such powers and duties as may from time to time be specifically decided by the Board. The President shall be the chief executive officer of the Corporation.

Section 5 - Compensation. The officers of the Corporation shall be entitled to such compensation as the Board shall from time to time determine.

Section 6 - Delegation of Duties. In the absence or disability of any Officer of the Corporation or for any other reason deemed sufficient by the Board of Directors, the Board may delegate his powers or duties to any other Officer or to any other Director.

Section 7 - Shares of Other Corporations. Whenever the Corporation is the holder of shares of any other Corporation, any right or power of the Corporation as such shareholder (including the attendance, acting and voting at shareholders' meetings and execution of waivers, consents, proxies, or other instruments) may be exercised on behalf of the Corporation by the President, any Vice President, or such other person as the Board may authorize.

Section 8 - Liability. No officer shall be liable for any debt, obligation, or liability of the corporation.

ARTICLE VI - COMMITTEES

Section 1 - Committees. The Board of Directors may, by resolution, designate an Executive Committee and one or more other committees. Such committees shall have such functions and may exercise such power of the Board of Directors as can be lawfully delegated, and to the extent provided in the resolution or resolutions creating such committee or committees. Meetings of committees may be held without notice at such time and at such place as shall from time to time be determined by the committees. The committees of the corporation shall keep regular minutes of their proceedings, and report these minutes to the Board of Directors when required.

ARTICLE VII - BOOKS, RECORDS AND REPORTS

Section 1 - Annual Report. The President of the Corporation shall cause to be prepared annual or other reports required by law and shall provide copies to the Board of Directors.

Section 2 - Permanent Records. The corporation shall keep current and correct records of the accounts, minutes of the meetings and proceedings, and membership records (if any) of the corporation. Such records shall be kept at the registered office or the principal place of business of the corporation. Any such records shall be in written form or in a form capable of being converted into written form.

Section 3 - Inspection of Corporate Records. If this corporation has members, then those members shall have the right at any reasonable time, and on written demand stating the purpose thereof, to examine and make copies from the relevant books and records of accounts, minutes, and records of the Corporation.

ARTICLE VIII - FISCAL YEAR

Section 1 - Fiscal Year. The fiscal year of the Corporation shall be the period selected by the Board of Directors as the tax year of the Corporation for federal income tax purposes.

ARTICLE IX - CORPORATE SEAL

Section 1 - Seal. The Board of Directors may adopt, use, and modify a corporate seal. Failure to affix the seal to corporate documents shall not affect the validity of such document.

ARTICLE X - AMENDMENTS

Section 1 - Articles of Incorporation. The Articles of Incorporation may be amended by the Board of Directors unless this corporation has members, in which case they can be amended as provided by law.

Section 2 - Bylaws. These Bylaws may be amended by the Board of Directors.

ARTICLE XI - INDEMNIFICATION

Section 1 - Indemnification. Any officer, director, or employee of the Corporation shall be indemnified and held harmless to the full extent allowed by law.

Section 2 - Insurance. The corporation may but is not required to obtain insurance providing for indemnification of directors, officers, and employees.

Certified to be the Bylaws of the corporation adopted by the Board of Directors on _____, 20____.

_____

Secretary

ADDENDUM TO BYLAWS OF

_____

A NONPROFIT CORPORATION

MEMBERS

Section l - Members. The corporation shall have one class of members and each member shall have one vote. The Corporation shall keep a list of all active members. Memberships shall not be transferable.

Section 2 - Admission and Termination. Any person may be admitted to membership in the corporation upon payment of such application fee and dues as shall be determined by the board of directors. A member may terminate his or her membership at any time by giving notice to an officer or director of the corporation. The Board of Directors may terminate a member who is delinquent in paying dues or who has acted contrary to the interests of the Corporation. Prior to termination of a member, the Corporation shall give said member thirty (30) days written notice to pay the dues or to explain satisfactorily to the Board alleged to be contrary to the interests of the Corporation.

Section 3 - Annual Meetings. The annual meeting of the members of the Corporation shall be held each year on the _____ day of _____ at the principal office of the Corporation or at such other date and place as the Board may authorize, for the purpose of electing directors, and transacting such other business as may properly come before the meeting.

Section 4 - Special Meetings. Special meetings of the members may be called at any time by the Board, the President, or by the holders of twenty-five percent (25%) of the shares then outstanding and entitled to vote.

Section 5 - Notice of Meetings. Written or printed notice stating the place, day, and hour of the meeting and, in the case of a special meeting, the purpose of the meeting, shall be delivered personally or by mail not less than ten days, nor more than sixty days, before the date of the meeting. Notice shall be given to each Member of record entitled to vote at the meeting. If mailed, such notice shall be deemed to have been delivered when deposited in the United States Mail with postage paid and addressed to the Member at his or her address as it appears on the records of the Corporation.

Section 6 - Waiver of Notice. A written waiver of notice signed by a Member, whether before or after a meeting, shall be equivalent to the giving of such notice. Attendance of a Member at a meeting shall constitute a waiver of notice of such meeting, except when the Member attends for the express purpose of objecting, at the beginning of the meeting, to the transaction of any business because the meeting is not lawfully called or convened.

Section 7 - Quorum. Except as otherwise provided by Statute, or the Articles of Incorporation, at all meetings of Members of the Corporation, the presence at the commencement of such meetings in person or by proxy of a majority of the total membership of the Corporation entitled to vote, but in no event less than one-third of the Members entitled to vote at the meeting, shall constitute a quorum for the transaction of any business. If any Member leaves after the commencement of a meeting, this shall have no effect on the existence of a quorum, after a quorum has been established at such meeting.

Despite the absence of a quorum at any annual or special meeting of members, the members, by a majority of the votes cast by those entitled to vote thereon, may adjourn the meeting. At any such adjourned meeting at which a quorum is present, any business may be transacted at the meeting as originally called as if a quorum had been present.

Section 8 - Voting. Except as otherwise provided by Statute or by the Articles of Incorporation, any corporate action, other than the election of directors, to be taken by vote of the members, shall be authorized by a majority of votes cast at a meeting of Members.

Except as otherwise provided by Statute or by the Articles of Incorporation, at each meeting of Members, active Member of the Corporation shall be entitled to one vote.

Each Member entitled to vote may do so by proxy; provided, however, that the instrument authorizing such proxy to act shall have been executed in writing by the member him- or herself. No proxy shall be valid after the expiration of eleven months from the date of its execution, unless the person executing it shall have specified therein, the length of time it is to continue in force. Such instrument shall be exhibited to the Secretary at the meeting and shall be filed with the records of the corporation.

Any resolution in writing, signed by all of the Members entitled to vote thereon, shall be and constitute action by such Members to the effect therein expressed, with the same force and effect as if the same had been duly passed by unanimous vote at a duly called meeting of Members and such resolution so signed shall be inserted in the Minute Book of the Corporation under its proper date.

Form **SS-4**	**Application for Employer Identification Number**	OMB No. 1545-0003
(Rev. February 2006)	**(For use by employers, corporations, partnerships, trusts, estates, churches, government agencies, Indian tribal entities, certain individuals, and others.)**	**EIN**
Department of the Treasury Internal Revenue Service	▶ **See separate instructions for each line.** ▶ **Keep a copy for your records.**	

Type or print clearly.

1 Legal name of entity (or individual) for whom the EIN is being requested

2 Trade name of business (if different from name on line 1)

3 Executor, administrator, trustee, "care of" name

4a Mailing address (room, apt., suite no. and street, or P.O. box)

5a Street address (if different) (Do not enter a P.O. box.)

4b City, state, and ZIP code

5b City, state, and ZIP code

6 County and state where principal business is located

7a Name of principal officer, general partner, grantor, owner, or trustor

7b SSN, ITIN, or EIN

8a **Type of entity** (check only one box)
- ☐ Sole proprietor (SSN) _____
- ☐ Partnership
- ☐ Corporation (enter form number to be filed) ▶ _____
- ☐ Personal service corporation
- ☐ Church or church-controlled organization
- ☐ Other nonprofit organization (specify) ▶ _____
- ☐ Other (specify) ▶

- ☐ Estate (SSN of decedent) _____
- ☐ Plan administrator (SSN) _____
- ☐ Trust (SSN of grantor) _____
- ☐ National Guard   ☐ State/local government
- ☐ Farmers' cooperative   ☐ Federal government/military
- ☐ REMIC   ☐ Indian tribal governments/enterprises
- Group Exemption Number (GEN) ▶ _____

8b If a corporation, name the state or foreign country (if applicable) where incorporated

State	Foreign country

9 **Reason for applying** (check only one box)
- ☐ Started new business (specify type) ▶_____
- ☐ Hired employees (Check the box and see line 12.)
- ☐ Compliance with IRS withholding regulations
- ☐ Other (specify) ▶

- ☐ Banking purpose (specify purpose) ▶ _____
- ☐ Changed type of organization (specify new type) ▶ _____
- ☐ Purchased going business
- ☐ Created a trust (specify type) ▶ _____
- ☐ Created a pension plan (specify type) ▶ _____

10 Date business started or acquired (month, day, year). See instructions.

11 Closing month of accounting year

12 First date wages or annuities were paid (month, day, year). **Note.** If applicant is a withholding agent, enter date income will first be paid to nonresident alien. (month, day, year)   . . . . ▶

13 Highest number of employees expected in the next 12 months (enter -0- if none).

Do you expect to have $1,000 or less in employment tax liability for the calendar year? ☐ **Yes** ☐ **No**. (If you expect to pay $4,000 or less in wages, you can mark yes.)

Agricultural	Household	Other

14 Check **one** box that best describes the principal activity of your business.
- ☐ Construction ☐ Rental & leasing ☐ Transportation & warehousing
- ☐ Real estate ☐ Manufacturing ☐ Finance & insurance
- ☐ Health care & social assistance ☐ Wholesale–agent/broker
- ☐ Accommodation & food service ☐ Wholesale–other ☐ Retail
- ☐ Other (specify)

15 Indicate principal line of merchandise sold, specific construction work done, products produced, or services provided.

16a Has the applicant ever applied for an employer identification number for this or any other business? . . . . ☐ **Yes** ☐ **No**
Note. If "Yes," please complete lines 16b and 16c.

16b If you checked "Yes" on line 16a, give applicant's legal name and trade name shown on prior application if different from line 1 or 2 above.
Legal name ▶   Trade name ▶

16c Approximate date when, and city and state where, the application was filed. Enter previous employer identification number if known.
Approximate date when filed (mo., day, year)   City and state where filed   Previous EIN

Third Party Designee	Complete this section **only** if you want to authorize the named individual to receive the entity's EIN and answer questions about the completion of this form.	
	Designee's name	Designee's telephone number (include area code) ( )
	Address and ZIP code	Designee's fax number (include area code) ( )

Under penalties of perjury, I declare that I have examined this application, and to the best of my knowledge and belief, it is true, correct, and complete.

	Applicant's telephone number (include area code) ( )
Name and title (type or print clearly) ▶	
	Applicant's fax number (include area code) ( )
Signature ▶ Date ▶	

For Privacy Act and Paperwork Reduction Act Notice, see separate instructions.   Cat. No. 16055N   Form **SS-4** (Rev. 2-2006)

Do I Need an EIN?

File Form SS-4 if the applicant entity does not already have an EIN but is required to show an EIN on any return, statement, or other document.[1] See also the separate instructions for each line on Form SS-4.

IF the applicant...	AND...	THEN...
Started a new business	Does not currently have (nor expect to have) employees	Complete lines 1, 2, 4a–8a, 8b (if applicable), and 9–16c.
Hired (or will hire) employees, including household employees	Does not already have an EIN	Complete lines 1, 2, 4a–6, 7a–b (if applicable), 8a, 8b (if applicable), and 9–16c.
Opened a bank account	Needs an EIN for banking purposes only	Complete lines 1–5b, 7a–b (if applicable), 8a, 9, and 16a–c.
Changed type of organization	Either the legal character of the organization or its ownership changed (for example, you incorporate a sole proprietorship or form a partnership)[2]	Complete lines 1–16c (as applicable).
Purchased a going business[3]	Does not already have an EIN	Complete lines 1–16c (as applicable).
Created a trust	The trust is other than a grantor trust or an IRA trust[4]	Complete lines 1–16c (as applicable).
Created a pension plan as a plan administrator[5]	Needs an EIN for reporting purposes	Complete lines 1, 3, 4a–b, 8a, 9, and 16a–c.
Is a foreign person needing an EIN to comply with IRS withholding regulations	Needs an EIN to complete a Form W-8 (other than Form W-8ECI), avoid withholding on portfolio assets, or claim tax treaty benefits[6]	Complete lines 1–5b, 7a–b (SSN or ITIN optional), 8a–9, and 16a–c.
Is administering an estate	Needs an EIN to report estate income on Form 1041	Complete lines 1, 2, 3, 4a–6, 8a, 9-11, 12-15 (if applicable), and 16a–c.
Is a withholding agent for taxes on non-wage income paid to an alien (i.e., individual, corporation, or partnership, etc.)	Is an agent, broker, fiduciary, manager, tenant, or spouse who is required to file Form 1042, Annual Withholding Tax Return for U.S. Source Income of Foreign Persons	Complete lines 1, 2, 3 (if applicable), 4a–5b, 7a–b (if applicable), 8a, 9, and 16a–c.
Is a state or local agency	Serves as a tax reporting agent for public assistance recipients under Rev. Proc. 80-4, 1980-1 C.B. 581[7]	Complete lines 1, 2, 4a–5b, 8a, 9, and 16a–c.
Is a single-member LLC	Needs an EIN to file Form 8832, Entity Classification Election, for filing employment tax returns, **or** for state reporting purposes[8]	Complete lines 1–16c (as applicable).
Is an S corporation	Needs an EIN to file Form 2553, Election by a Small Business Corporation[9]	Complete lines 1–16c (as applicable).

[1] For example, a sole proprietorship or self-employed farmer who establishes a qualified retirement plan, or is required to file excise, employment, alcohol, tobacco, or firearms returns, must have an EIN. A partnership, corporation, REMIC (real estate mortgage investment conduit), nonprofit organization (church, club, etc.), or farmers' cooperative must use an EIN for any tax-related purpose even if the entity does not have employees.

[2] However, do not apply for a new EIN if the existing entity only (a) changed its business name, (b) elected on Form 8832 to change the way it is taxed (or is covered by the default rules), or (c) terminated its partnership status because at least 50% of the total interests in partnership capital and profits were sold or exchanged within a 12-month period. The EIN of the terminated partnership should continue to be used. See Regulations section 301.6109-1(d)(2)(iii).

[3] Do not use the EIN of the prior business unless you became the "owner" of a corporation by acquiring its stock.

[4] However, grantor trusts that do not file using Optional Method 1 and IRA trusts that are required to file Form 990-T, Exempt Organization Business Income Tax Return, must have an EIN. For more information on grantor trusts, see the Instructions for Form 1041.

[5] A plan administrator is the person or group of persons specified as the administrator by the instrument under which the plan is operated.

[6] Entities applying to be a Qualified Intermediary (QI) need a QI-EIN even if they already have an EIN. See Rev. Proc. 2000-12.

[7] See also Household employer on page 3. **Note.** State or local agencies may need an EIN for other reasons, for example, hired employees.

[8] Most LLCs do not need to file Form 8832. See Limited liability company (LLC) on page 4 for details on completing Form SS-4 for an LLC.

[9] An existing corporation that is electing or revoking S corporation status should use its previously-assigned EIN.

Instructions for Form SS-4

Department of the Treasury
Internal Revenue Service

(Rev. February 2006)

Application for Employer Identification Number

Section references are to the Internal Revenue Code unless otherwise noted.

General Instructions

Use these instructions to complete Form SS-4, Application for Employer Identification Number. Also see *Do I Need an EIN?* on page 2 of Form SS-4.

Purpose of Form

Use Form SS-4 to apply for an employer identification number (EIN). An EIN is a nine-digit number (for example, 12-3456789) assigned to sole proprietors, corporations, partnerships, estates, trusts, and other entities for tax filing and reporting purposes. The information you provide on this form will establish your business tax account.

 An EIN is for use in connection with your business activities only. Do not use your EIN in place of your social security number (SSN).

Reminders

Apply online. Generally, you can apply for and receive an EIN online using the Internet. See *How To Apply* below.

File only one Form SS-4. Generally, a sole proprietor should file only one Form SS-4 and needs only one EIN, regardless of the number of businesses operated as a sole proprietorship or trade names under which a business operates. However, if the proprietorship incorporates or enters into a partnership, a new EIN is required. Also, each corporation in an affiliated group must have its own EIN.

EIN applied for, but not received. If you do not have an EIN by the time a return is due, write "Applied For" and the date you applied in the space shown for the number. Do not show your SSN as an EIN on returns.

If you do not have an EIN by the time a tax deposit is due, send your payment to the Internal Revenue Service Center for your filing area as shown in the instructions for the form that you are filing. Make your check or money order payable to the "United States Treasury" and show your name (as shown on Form SS-4), address, type of tax, period covered, and date you applied for an EIN.

Federal tax deposits. New employers that have a federal tax obligation will be pre-enrolled in the Electronic Federal Tax Payment System (EFTPS). EFTPS allows you to make all of your federal tax payments online at *www.eftps.gov* or by telephone. Shortly after we have assigned you your EIN, you will receive instructions by mail for activating your EFTPS enrollment. You will also receive an EFTPS Personal Identification Number (PIN) that you will use to make your payments, as well as instructions for obtaining an Internet password you will need to make payments online.

If you are not required to make deposits by EFTPS, you can use Form 8109, Federal Tax Deposit (FTD) Coupon, to make deposits at an authorized depositary. If

you would like to receive Form 8109, call 1-800-829-4933. Allow 5 to 6 weeks for delivery. For more information on federal tax deposits, see Pub. 15 (Circular E).

How To Apply

You can apply for an EIN online, by telephone, by fax, or by mail depending on how soon you need to use the EIN. Use only one method for each entity so you do not receive more than one EIN for an entity.

Online. Generally, you can receive your EIN by Internet and use it immediately to file a return or make a payment. Go to the IRS website at *www.irs.gov/businesses* and click on Employer ID Numbers.

Applicants that may not apply online. The online application process is not yet available to:
● Applicants with foreign addresses (including Puerto Rico),
● Limited Liability Companies (LLCs) that have not yet determined their entity classification for federal tax purposes (see *Limited liability company (LLC)* on page 4),
● Real Estate Investment Conduits (REMICs),
● State and local governments,
● Federal Government/Military, and
● Indian Tribal Governments/Enterprises.

Telephone. You can receive your EIN by telephone and use it immediately to file a return or make a payment. Call the IRS at 1-800-829-4933. (International applicants must call 215-516-6999.) The hours of operation are 7:00 a.m. to 10:00 p.m. local time (Pacific time for Alaska and Hawaii). The person making the call must be authorized to sign the form or be an authorized designee. See *Signature* and *Third Party Designee* on page 6. Also see the *TIP* below.

If you are applying by telephone, it will be helpful to complete Form SS-4 before contacting the IRS. An IRS representative will use the information from the Form SS-4 to establish your account and assign you an EIN. Write the number you are given on the upper right corner of the form and sign and date it. Keep this copy for your records.

If requested by an IRS representative, mail or fax (facsimile) the signed Form SS-4 (including any Third Party Designee authorization) within 24 hours to the IRS address provided by the IRS representative.

 Taxpayer representatives can apply for an EIN on behalf of their client and request that the EIN be faxed to their client on the same day. **Note.** By using this procedure, you are authorizing the IRS to fax the EIN without a cover sheet.

Fax. Under the Fax-TIN program, you can receive your EIN by fax within 4 business days. Complete and fax Form SS-4 to the IRS using the Fax-TIN number listed on page 2 for your state. A long-distance charge to callers outside of the local calling area will apply. Fax-TIN numbers can only be used to apply for an EIN. The numbers may change without notice. Fax-TIN is available 24 hours a day, 7 days a week.

Be sure to provide your fax number so the IRS can fax the EIN back to you.

Note. By using this procedure, you are authorizing the IRS to fax the EIN without a cover sheet.

Mail. Complete Form SS-4 at least 4 to 5 weeks before you will need an EIN. Sign and date the application and mail it to the service center address for your state. You will receive your EIN in the mail in approximately 4 weeks. See also *Third Party Designee* on page 6.

Call 1-800-829-4933 to verify a number or to ask about the status of an application by mail.

Where to Fax or File

If your principal business, office or agency, or legal residence in the case of an individual, is located in:	Fax or file with the "Internal Revenue Service Center" at:
Connecticut, Delaware, District of Columbia, Florida, Georgia, Maine, Maryland, Massachusetts, New Hampshire, New Jersey, New York, North Carolina, Ohio, Pennsylvania, Rhode Island, South Carolina, Vermont, Virginia, West Virginia	Attn: EIN Operation Holtsville, NY 11742 Fax-TIN: 631-447-8960
Illinois, Indiana, Kentucky, Michigan	Attn: EIN Operation Cincinnati, OH 45999 Fax-TIN: 859-669-5760
Alabama, Alaska, Arizona, Arkansas, California, Colorado, Hawaii, Idaho, Iowa, Kansas, Louisiana, Minnesota, Mississippi, Missouri, Montana, Nebraska, Nevada, New Mexico, North Dakota, Oklahoma, Oregon, South Dakota, Tennessee, Texas, Utah, Washington, Wisconsin, Wyoming	Attn: EIN Operation Philadelphia, PA 19255 Fax-TIN: 859-669-5760
If you have no legal residence, principal place of business, or principal office or agency in any state:	Attn: EIN Operation Philadelphia, PA 19255 Fax-TIN: 215-516-1040

How To Get Forms and Publications

Phone. Call 1-800-TAX-FORM (1-800-829-3676) to order forms, instructions, and publications. You should receive your order or notification of its status within 10 workdays.

Internet. You can access the IRS website 24 hours a day, 7 days a week at *www.irs.gov* to download forms, instructions, and publications.

CD-ROM. For small businesses, return preparers, or others who may frequently need tax forms or publications, a CD-ROM containing over 2,000 tax products (including many prior year forms) can be purchased from the National Technical Information Service (NTIS).

To order Pub. 1796, IRS Tax Products CD, call 1-877-CDFORMS (1-877-233-6767) toll free or connect to *www.irs.gov/cdorders*.

Tax Help for Your Business

IRS-sponsored Small Business Workshops provide information about your federal and state tax obligations. For information about workshops in your area, call 1-800-829-4933.

Related Forms and Publications

The following forms and instructions may be useful to filers of Form SS-4.
- Form 990-T, Exempt Organization Business Income Tax Return.
- Instructions for Form 990-T.
- Schedule C (Form 1040), Profit or Loss From Business.
- Schedule F (Form 1040), Profit or Loss From Farming.
- Instructions for Form 1041 and Schedules A, B, D, G, I, J, and K-1, U.S. Income Tax Return for Estates and Trusts.
- Form 1042, Annual Withholding Tax Return for U.S. Source Income of Foreign Persons.
- Instructions for Form 1065, U.S. Return of Partnership Income.
- Instructions for Form 1066, U.S. Real Estate Mortgage Investment Conduit (REMIC) Income Tax Return.
- Instructions for Forms 1120 and 1120-A.
- Form 2553, Election by a Small Business Corporation.
- Form 2848, Power of Attorney and Declaration of Representative.
- Form 8821, Tax Information Authorization.
- Form 8832, Entity Classification Election.

For more information about filing Form SS-4 and related issues, see:
- Pub. 51 (Circular A), Agricultural Employer's Tax Guide;
- Pub. 15 (Circular E), Employer's Tax Guide;
- Pub. 538, Accounting Periods and Methods;
- Pub. 542, Corporations;
- Pub. 557, Tax-Exempt Status for Your Organization;
- Pub. 583, Starting a Business and Keeping Records;
- Pub. 966, The Secure Way to Pay Your Federal Taxes for Business and Individual Taxpayers;
- Pub. 1635, Understanding Your EIN;
- Package 1023, Application for Recognition of Exemption Under Section 501(c)(3) of the Internal Revenue Code; and
- Package 1024, Application for Recognition of Exemption Under Section 501(a).

Specific Instructions

Print or type all entries on Form SS-4. Follow the instructions for each line to expedite processing and to avoid unnecessary IRS requests for additional information. Enter "N/A" (nonapplicable) on the lines that do not apply.

Line 1 — Legal name of entity (or individual) for whom the EIN is being requested. Enter the legal name of the entity (or individual) applying for the EIN exactly as it appears on the social security card, charter, or other applicable legal document. An entry is required.

Individuals. Enter your first name, middle initial, and last name. If you are a sole proprietor, enter your individual name, not your business name. Enter your business name on line 2. Do not use abbreviations or nicknames on line 1.

Trusts. Enter the name of the trust.

Estate of a decedent. Enter the name of the estate. For an estate that has no legal name, enter the name of the decedent followed by "Estate."

Partnerships. Enter the legal name of the partnership as it appears in the partnership agreement.

Corporations. Enter the corporate name as it appears in the corporate charter or other legal document creating it.

Plan administrators. Enter the name of the plan administrator. A plan administrator who already has an EIN should use that number.

Line 2 — Trade name of business. Enter the trade name of the business if different from the legal name. The trade name is the "doing business as " (DBA) name.

 Use the full legal name shown on line 1 on all tax returns filed for the entity. (However, if you enter a trade name on line 2 and choose to use the trade name instead of the legal name, enter the trade name on all returns you file.) To prevent processing delays and errors, always use the legal name only (or the trade name only) on all tax returns.

Line 3 — Executor, administrator, trustee, "care of" name. Trusts enter the name of the trustee. Estates enter the name of the executor, administrator, or other fiduciary. If the entity applying has a designated person to receive tax information, enter that person's name as the "care of" person. Enter the individual's first name, middle initial, and last name.

Lines 4a-b — Mailing address. Enter the mailing address for the entity's correspondence. If line 3 is completed, enter the address for the executor, trustee or "care of" person. Generally, this address will be used on all tax returns.

 File Form 8822, Change of Address, to report any subsequent changes to the entity's mailing address.

Lines 5a-b — Street address. Provide the entity's physical address only if different from its mailing address shown in lines 4a-b. Do not enter a P.O. box number here.

Line 6 — County and state where principal business is located. Enter the entity's primary physical location.

Lines 7a-b — Name of principal officer, general partner, grantor, owner, or trustor. Enter the first name, middle initial, last name, and SSN of (a) the principal officer if the business is a corporation, (b) a general partner if a partnership, (c) the owner of an entity that is disregarded as separate from its owner (disregarded entities owned by a corporation enter the corporation's name and EIN), or (d) a grantor, owner, or trustor if a trust.

If the person in question is an alien individual with a previously assigned individual taxpayer identification number (ITIN), enter the ITIN in the space provided and submit a copy of an official identifying document. If necessary, complete Form W-7, Application for IRS Individual Taxpayer Identification Number, to obtain an ITIN.

You must enter an SSN, ITIN, or EIN unless the only reason you are applying for an EIN is to make an entity classification election (see Regulations sections 301.7701-1 through 301.7701-3) and you are a nonresident alien or other foreign entity with no effectively connected income from sources within the United States.

Line 8a — Type of entity. Check the box that best describes the type of entity applying for the EIN. If you are an alien individual with an ITIN previously assigned to you, enter the ITIN in place of a requested SSN.

 This is not an election for a tax classification of an entity. See Limited liability company (LLC) *on page 4.*

Other. If not specifically listed, check the "Other" box, enter the type of entity and the type of return, if any, that will be filed (for example, "Common Trust Fund, Form 1065" or "Created a Pension Plan"). Do not enter "N/A." If you are an alien individual applying for an EIN, see the *Lines 7a-b* instructions above.

- **Household employer.** If you are an individual, check the "Other" box and enter "Household Employer" and your SSN. If you are a state or local agency serving as a tax reporting agent for public assistance recipients who become household employers, check the "Other" box and enter "Household Employer Agent." If you are a trust that qualifies as a household employer, you do not need a separate EIN for reporting tax information relating to household employees; use the EIN of the trust.
- **QSub.** For a qualified subchapter S subsidiary (QSub) check the "Other" box and specify "QSub."
- **Withholding agent.** If you are a withholding agent required to file Form 1042, check the "Other" box and enter "Withholding Agent."

Sole proprietor. Check this box if you file Schedule C, C-EZ, or F (Form 1040) and have a qualified plan, or are required to file excise, employment, alcohol, tobacco, or firearms returns, or are a payer of gambling winnings. Enter your SSN (or ITIN) in the space provided. If you are a nonresident alien with no effectively connected income from sources within the United States, you do not need to enter an SSN or ITIN.

Corporation. This box is for any corporation other than a personal service corporation. If you check this box, enter the income tax form number to be filed by the entity in the space provided.

 If you entered "1120S" after the "Corporation" checkbox, the corporation must file Form 2553 no later than the 15th day of the 3rd month of the tax year the election is to take effect. Until Form 2553 has been received and approved, you will be considered a Form 1120 filer. See the Instructions for Form 2553.

Personal service corporation. Check this box if the entity is a personal service corporation. An entity is a personal service corporation for a tax year only if:
- The principal activity of the entity during the testing period (prior tax year) for the tax year is the performance of personal services substantially by employee-owners, and
- The employee-owners own at least 10% of the fair market value of the outstanding stock in the entity on the last day of the testing period.

Personal services include performance of services in such fields as health, law, accounting, or consulting. For more information about personal service corporations, see the Instructions for Forms 1120 and 1120-A and Pub. 542.

Other nonprofit organization. Check this box if the nonprofit organization is other than a church or church-controlled organization and specify the type of nonprofit organization (for example, an educational organization).

 If the organization also seeks tax-exempt status, you must file either Package 1023 or Package 1024. See Pub. 557 for more information.

If the organization is covered by a group exemption letter, enter the four-digit group exemption number (GEN). (Do not confuse the GEN with the nine-digit EIN.) If you do not know the GEN, contact the parent organization. Get Pub. 557 for more information about group exemption numbers.

If the organization is a section 527 political organization, check the box for *Other nonprofit organization* and specify "section 527 organization" in the space to the right. To be recognized as exempt from tax, a section 527 political organization must electronically file Form 8871, Political Organization Notice of Section 527 Status, within 24 hours of the date on which the organization was established. The organization may also have to file Form 8872, Political Organization Report of Contributions and Expenditures. See *www.irs.gov/ polorgs* for more information.

Plan administrator. If the plan administrator is an individual, enter the plan administrator's SSN in the space provided.

REMIC. Check this box if the entity has elected to be treated as a real estate mortgage investment conduit (REMIC). See the Instructions for Form 1066 for more information.

State/local government. If you are a government employer and you are not sure of your social security and Medicare coverage options, go to *www.ncsssa.org/ ssaframes.html* to obtain the contact information for your state's Social Security Administrator.

Limited liability company (LLC). An LLC is an entity organized under the laws of a state or foreign country as a limited liability company. For federal tax purposes, an LLC may be treated as a partnership or corporation or be disregarded as an entity separate from its owner.

By default, a domestic LLC with only one member is disregarded as an entity separate from its owner and must include all of its income and expenses on the owner's tax return (for example, Schedule C (Form 1040)). Also by default, a domestic LLC with two or more members is treated as a partnership. A domestic LLC may file Form 8832 to avoid either default classification and elect to be classified as an association taxable as a corporation. For more information on entity classifications (including the rules for foreign entities), see the instructions for Form 8832.

 Do not file Form 8832 if the LLC accepts the default classifications above. If the LLC is eligible to be treated as a corporation that meets certain tests and it will be electing S corporation status, it must timely file Form 2553. The LLC will be treated as a corporation as of the effective date of the S corporation election and does not need to file Form 8832. See the Instructions for Form 2553.

Complete Form SS-4 for LLCs as follows.

• A single-member domestic LLC that accepts the default classification (above) does not need an EIN and generally should not file Form SS-4. Generally, the LLC should use the name and EIN of its owner for all federal tax purposes. However, the reporting and payment of employment taxes for employees of the LLC may be made using the name and EIN of either the owner or the LLC as explained in Notice 99-6. You can find Notice 99-6 on page 12 of Internal Revenue Bulletin 1999-3 at *www.irs.gov/pub/irs-irbs/irb99-03.pdf.* (**Note.** If the LLC applicant indicates in box 13 that it has employees or expects to have employees, the owner (whether an individual or other entity) of a single-member domestic LLC will also be assigned its own EIN (if it does not already have one) even if the LLC will be filing the employment tax returns.)

• A single-member, domestic LLC that accepts the default classification (above) and wants an EIN for filing employment tax returns (see above) or non-federal purposes, such as a state requirement, must check the "Other" box and write "Disregarded Entity" or, when applicable, "Disregarded Entity — Sole Proprietorship" in the space provided.

• A multi-member, domestic LLC that accepts the default classification (above) must check the "Partnership" box.

• A domestic LLC that will be filing Form 8832 to elect corporate status must check the "Corporation" box and write in "Single-Member" or "Multi-Member" immediately below the "form number" entry line.

Line 9 — Reason for applying. Check only one box. Do not enter "N/A."

Started new business. Check this box if you are starting a new business that requires an EIN. If you check this box, enter the type of business being started. Do not apply if you already have an EIN and are only adding another place of business.

Hired employees. Check this box if the existing business is requesting an EIN because it has hired or is hiring employees and is therefore required to file employment tax returns. Do not apply if you already have an EIN and are only hiring employees. For information on employment taxes (for example, for family members), see Pub. 15 (Circular E).

 You may have to make electronic deposits of all depository taxes (such as employment tax, excise tax, and corporate income tax) using the Electronic Federal Tax Payment System (EFTPS). See Federal tax deposits on page 1; section 11, Depositing Taxes, of Pub. 15 (Circular E); and Pub. 966.

Created a pension plan. Check this box if you have created a pension plan and need an EIN for reporting purposes. Also, enter the type of plan in the space provided.

Check this box if you are applying for a trust EIN when a new pension plan is established. In addition, check the "Other" box in line 8a and write "Created a Pension Plan" in the space provided.

Banking purpose. Check this box if you are requesting an EIN for banking purposes only, and enter the banking purpose (for example, a bowling league for depositing dues or an investment club for dividend and interest reporting).

Changed type of organization. Check this box if the business is changing its type of organization. For example, the business was a sole proprietorship and has been incorporated or has become a partnership. If you check this box, specify in the space provided (including available space immediately below) the type of change made. For example, "From Sole Proprietorship to Partnership."

Purchased going business. Check this box if you purchased an existing business. Do not use the former owner's EIN unless you became the "owner" of a corporation by acquiring its stock.

Created a trust. Check this box if you created a trust, and enter the type of trust created. For example, indicate if the trust is a nonexempt charitable trust or a split-interest trust.

Exception. Do not file this form for certain grantor-type trusts. The trustee does not need an EIN for the trust if the trustee furnishes the name and TIN of the grantor/owner and the address of the trust to all payors. However, grantor trusts that do not file using Optional Method 1 and IRA trusts that are required to file Form 990-T, Exempt Organization Business Income Tax Return, must have an EIN. For more information on grantor trusts, see the Instructions for Form 1041.

 Do not check this box if you are applying for a trust EIN when a new pension plan is established. Check "Created a pension plan."

Other. Check this box if you are requesting an EIN for any other reason; and enter the reason. For example, a newly-formed state government entity should enter "Newly-Formed State Government Entity" in the space provided.

Line 10 — Date business started or acquired. If you are starting a new business, enter the starting date of the business. If the business you acquired is already operating, enter the date you acquired the business. If you are changing the form of ownership of your business, enter the date the new ownership entity began. Trusts should enter the date the trust was funded. Estates should enter the date of death of the decedent whose name appears on line 1 or the date when the estate was legally funded.

Line 11 — Closing month of accounting year. Enter the last month of your accounting year or tax year. An accounting or tax year is usually 12 consecutive months, either a calendar year or a fiscal year (including a period of 52 or 53 weeks). A calendar year is 12 consecutive months ending on December 31. A fiscal year is either 12 consecutive months ending on the last day of any month other than December or a 52-53 week year. For more information on accounting periods, see Pub. 538.

Individuals. Your tax year generally will be a calendar year.

Partnerships. Partnerships must adopt one of the following tax years.
• The tax year of the majority of its partners.
• The tax year common to all of its principal partners.
• The tax year that results in the least aggregate deferral of income.
• In certain cases, some other tax year.

See the Instructions for Form 1065 for more information.

REMICs. REMICs must have a calendar year as their tax year.

Personal service corporations. A personal service corporation generally must adopt a calendar year unless it meets one of the following requirements.
• It can establish a business purpose for having a different tax year.
• It elects under section 444 to have a tax year other than a calendar year.

Trusts. Generally, a trust must adopt a calendar year except for the following trusts.
• Tax-exempt trusts.
• Charitable trusts.
• Grantor-owned trusts.

Line 12 — First date wages or annuities were paid. If the business has employees, enter the date on which the business began to pay wages. If the business does not plan to have employees, enter "N/A."

Withholding agent. Enter the date you began or will begin to pay income (including annuities) to a nonresident alien. This also applies to individuals who are required to file Form 1042 to report alimony paid to a nonresident alien.

Line 13 — Highest number of employees expected in the next 12 months. Complete each box by entering the number (including zero ("-0-")) of "Agricultural," "Household," or "Other" employees expected by the applicant in the next 12 months. Check the appropriate box to indicate if you expect your annual employment tax liability to be $1,000 or less. Generally, if you pay $4,000 or less in wages subject to social security and Medicare taxes and federal income tax withholding, you are likely to pay $1,000 or less in employment taxes.

For more information on employment taxes, see Pub. 15 (Circular E); or Pub. 51 (Circular A) if you have agricultural employees (farmworkers).

Lines 14 and 15. Check the one box in line 14 that best describes the principal activity of the applicant's business. Check the "Other" box (and specify the applicant's principal activity) if none of the listed boxes applies. You must check a box.

Use line 15 to describe the applicant's principal line of business in more detail. For example, if you checked the "Construction" box in line 14, enter additional detail such as "General contractor for residential buildings" in line 15. An entry is required.

Construction. Check this box if the applicant is engaged in erecting buildings or engineering projects, (for example, streets, highways, bridges, tunnels). The term "Construction" also includes special trade contractors, (for example, plumbing, HVAC, electrical, carpentry, concrete, excavation, etc. contractors).

Real estate. Check this box if the applicant is engaged in renting or leasing real estate to others; managing, selling, buying or renting real estate for others; or providing related real estate services (for example, appraisal services).

Rental and leasing. Check this box if the applicant is engaged in providing tangible goods such as autos, computers, consumer goods, or industrial machinery and equipment to customers in return for a periodic rental or lease payment.

Manufacturing. Check this box if the applicant is engaged in the mechanical, physical, or chemical transformation of materials, substances, or components into new products. The assembling of component parts of manufactured products is also considered to be manufacturing.

Transportation & warehousing. Check this box if the applicant provides transportation of passengers or cargo; warehousing or storage of goods; scenic or sight-seeing transportation; or support activities related to transportation.

Finance & insurance. Check this box if the applicant is engaged in transactions involving the creation, liquidation, or change of ownership of financial assets and/or facilitating such financial transactions; underwriting annuities/insurance policies; facilitating such underwriting by selling insurance policies; or by providing other insurance or employee-benefit related services.

Health care and social assistance. Check this box if the applicant is engaged in providing physical, medical, or psychiatric care or providing social assistance activities such as youth centers, adoption agencies, individual/family services, temporary shelters, daycare, etc.

Accommodation & food services. Check this box if the applicant is engaged in providing customers with lodging, meal preparation, snacks, or beverages for immediate consumption.

Wholesale–agent/broker. Check this box if the applicant is engaged in arranging for the purchase or sale of goods owned by others or purchasing goods on a commission basis for goods traded in the wholesale market, usually between businesses.

Wholesale–other. Check this box if the applicant is engaged in selling goods in the wholesale market generally to other businesses for resale on their own account, goods used in production, or capital or durable nonconsumer goods.

Retail. Check this box if the applicant is engaged in selling merchandise to the general public from a fixed store; by direct, mail-order, or electronic sales; or by using vending machines.

Other. Check this box if the applicant is engaged in an activity not described above. Describe the applicant's principal business activity in the space provided.

Lines 16a-c. Check the applicable box in line 16a to indicate whether or not the entity (or individual) applying for an EIN was issued one previously. Complete lines 16b and 16c only if the "Yes" box in line 16a is checked. If the applicant previously applied for more than one EIN, write "See Attached" in the empty space in line 16a and attach a separate sheet providing the line 16b and 16c information for each EIN previously requested.

Third Party Designee. Complete this section only if you want to authorize the named individual to receive the entity's EIN and answer questions about the completion of Form SS-4. The designee's authority terminates at the time the EIN is assigned and released to the designee. You must complete the signature area for the authorization to be valid.

Signature. When required, the application must be signed by (a) the individual, if the applicant is an individual, (b) the president, vice president, or other principal officer, if the applicant is a corporation, (c) a responsible and duly authorized member or officer having knowledge of its affairs, if the applicant is a partnership, government entity, or other unincorporated organization, or (d) the fiduciary, if the applicant is a trust or an estate. Foreign applicants may have any duly-authorized person, (for example, division manager), sign Form SS-4.

Privacy Act and Paperwork Reduction Act Notice. We ask for the information on this form to carry out the Internal Revenue laws of the United States. We need it to comply with section 6109 and the regulations thereunder, which generally require the inclusion of an employer identification number (EIN) on certain returns, statements, or other documents filed with the Internal Revenue Service. If your entity is required to obtain an EIN, you are required to provide all of the information requested on this form. Information on this form may be used to determine which federal tax returns you are required to file and to provide you with related forms and publications.

We disclose this form to the Social Security Administration (SSA) for their use in determining compliance with applicable laws. We may give this information to the Department of Justice for use in civil and criminal litigation, and to the cities, states, and the District of Columbia for use in administering their tax laws. We may also disclose this information to other countries under a tax treaty, to federal and state agencies to enforce federal nontax criminal laws, and to federal law enforcement and intelligence agencies to combat terrorism.

We will be unable to issue an EIN to you unless you provide all of the requested information that applies to your entity. Providing false information could subject you to penalties.

You are not required to provide the information requested on a form that is subject to the Paperwork Reduction Act unless the form displays a valid OMB control number. Books or records relating to a form or its instructions must be retained as long as their contents may become material in the administration of any Internal Revenue law. Generally, tax returns and return information are confidential, as required by section 6103.

The time needed to complete and file this form will vary depending on individual circumstances. The estimated average time is:

Recordkeeping	8 hrs., 22 min.
Learning about the law or the form	42 min.
Preparing the form	52 min.
Copying, assembling, and sending the form to the IRS	- - - - -

If you have comments concerning the accuracy of these time estimates or suggestions for making this form simpler, we would be happy to hear from you. You can write to Internal Revenue Service, Tax Products Coordinating Committee, SE:W:CAR:MP:T:T:SP, IR-6406, 1111 Constitution Avenue, NW, Washington, DC 20224. Do not send the form to this address. Instead, see *Where to Fax or File* on page 2.

Form 8718
(Rev. June 2006)
Department of the Treasury
Internal Revenue Service

User Fee for Exempt Organization Determination Letter Request
▶ Attach this form to determination letter application.
(Form 8718 is NOT a determination letter application.)

For IRS Use Only	OMB No. 1545-1798
	Control number _____
	Amount paid _____
	User fee screener

1 Name of organization

2 Employer Identification Number

Caution. Do not attach Form 8718 to an application for a pension plan determination letter. Use Form 8717 instead.

3   Type of request   **Fee**

a ☐ Initial request for a determination letter for:

● An exempt organization that has had annual gross receipts averaging not more than $10,000 during the preceding 4 years or

● A new organization that anticipates gross receipts averaging not more than $10,000 during its first 4 years ▶ $300

Note. If you checked box 3a, you must complete the *Certification* below.

Certification

I certify that the annual gross receipts of --
                                                                        name of organization
have averaged (or are expected to average) not more than $10,000 during the preceding 4 (or the first 4) years of operation.

Signature ▶   Title ▶

b ☐ Initial request for a determination letter for:

● An exempt organization that has had annual gross receipts averaging more than $10,000 during the preceding 4 years or

● A new organization that anticipates gross receipts averaging more than $10,000 during its first 4 years . ▶ $750

c ☐ Group exemption letters . . . . ▶ $900

Instructions

The law requires payment of a user fee with each application for a determination letter. The user fees are listed on line 3 above. For more information, see Rev. Proc. 2006-8, 2006-1 I.R.B. 245, or latest annual update.

Check the box or boxes on line 3 for the type of application you are submitting. If you check box 3a, you must complete and sign the certification statement that appears under line 3a.

Attach to Form 8718 a check or money order payable to the "United States Treasury" for the full amount of the user fee. If you do not include the full amount, your application will be returned. Attach Form 8718 to your determination letter application.

Generally, the user fee will be refunded only if the Internal Revenue Service declines to issue a determination.

Where To File

Send the determination letter application and Form 8718 to:

Internal Revenue Service
P.O. Box 192
Covington, KY 41012-0192

Paperwork Reduction Act Notice. We ask for the information on this form to carry out the Internal Revenue laws of the United States. If you want your organization to be recognized as tax-exempt by the IRS, you are required to give us this information. We need it to determine whether the organization meets the legal requirements for tax-exempt status.

You are not required to provide the information requested on a form that is subject to the Paperwork Reduction Act unless the form displays a valid OMB control number. Books or records relating

to a form or its instructions must be retained as long as their contents may become material in the administration of any Internal Revenue law. The rules governing the confidentiality of Form 8718 are covered in section 6104.

The time needed to complete and file this form will vary depending on individual circumstances. The estimated average time is 5 minutes. If you have comments concerning the accuracy of this time estimate or suggestions for making this form simpler, we would be happy to hear from you. You can write to the Internal Revenue Service, Tax Products Coordinating Committee, SE:W:CAR:MP:T:T:SP, 1111 Constitution Ave. NW, IR-6406, Washington, DC 20224. Do not send this form to this address. Instead, see *Where To File* above.

Attach Check or Money Order Here

Cat. No. 64728Z

Printed on Recycled Paper

Form **8718** (6-2006)

This page intentionally left blank.

WAIVER OF NOTICE
OF THE ORGANIZATIONAL MEETING

of

_____

We, the undersigned incorporators named in the articles or certificate of incorporation of the above-named corporation, hereby agree and consent that the organization meeting of the corporation be held on the date and time and place stated below and hereby waive all notice of such meeting and of any adjournment thereof.

Place of meeting: _____

Date of Meeting: _____

Time of meeting: _____

Dated: _____

_____
Incorporator

_____
Incorporator

_____
Incorporator

This page intentionally left blank.

MINUTES OF THE ORGANIZATIONAL MEETING OF

INCORPORATORS AND DIRECTORS OF

_____

The organization meeting of the above corporation was held on _____, 20_____ at
_____ at _____ o'clock ___m.

The following persons were present:

_____   _____

_____   _____

_____   _____

The Waiver of Notice of this meeting was signed by all directors and incorporators named in the Articles of Incorporation and filed in the minute book.

The meeting was called to order by _____, an Incorporator named in the Articles of Incorporation. _____ was nominated and elected chairman and acted as such until relieved by the president. _____ was nominated and elected temporary secretary, and acted as such until relieved by the permanent secretary.

A copy of the Articles of Incorporation, which was filed with the Secretary of State of the State of _____ on _____, 20____, was examined by the Directors and Incorporators and filed in the minute book.

The election of officers for the coming year was then held and the following were duly nominated and elected by the Board of Directors to be the officers of the corporation, to serve until such time as their successors are elected and qualified:

President: _____

Vice President: _____

Secretary: _____

Treasurer: _____

The proposed Bylaws for the corporation were then presented to the meeting and discussed. Upon motion duly made, seconded, and carried, the Bylaws were adopted and added to the minute book.

A corporate seal for the corporation was then presented to the meeting and upon motion duly made, seconded, and carried, it was adopted as the seal of the corporation. An impression thereof was then made in the margin of these minutes.

The necessity of opening a bank account was then discussed and upon motion duly made, seconded, and carried, the following resolution was adopted:

RESOLVED that the corporation open bank accounts with _____ _____ and that the officers of the corporation are authorized to take such action as is necessary to open such accounts; that the bank's printed form of resolution is hereby adopted and incorporated into these minutes by reference and shall be placed in the minute book; that any _____ of the following persons shall have signature authority over the account:

_____   _____
_____   _____
_____   _____

The tax status of the corporation was then discussed and it was moved, seconded, and carried that the officers of the corporation take the necessary action to:

1.   Obtain an employer tax number by filing form SS-4,

2.   Apply for exemption from taxation under IRC § 501(c)(___).

The expenses of organizing the corporation were then discussed and it was moved, seconded, and carried that the corporation pay in full from the corporate funds the expenses and reimburse any advances made by the incorporators upon proof of payment.

The Directors named in the Articles of Incorporation then tendered their resignations, effective upon the adjournment of this meeting. Upon motion duly made, seconded, and carried, the following named persons were elected as Directors of the corporation, each to hold office until the next election of Directors, and until a successor of each shall have been elected and qualified.

_____
_____
_____
_____

There being no further business before the meeting, on motion duly made, seconded, and carried, the meeting adjourned.

DATED: _____

_____
President

_____
Secretary

RESOLUTION TO REIMBURSE EXPENSES

OF

_____

A _____ **CORPORATION**

RESOLVED that the corporation shall reimburse the following parties for the organizational expenses of the organizers of this corporation and that the corporation shall amortize these expenses as allowed by IRS regulations.

Name	Expense	Amount
_____	_____	$_____
_____	_____	$_____
_____	_____	$_____
_____	_____	$_____
_____	_____	$_____

Date: _____

_____

_____

_____

_____

This page intentionally left blank.

BANKING RESOLUTION OF

_____

The undersigned, being the corporate secretary of the above corporation, hereby certifies that on the _____ day of _____, 20___, the Board of Directors of the corporation adopted the following resolution:

RESOLVED that the corporation open bank accounts with _____ _____ and that the officers of the corporation are authorized to take such action as is necessary to open such accounts; that the bank's printed form of resolution is hereby adopted and incorporated into these minutes by reference and shall be placed in the minute book; and that any of the following persons shall have signature authority over the account:

_____   _____

_____   _____

and that said resolution has not been modified or rescinded.

Date: _____

_____
Corporate Secretary

(Seal)

This page intentionally left blank.

WAIVER OF NOTICE OF THE ANNUAL MEETING OF
THE BOARD OF DIRECTORS OF

_____

The undersigned, being all the Directors of the Corporation, hereby agree and consent that an annual meeting of the Board of Directors of the Corporation be held on the _____ day of _____, 20_____ at _____ o'clock ___m. at _____ and do hereby waive all notice whatsoever of such meeting and of any adjournment or adjournments thereof.

We do further agree and consent that any and all lawful business may be transacted at such meeting or at any adjournment or adjournments thereof as may be deemed advisable by the Directors present. Any business transacted at such meeting or at any adjournment or adjournments thereof shall be as valid and legal as if such meeting or adjourned meeting were held after notice.

Date: _____

_____
Director

_____
Director

_____
Director

_____
Director

This page intentionally left blank.

Minutes of the Annual Meeting of
the Board of Directors of

_____

The annual meeting of the Board of Directors of the Corporation was held on the date and at the time and place set forth in the written waiver of notice signed by the Directors, and attached to the Minutes of this meeting.

The following were present, being all the directors of the Corporation:

_____   _____

_____   _____

The meeting was called to order and it was moved, seconded, and unanimously carried that _____ act as Chairman and that _____ act as Secretary.

The minutes of the last meeting of the Board of Directors, which was held on _____, 20___, were read and approved by the Board.

Upon motion duly made, seconded, and carried, the following were elected officers for the following year and until their successors are elected and qualify:

President: _____
Vice President: _____
Secretary: _____
Treasurer: _____

There being no further business to come before the meeting, upon motion duly made, seconded, and unanimously carried, it was adjourned.

_____
Secretary

Directors:

_____

_____

_____

_____

This page intentionally left blank.

WAIVER OF NOTICE OF SPECIAL MEETING OF
THE BOARD OF DIRECTORS OF

_____

The undersigned, being all the Directors of the Corporation, hereby agree and consent that a special meeting of the Board of Directors of the Corporation be held on the _____ day of _____, 20___ at ___ o'clock ___m. at _____ and do hereby waive all notice whatsoever of such meeting and of any adjournment or adjournments thereof.

The purpose of the meeting is:

We do further agree and consent that any and all lawful business may be transacted at such meeting or at any adjournment or adjournments thereof as may be deemed advisable by the Directors present. Any business transacted at such meeting or at any adjournment or adjournments thereof shall be as valid and legal as if such meeting or adjourned meeting were held after notice.

Date: _____

_____
Director

_____
Director

_____
Director

_____
Director

This page intentionally left blank.

MINUTES OF SPECIAL MEETING OF
THE BOARD OF DIRECTORS OF

_____

A special meeting of the Board of Directors of the Corporation was held on the date and at the time and place set forth in the written waiver of notice signed by the directors and attached to the Minutes of this meeting.

The following were present, being all the directors of the Corporation:

_____   _____

_____   _____

The meeting was called to order and it was moved, seconded, and unanimously carried that _____ act as Chairman and that _____ act as Secretary.

The minutes of the last meeting of the Board of Directors, which was held on _____, 20___, were read and approved by the Board.

Upon motion duly made, seconded, and carried, the following resolution was adopted:

There being no further business to come before the meeting, upon motion duly made, seconded, and unanimously carried, it was adjourned.

_____
Secretary

Directors:

_____

_____

_____

_____

This page intentionally left blank.

CHANGE OF REGISTERED AGENT AND/OR REGISTERED OFFICE

1. The name of the corporation is:

2. The street address of the current registered office is:

3. The new address of the registered office is to be:

4. The current registered agent is:

5. The new registered agent is:

6. The street address of the registered office and the street address of the business address of the registered agent are identical.

7. Such change was authorized by resolution duly adopted by the Board of Directors of the corporation or by an officer of the corporation so authorized by the board of directors.

_____
Secretary

Having been named as registered agent and to accept service of process for the above stated corporation at the place designated in this certificate, I hereby accept the appointment as registered agent and agree to act in this capacity. I further agree to comply with the provisions of all statutes relating to the proper and complete performance of my duties, and am familiar with and accept the obligations of my position as registered agent.

_____
Registered Agent

This page intentionally left blank.

APPLICATION FOR EMPLOYMENT

We consider applicants for all positions without regard to race, color, religion, sex, national origin, age, marital or veteran status, the presence of a non-job-related medical condition or handicap, or any other legally protected status. Proof of citizenship or immigration status will be required upon employment.

(PLEASE TYPE OR PRINT)

Position Applied For   Date of Application

Last Name   First Name   Middle Name or Initial

Is there any other information regarding your name that will be needed to check work or school records? ❑ Yes ❑ No

Address   *Number Street*   *City*   *State*   *Zip Code*

Telephone Number(s) [indicate home or work]   Social Security Number

Date Available:_____   Are you available: ❑ Full Time   ❑ Part Time   ❑ Weekends

Are you 18 years of age or older?   ❑   Yes   ❑   No

Have you been convicted of a felony within the past 7 years?   ❑   Yes   ❑   No

Conviction will not necessarily disqualify an applicant from employment.
If Yes, attach explanation.
Can you produce documents proving you are authorized to work in the United States? ❑ Yes   ❑ No

Education

	High School	Undergraduate	Graduate
School Name & Location			
Years Completed	1 2 3 4	1 2 3 4	1 2 3 4
Diploma / Degree			
Course of Study			

State any additional information you feel may be helpful to us in considering your application (such as any specialized training; skills; apprenticeships; honors received; professional, trade, business or civic organizations or activities; job-related military training or experience; foreign language abilities; etc.)

_____

_____

_____

_____

Employment Experience

Start with your present or last job. Include any job-related military service assignments and voluntary activities. You may exclude organizations which indicate race, color, religion, gender, national origin, handicap, or other protected status.

1.	Employer Name & Address	Dates Employed	Job Title/Duties
		Hourly Rate/Salary	
	May we contact this employer? ❑ Yes ❑ No	Hours Per Week	
	Employer Phone		
	Supervisor		
	Reason for Leaving		
2.	Employer Name & Address	Dates Employed	Job Title/Duties
		Hourly Rate/Salary	
	Employer Phone	Hours Per Week	
	Supervisor		
	Reason for Leaving		
3.	Employer Name & Address	Dates Employed	Job Title/Duties
		Hourly Rate/Salary	
	Employer Phone	Hours Per Week	
	Supervisor		
	Reason for Leaving		

References: Name   Occupation   Address   Phone #   Relationship   Years known

1. _____

2. _____

3. _____

If you need additional space, continue on a separate sheet of paper.

Applicant's Statement

I certify that the information given on this application is true and complete to the best of my knowledge. I authorize investigation of all statements contained in this application, and understand that false or misleading information given in my application or interview(s) may result in discharge.

I understand and acknowledge that, unless otherwise defined by applicable law, any employment relationship with this organization is "at will," which means that I may resign at any time and the employer may discharge me at any time with or without cause. I further understand that this "at will" employment relationship may not be changed orally, by any written document, or by conduct, unless such change is specifically acknowledged in writing by an authorized executive of this organization.

_____   _____

Signature of Applicant   Date

AUTHORIZATION TO RELEASE EMPLOYMENT INFORMATION

To:

The undersigned applicant hereby authorizes you to release records of his/her dates of employment, job title, salary, and reason for leaving your company to:

_____

_____

_____

_____

Applicant's signature

This page intentionally left blank.

VERIFICATION OF EDUCATION

To:

The undersigned applicant hereby authorizes you to release records verifying his/her education at your institution to:

_____

_____

_____

_____

Applicant's signature

This page intentionally left blank.

VERIFICATION OF LICENSURE

To:

The undersigned applicant hereby authorizes you to verify that he/she is licensed as a _____

that such license has been valid since _____ and is still valid.

_____

_____

_____

_____

Applicant's signature

This page intentionally left blank.

U.S. Department of Justice
Immigration and Naturalization Service

OMB No. 1115-0136

Employment Eligibility Verification

Please read instructions carefully before completing this form. The instructions must be available during completion of this form. ANTI-DISCRIMINATION NOTICE: It is illegal to discriminate against work eligible individuals. Employers CANNOT specify which document(s) they will accept from an employee. The refusal to hire an individual because of a future expiration date may also constitute illegal discrimination.

Section 1. Employee Information and Verification. To be completed and signed by employee at the time employment begins.

Print Name: Last	First	Middle Initial	Maiden Name

Address (Street Name and Number)	Apt. #	Date of Birth (month/day/year)

City	State	Zip Code	Social Security #

I am aware that federal law provides for imprisonment and/or fines for false statements or use of false documents in connection with the completion of this form.

I attest, under penalty of perjury, that I am (check one of the following):

☐ A citizen or national of the United States
☐ A Lawful Permanent Resident (Alien # A
☐ An alien authorized to work until ___/___/___
(Alien # or Admission #)

Employee's Signature
[signature]

Date (month/day/year)

Preparer and/or Translator Certification. (To be completed and signed if Section 1 is prepared by a person other than the employee.) I attest, under penalty of perjury, that I have assisted in the completion of this form and that to the best of my knowledge the information is true and correct.

Preparer's/Translator's Signature [signature]	Print Name
Address (Street Name and Number, City, State, Zip Code)	Date (month/day/year)

Section 2. Employer Review and Verification. To be completed and signed by employer. Examine one document from List A OR examine one document from List B and one from List C, as listed on the reverse of this form, and record the title, number and expiration date, if any, of the document(s)

List A	OR	List B	AND	List C
Document title:_____		_____		_____
Issuing authority: _____		_____		_____
Document #: _____		_____		_____
Expiration Date (if any): ___/___/___		___/___/___		___/___/___
Document #: _____				
Expiration Date (if any): ___/___/___				

CERTIFICATION - I attest, under penalty of perjury, that I have examined the document(s) presented by the above-named employee, that the above-listed document(s) appear to be genuine and to relate to the employee named, that the employee began employment on (month/day/year) ___/___/___ **and that to the best of my knowledge the employee is eligible to work in the United States. (State employment agencies may omit the date the employee began employment.)**

Signature of Employer or Authorized Representative [signature	Print Name	Title
Business or Organization Name	Address (Street Name and Number, City, State, Zip Code)	Date (month/day/year)

Section 3. Updating and Reverification. To be completed and signed by employer.

A. New Name (if applicable)	B. Date of rehire (month/day/year) (if applicable)

C. If employee's previous grant of work authorization has expired, provide the information below for the document that establishes current employment eligibility.

Document Title:_____   Document #: _____   Expiration Date (if any): ___/___/___

I attest, under penalty of perjury, that to the best of my knowledge, this employee is eligible to work in the United States, and if the employee presented document(s), the document(s) I have examined appear to be genuine and to relate to the individual.

Signature of Employer or Authorized Representative [signature]	Date (month/day/year)

U.S. Department of Justice
Immigration and Naturalization Service

OMB No. 1115-0136

Employment Eligibility Verification

INSTRUCTIONS
PLEASE READ ALL INSTRUCTIONS CAREFULLY BEFORE COMPLETING THIS FORM.

Anti-Discrimination Notice. It is illegal to discriminate against any individual (other than an alien not authorized to work in the U.S.) in hiring, discharging, or recruiting or referring for a fee because of that individual's national origin or citizenship status. It is illegal to discriminate against work eligible individuals. Employers **CANNOT** specify which document(s) they will accept from an employee. The refusal to hire an individual because of a future expiration date may also constitute illegal discrimination.

Section 1 - Employee.
All employees, citizens and noncitizens, hired after November 6, 1986, must complete Section 1 of this form at the time of hire, which is the actual beginning of employment. **The employer is responsible for ensuring that Section 1 is timely and properly completed.**

Preparer/Translator Certification. The Preparer/Translator Certification must be completed if Section 1 is prepared by a person other than the employee. A preparer/translator may be used only when the employee is unable to complete Section 1 on his/her own. However, the employee must still sign Section 1.

Section 2 - Employer.
For the purpose of completing this form, the term "employer" includes those recruiters and referrers for a fee who are agricultural associations, agricultural employers or farm labor contractors.

Employers must complete Section 2 by examining evidence of identity and employment eligibility within three (3) business days of the date employment begins. If employees are authorized to work, but are unable to present the required document(s) within three business days, they must present a receipt for the application of the document(s) within three business days and the actual document(s) within ninety (90) days. However, if employers hire individuals for a duration of less than three business days, Section 2 must be completed at the time employment begins. **Employers must record: 1)** document title; **2)** issuing authority; **3)** document number, **4)** expiration date, if any; and **5)** the date employment begins. Employers must sign and date the certification. Employees must present original documents. Employers may, but are not required to, photocopy the document(s) presented. These photocopies may only be used for the verification process and must be retained with the I-9. **However, employers are still responsible for completing the I-9.**

Section 3 - Updating and Reverification.
Employers must complete Section 3 when updating and/or reverifying the I-9. Employers must reverify employment eligibility of their employees on or before the expiration date recorded in Section 1. Employers **CANNOT** specify which document(s) they will accept from an employee.

- If an employee's name has changed at the time this form is being updated/ reverified, complete Block A.

- If an employee is rehired within three (3) years of the date this form was originally completed and the employee is still eligible to be employed on the same basis as previously indicated on this form (updating), complete Block B and the signature block.

- If an employee is rehired within three (3) years of the date this form was originally completed and the employee's work authorization has expired **or** if a current employee's work authorization is about to expire (reverification), complete Block B and:
  - examine any document that reflects that the employee is authorized to work in the U.S. (see List A or C),
  - record the document title, document number and expiration date (if any) in Block C, and complete the signature block.

Photocopying and Retaining Form I-9. A blank I-9 may be reproduced, provided both sides are copied. The Instructions must be available to all employees completing this form. Employers must retain completed I-9s for three (3) years after the date of hire or one (1) year after the date employment ends, whichever is later.

For more detailed information, you may refer to the INS Handbook for Employers, (Form M-274). You may obtain the handbook at your local INS office.

Privacy Act Notice. The authority for collecting this information is the Immigration Reform and Control Act of 1986, Pub. L. 99-603 (8 USC 1324a).

This information is for employers to verify the eligibility of individuals for employment to preclude the unlawful hiring, or recruiting or referring for a fee, of aliens who are not authorized to work in the United States.

This information will be used by employers as a record of their basis for determining eligibility of an employee to work in the United States. The form will be kept by the employer and made available for inspection by officials of the U.S. Immigration and Naturalization Service, the Department of Labor and the Office of Special Counsel for Immigration Related Unfair Employment Practices.

Submission of the information required in this form is voluntary. However, an individual may not begin employment unless this form is completed, since employers are subject to civil or criminal penalties if they do not comply with the Immigration Reform and Control Act of 1986.

Reporting Burden. We try to create forms and instructions that are accurate, can be easily understood and which impose the least possible burden on you to provide us with information. Often this is difficult because some immigration laws are very complex. Accordingly, the reporting burden for this collection of information is computed as follows: **1)** learning about this form, 5 minutes; **2)** completing the form, 5 minutes; and **3)** assembling and filing (recordkeeping) the form, 5 minutes, for an average of 15 minutes per response. If you have comments regarding the accuracy of this burden estimate, or suggestions for making this form simpler, you can write to the Immigration and Naturalization Service, HQPDI, 425 I Street, N.W., Room 4307r, Washington, DC 20536. OMB No. 1115-0136.

Form SS-8
(Rev. June 2003)
Department of the Treasury
Internal Revenue Service

Determination of Worker Status for Purposes of Federal Employment Taxes and Income Tax Withholding

OMB No. 1545-0004

Name of firm (or person) for whom the worker performed services	Worker's name

Firm's address (include street address, apt. or suite no., city, state, and ZIP code)	Worker's address (include street address, apt. or suite no., city, state, and ZIP code)

Trade name	Telephone number (include area code) ( )	Worker's social security number

Telephone number (include area code) ( )	Firm's employer identification number	Worker's employer identification number (if any)

If the worker is paid by a firm other than the one listed on this form for these services, enter the name, address, and employer identification number of the payer.

Important Information Needed To Process Your Request

We must have your permission to disclose your name and the information on this form and any attachments to other parties involved with this request. **Do we have your permission to disclose this information?** . . . . ☐ Yes ☐ No
If you answered "No" or did not mark a box, we will not process your request and will not issue a determination.

You must answer ALL items OR mark them "Unknown" or "Does not apply." If you need more space, attach another sheet.

A This form is being completed by: ☐ Firm ☐ Worker; for services performed _____ to _____ .
(beginning date)   (ending date)

B Explain your reason(s) for filing this form (e.g., you received a bill from the IRS, you believe you received a Form 1099 or Form W-2 erroneously, you are unable to get worker's compensation benefits, you were audited or are being audited by the IRS). ----------------------
----

C Total number of workers who performed or are performing the same or similar services _____ .

D How did the worker obtain the job? ☐ Application ☐ Bid ☐ Employment Agency ☐ Other (specify) _____ .

E Attach copies of all supporting documentation (contracts, invoices, memos, Forms W-2, Forms 1099, IRS closing agreements, IRS rulings, etc.). In addition, please inform us of any current or past litigation concerning the worker's status. If no income reporting forms (Form 1099-MISC or W-2) were furnished to the worker, enter the amount of income earned for the year(s) at issue $ _____ .

F Describe the firm's business. --

G Describe the work done by the worker and provide the worker's job title. ---------------------
----

H Explain why you believe the worker is an employee or an independent contractor. ------------------
----

I Did the worker perform services for the firm before getting this position? . . . . ☐ Yes ☐ No ☐ N/A
If "Yes," what were the dates of the prior service? ----------------------------
If "Yes," explain the differences, if any, between the current and prior service. --------------------
----

J If the work is done under a written agreement between the firm and the worker, attach a copy (preferably signed by both parties). Describe the terms and conditions of the work arrangement. ------------------------
----

Part I   Behavioral Control

1 What specific training and/or instruction is the worker given by the firm? ....

2 How does the worker receive work assignments? ....

3 Who determines the methods by which the assignments are performed? ....

4 Who is the worker required to contact if problems or complaints arise and who is responsible for their resolution? ....

5 What types of reports are required from the worker? Attach examples. ....

6 Describe the worker's daily routine (i.e., schedule, hours, etc.). ....

7 At what location(s) does the worker perform services (e.g., firm's premises, own shop or office, home, customer's location, etc.)? ....

8 Describe any meetings the worker is required to attend and any penalties for not attending (e.g., sales meetings, monthly meetings, staff meetings, etc.). ....

9 Is the worker required to provide the services personally?   . . . . ☐ **Yes**   ☐ **No**

10 If substitutes or helpers are needed, who hires them? ....

11 If the worker hires the substitutes or helpers, is approval required?   . . . . ☐ **Yes**   ☐ **No**
    If "Yes," by whom? ....

12 Who pays the substitutes or helpers? ....

13 Is the worker reimbursed if the worker pays the substitutes or helpers?   . . . . ☐ **Yes**   ☐ **No**
    If "Yes," by whom?

Part II   Financial Control

1 List the supplies, equipment, materials, and property provided by each party:
    The firm ....
    The worker ....
    Other party ....

2 Does the worker lease equipment?   . . . . ☐ **Yes**   ☐ **No**
    If "Yes," what are the terms of the lease? (Attach a copy or explanatory statement.) ....

3 What expenses are incurred by the worker in the performance of services for the firm? ....

4 Specify which, if any, expenses are reimbursed by:
    The firm ....
    Other party ....

5 Type of pay the worker receives: ☐ Salary   ☐ Commission   ☐ Hourly Wage   ☐ Piece Work
    ☐ Lump Sum   ☐ Other (specify) ....
    If type of pay is commission, and the firm guarantees a minimum amount of pay, specify amount $ _____ .

6 Is the worker allowed a drawing account for advances? . . . . ☐ **Yes**   ☐ **No**
    If "Yes," how often? ....
    Specify any restrictions. ....

7 Whom does the customer pay? . . . . ☐ Firm   ☐ Worker
    If worker, does the worker pay the total amount to the firm?   ☐ **Yes**   ☐ **No**   If "No," explain. ....

8 Does the firm carry worker's compensation insurance on the worker?   . . . . ☐ **Yes**   ☐ **No**

9 What economic loss or financial risk, if any, can the worker incur beyond the normal loss of salary (e.g., loss or damage of equipment, material, etc.)? ....

Part III **Relationship of the Worker and Firm**

1 List the benefits available to the worker (e.g., paid vacations, sick pay, pensions, bonuses). ─────────────────────

2 Can the relationship be terminated by either party without incurring liability or penalty? . . . . ☐ **Yes** ☐ **No**
If "No," explain your answer. ──

3 Does the worker perform similar services for others? . . . . ☐ **Yes** ☐ **No**
If "Yes," is the worker required to get approval from the firm? . . . . ☐ **Yes** ☐ **No**

4 Describe any agreements prohibiting competition between the worker and the firm while the worker is performing services or during any later period. Attach any available documentation. ──────────────────────────────

5 Is the worker a member of a union? . . . . ☐ **Yes** ☐ **No**

6 What type of advertising, if any, does the worker do (e.g., a business listing in a directory, business cards, etc.)? Provide copies, if applicable. ───────────────────

7 If the worker assembles or processes a product at home, who provides the materials and instructions or pattern? ──────

8 What does the worker do with the finished product (e.g., return it to the firm, provide it to another party, or sell it)? ──────

9 How does the firm represent the worker to its customers (e.g., employee, partner, representative, or contractor)? ──────

10 If the worker no longer performs services for the firm, how did the relationship end? ──────────────────────

Part IV **For Service Providers or Salespersons-** Complete this part if the worker provided a service directly to customers or is a salesperson.

1 What are the worker's responsibilities in soliciting new customers? ──────────────────────────

2 Who provides the worker with leads to prospective customers? ───────────────────────────

3 Describe any reporting requirements pertaining to the leads. ───────────────────────────

4 What terms and conditions of sale, if any, are required by the firm? ─────────────────────────

5 Are orders submitted to and subject to approval by the firm? . . . . ☐ **Yes** ☐ **No**

6 Who determines the worker's territory? ─────────────────────────────────────

7 Did the worker pay for the privilege of serving customers on the route or in the territory? . . . . ☐ **Yes** ☐ **No**
If "Yes," whom did the worker pay? ──────────────────────────────────────
If "Yes," how much did the worker pay? . . . . $ ──────── .

8 Where does the worker sell the product (e.g., in a home, retail establishment, etc.)? ───────────────────

9 List the product and/or services distributed by the worker (e.g., meat, vegetables, fruit, bakery products, beverages, or laundry or dry cleaning services). If more than one type of product and/or service is distributed, specify the principal one. ──────────

10 Does the worker sell life insurance full time? . . . . ☐ **Yes** ☐ **No**

11 Does the worker sell other types of insurance for the firm? . . . . ☐ **Yes** ☐ **No**
If "Yes," enter the percentage of the worker's total working time spent in selling other types of insurance. . . . ──────── %

12 If the worker solicits orders from wholesalers, retailers, contractors, or operators of hotels, restaurants, or other similar establishments, enter the percentage of the worker's time spent in the solicitation. . . . . ──────── %

13 Is the merchandise purchased by the customers for resale or use in their business operations? . . . . ☐ **Yes** ☐ **No**
Describe the merchandise and state whether it is equipment installed on the customers' premises. ─────────────

Part V **Signature** (see page 4)

Under penalties of perjury, I declare that I have examined this request, including accompanying documents, and to the best of my knowledge and belief, the facts presented are true, correct, and complete.

Signature ▶ ────────────── Title ▶ ────────────── Date ▶ ──────────
(Type or print name below)

This page intentionally left blank.

Form **1023** (Rev. June 2006) Department of the Treasury Internal Revenue Service	**Application for Recognition of Exemption** **Under Section 501(c)(3) of the Internal Revenue Code**	OMB No. 1545-0056 **Note:** *If exempt status is approved, this application will be open for public inspection.*

*Use the instructions to complete this application and for a definition of all **bold** items.* For additional help, call IRS Exempt Organizations Customer Account Services toll-free at 1-877-829-5500. Visit our website at **www.irs.gov** for forms and publications. If the required information and documents are not submitted with payment of the appropriate user fee, the application may be returned to you.

Attach additional sheets to this application if you need more space to answer fully. Put your name and EIN on each sheet and identify each answer by Part and line number. Complete Parts I - XI of Form 1023 and submit only those Schedules (A through H) that apply to you.

Part I   Identification of Applicant

1 Full name of organization (exactly as it appears in your **organizing document**)

2 c/o Name (if applicable)

3 **Mailing address** (Number and street) (see instructions)   Room/Suite

4 Employer Identification Number (EIN)

City or town, state or country, and ZIP + 4

5 Month the annual accounting period ends (01 – 12)

6 Primary contact (officer, director, trustee, or **authorized representative**)

  a Name:

  b Phone:

  c Fax: (optional)

7 Are you represented by an authorized representative, such as an attorney or accountant? If "Yes," provide the authorized representative's name, and the name and address of the authorized representative's firm. Include a completed Form 2848, *Power of Attorney and Declaration of Representative,* with your application if you would like us to communicate with your representative.   ☐ Yes   ☐ No

8 Was a person who is not one of your officers, directors, trustees, employees, or an authorized representative listed in line 7, paid, or promised payment, to help plan, manage, or advise you about the structure or activities of your organization, or about your financial or tax matters? If "Yes," provide the person's name, the name and address of the person's firm, the amounts paid or promised to be paid, and describe that person's role.   ☐ Yes   ☐ No

9a Organization's website:

  b Organization's email: (optional)

10 Certain organizations are not required to file an information return (Form 990 or Form 990-EZ). If you are granted tax-exemption, are you claiming to be excused from filing Form 990 or Form 990-EZ? If "Yes," explain. See the instructions for a description of organizations not required to file Form 990 or Form 990-EZ.   ☐ Yes   ☐ No

11 Date incorporated if a corporation, or formed, if other than a corporation.   (MM/DD/YYYY)   /   /

12 Were you formed under the laws of a **foreign country?** If "Yes," state the country.   ☐ Yes   ☐ No

For Paperwork Reduction Act Notice, see page 24 of the instructions.   Cat. No. 17133K   Form **1023** (Rev. 6-2006)

Form 1023 (Rev. 6-2006)   Name: EIN: —   Page **2**

Part II   Organizational Structure

You must be a corporation (including a limited liability company), an unincorporated association, or a trust to be tax exempt. (See instructions.) **DO NOT file this form unless you can check "Yes" on lines 1, 2, 3, or 4.**

1   Are you a **corporation**? If "Yes," attach a copy of your articles of incorporation showing **certification of filing** with the appropriate state agency. Include copies of any amendments to your articles and be sure they also show state filing certification.   ☐ **Yes**   ☐ **No**

2   Are you a **limited liability company (LLC)**? If "Yes," attach a copy of your articles of organization showing certification of filing with the appropriate state agency. Also, if you adopted an operating agreement, attach a copy. Include copies of any amendments to your articles and be sure they show state filing certification. Refer to the instructions for circumstances when an LLC should not file its own exemption application.   ☐ **Yes**   ☐ **No**

3   Are you an **unincorporated association**? If "Yes," attach a copy of your articles of association, constitution, or other similar organizing document that is dated and includes at least two signatures. Include signed and dated copies of any amendments.   ☐ **Yes**   ☐ **No**

4a Are you a **trust**? If "Yes," attach a signed and dated copy of your trust agreement. Include signed and dated copies of any amendments.   ☐ **Yes**   ☐ **No**

b   Have you been funded? If "No," explain how you are formed without anything of value placed in trust.   ☐ **Yes**   ☐ **No**

5   Have you adopted **bylaws**? If "Yes," attach a current copy showing date of adoption. If "No," explain how your officers, directors, or trustees are selected.   ☐ **Yes**   ☐ **No**

Part III   Required Provisions in Your Organizing Document

The following questions are designed to ensure that when you file this application, your organizing document contains the required provisions to meet the organizational test under section 501(c)(3). Unless you can check the boxes in both lines 1 and 2, your organizing document does not meet the organizational test. **DO NOT file this application until you have amended your organizing document.** Submit your original and amended organizing documents (showing state filing certification if you are a corporation or an LLC) with your application.

1   Section 501(c)(3) requires that your organizing document state your exempt purpose(s), such as charitable, religious, educational, and/or scientific purposes. Check the box to confirm that your organizing document meets this requirement. Describe specifically where your organizing document meets this requirement, such as a reference to a particular article or section in your organizing document. Refer to the instructions for exempt purpose language. Location of Purpose Clause (Page, Article, and Paragraph): _____   ☐

2a Section 501(c)(3) requires that upon dissolution of your organization, your remaining assets must be used exclusively for exempt purposes, such as charitable, religious, educational, and/or scientific purposes. Check the box on line 2a to confirm that your organizing document meets this requirement by express provision for the distribution of assets upon dissolution. If you rely on state law for your dissolution provision, do not check the box on line 2a and go to line 2c.   ☐

2b If you checked the box on line 2a, specify the location of your dissolution clause (Page, Article, and Paragraph). Do not complete line 2c if you checked box 2a.   _____

2c See the instructions for information about the operation of state law in your particular state. Check this box if you rely on operation of state law for your dissolution provision and indicate the state: _____   ☐

Part IV   Narrative Description of Your Activities

Using an attachment, describe your *past, present,* and *planned* activities in a narrative. If you believe that you have already provided some of this information in response to other parts of this application, you may summarize that information here and refer to the specific parts of the application for supporting details. You may also attach representative copies of newsletters, brochures, or similar documents for supporting details to this narrative. Remember that if this application is approved, it will be open for public inspection. Therefore, your narrative description of activities should be thorough and accurate. Refer to the instructions for information that must be included in your description.

Part V   Compensation and Other Financial Arrangements With Your Officers, Directors, Trustees, Employees, and Independent Contractors

1a List the names, titles, and mailing addresses of all of your officers, directors, and trustees. For each person listed, state their total annual **compensation**, or proposed compensation, for all services to the organization, whether as an officer, employee, or other position. Use actual figures, if available. Enter "none" if no compensation is or will be paid. If additional space is needed, attach a separate sheet. Refer to the instructions for information on what to include as compensation.

Name	Title	Mailing address	Compensation amount (annual actual or estimated)

Form 1023 (Rev. 6-2006)   Name: EIN: –   Page **3**

| **Part V** | Compensation and Other Financial Arrangements With Your Officers, Directors, Trustees, Employees, and Independent Contractors *(Continued)* |

b List the names, titles, and mailing addresses of each of your five highest compensated employees who receive or will receive compensation of more than $50,000 per year. Use the actual figure, if available. Refer to the instructions for information on what to include as compensation. Do not include officers, directors, or trustees listed in line 1a.

Name	Title	Mailing address	Compensation amount (annual actual or estimated)

c List the names, names of businesses, and mailing addresses of your five highest compensated **independent contractors** that receive or will receive compensation of more than $50,000 per year. Use the actual figure, if available. Refer to the instructions for information on what to include as compensation.

Name	Title	Mailing address	Compensation amount (annual actual or estimated)

The following "Yes" or "No" questions relate to *past, present, or planned* relationships, transactions, or agreements with your officers, directors, trustees, highest compensated employees, and highest compensated independent contractors listed in lines 1a, 1b, and 1c.

2a Are any of your officers, directors, or trustees **related** to each other through **family** or **business relationships**? If "Yes," identify the individuals and explain the relationship.   ☐ **Yes**   ☐ **No**

b Do you have a business relationship with any of your officers, directors, or trustees other than through their position as an officer, director, or trustee? If "Yes," identify the individuals and describe the business relationship with each of your officers, directors, or trustees.   ☐ **Yes**   ☐ **No**

c Are any of your officers, directors, or trustees related to your highest compensated employees or highest compensated independent contractors listed on lines 1b or 1c through family or business relationships? If "Yes," identify the individuals and explain the relationship.   ☐ **Yes**   ☐ **No**

3a For each of your officers, directors, trustees, highest compensated employees, and highest compensated independent contractors listed on lines 1a, 1b, or 1c, attach a list showing their name, qualifications, average hours worked, and duties.

b Do any of your officers, directors, trustees, highest compensated employees, and highest compensated independent contractors listed on lines 1a, 1b, or 1c receive compensation from any other organizations, whether tax exempt or taxable, that are related to you through **common control**? If "Yes," identify the individuals, explain the relationship between you and the other organization, and describe the compensation arrangement.   ☐ **Yes**   ☐ **No**

4 In establishing the compensation for your officers, directors, trustees, highest compensated employees, and highest compensated independent contractors listed on lines 1a, 1b, and 1c, the following practices are recommended, although they are not required to obtain exemption. Answer "Yes" to all the practices you use.

a Do you or will the individuals that approve compensation arrangements follow a conflict of interest policy?   ☐ **Yes**   ☐ **No**
b Do you or will you approve compensation arrangements in advance of paying compensation?   ☐ **Yes**   ☐ **No**
c Do you or will you document in writing the date and terms of approved compensation arrangements?   ☐ **Yes**   ☐ **No**

Part V   **Compensation and Other Financial Arrangements With Your Officers, Directors, Trustees, Employees, and Independent Contractors** *(Continued)*

d Do you or will you record in writing the decision made by each individual who decided or voted on compensation arrangements? ☐ Yes ☐ No

e Do you or will you approve compensation arrangements based on information about compensation paid by **similarly situated** taxable or tax-exempt organizations for similar services, current compensation surveys compiled by independent firms, or actual written offers from similarly situated organizations? Refer to the instructions for Part V, lines 1a, 1b, and 1c, for information on what to include as compensation. ☐ Yes ☐ No

f Do you or will you record in writing both the information on which you relied to base your decision and its source? ☐ Yes ☐ No

g If you answered "No" to any item on lines 4a through 4f, describe how you set compensation that is **reasonable** for your officers, directors, trustees, highest compensated employees, and highest compensated independent contractors listed in Part V, lines 1a, 1b, and 1c.

5a Have you adopted a **conflict of interest policy** consistent with the sample conflict of interest policy in Appendix A to the instructions? If "Yes," provide a copy of the policy and explain how the policy has been adopted, such as by resolution of your governing board. If "No," answer lines 5b and 5c. ☐ Yes ☐ No

b What procedures will you follow to assure that persons who have a conflict of interest will not have influence over you for setting their own compensation?

c What procedures will you follow to assure that persons who have a conflict of interest will not have influence over you regarding business deals with themselves?

Note: A conflict of interest policy is recommended though it is not required to obtain exemption. Hospitals, see Schedule C, Section I, line 14.

6a Do you or will you compensate any of your officers, directors, trustees, highest compensated employees, and highest compensated independent contractors listed in lines 1a, 1b, or 1c through **non-fixed payments**, such as discretionary bonuses or revenue-based payments? If "Yes," describe all non-fixed compensation arrangements, including how the amounts are determined, who is eligible for such arrangements, whether you place a limitation on total compensation, and how you determine or will determine that you pay no more than reasonable compensation for services. Refer to the instructions for Part V, lines 1a, 1b, and 1c, for information on what to include as compensation. ☐ Yes ☐ No

b Do you or will you compensate any of your employees, other than your officers, directors, trustees, or your five highest compensated employees who receive or will receive compensation of more than $50,000 per year, through non-fixed payments, such as discretionary bonuses or revenue-based payments? If "Yes," describe all non-fixed compensation arrangements, including how the amounts are or will be determined, who is or will be eligible for such arrangements, whether you place or will place a limitation on total compensation, and how you determine or will determine that you pay no more than reasonable compensation for services. Refer to the instructions for Part V, lines 1a, 1b, and 1c, for information on what to include as compensation. ☐ Yes ☐ No

7a Do you or will you purchase any goods, services, or assets from any of your officers, directors, trustees, highest compensated employees, or highest compensated independent contractors listed in lines 1a, 1b, or 1c? If "Yes," describe any such purchase that you made or intend to make, from whom you make or will make such purchases, how the terms are or will be negotiated at **arm's length**, and explain how you determine or will determine that you pay no more than **fair market value**. Attach copies of any written contracts or other agreements relating to such purchases. ☐ Yes ☐ No

b Do you or will you sell any goods, services, or assets to any of your officers, directors, trustees, highest compensated employees, or highest compensated independent contractors listed in lines 1a, 1b, or 1c? If "Yes," describe any such sales that you made or intend to make, to whom you make or will make such sales, how the terms are or will be negotiated at arm's length, and explain how you determine or will determine you are or will be paid at least fair market value. Attach copies of any written contracts or other agreements relating to such sales. ☐ Yes ☐ No

8a Do you or will you have any leases, contracts, loans, or other agreements with your officers, directors, trustees, highest compensated employees, or highest compensated independent contractors listed in lines 1a, 1b, or 1c? If "Yes," provide the information requested in lines 8b through 8f. ☐ Yes ☐ No

b Describe any written or oral arrangements that you made or intend to make.

c Identify with whom you have or will have such arrangements.

d Explain how the terms are or will be negotiated at arm's length.

e Explain how you determine you pay no more than fair market value or you are paid at least fair market value.

f Attach copies of any signed leases, contracts, loans, or other agreements relating to such arrangements.

9a Do you or will you have any leases, contracts, loans, or other agreements with any organization in which any of your officers, directors, or trustees are also officers, directors, or trustees, or in which any individual officer, director, or trustee owns more than a 35% interest? If "Yes," provide the information requested in lines 9b through 9f. ☐ Yes ☐ No

Form 1023 (Rev. 6-2006)   Name: _____   EIN: _____ – _____   Page **5**

Part V   Compensation and Other Financial Arrangements With Your Officers, Directors, Trustees, Employees, and Independent Contractors (Continued)

b Describe any written or oral arrangements you made or intend to make.

c Identify with whom you have or will have such arrangements.

d Explain how the terms are or will be negotiated at arm's length.

e Explain how you determine or will determine you pay no more than fair market value or that you are paid at least fair market value.

f Attach a copy of any signed leases, contracts, loans, or other agreements relating to such arrangements.

Part VI   Your Members and Other Individuals and Organizations That Receive Benefits From You

The following "Yes" or "No" questions relate to goods, services, and funds you provide to individuals and organizations as part of your activities. Your answers should pertain to *past, present,* and *planned* activities. (See instructions.)

1a	In carrying out your exempt purposes, do you provide goods, services, or funds to individuals? If "Yes," describe each program that provides goods, services, or funds to individuals.	☐ Yes	☐ No
b	In carrying out your exempt purposes, do you provide goods, services, or funds to organizations? If "Yes," describe each program that provides goods, services, or funds to organizations.	☐ Yes	☐ No
2	Do any of your programs limit the provision of goods, services, or funds to a specific individual or group of specific individuals? For example, answer "Yes," if goods, services, or funds are provided only for a particular individual, your members, individuals who work for a particular employer, or graduates of a particular school. If "Yes," explain the limitation and how recipients are selected for each program.	☐ Yes	☐ No
3	Do any individuals who receive goods, services, or funds through your programs have a family or business relationship with any officer, director, trustee, or with any of your highest compensated employees or highest compensated independent contractors listed in Part V, lines 1a, 1b, and 1c? If "Yes," explain how these related individuals are eligible for goods, services, or funds.	☐ Yes	☐ No

Part VII   Your History

The following "Yes" or "No" questions relate to your history. (See instructions.)

1	Are you a **successor** to another organization? Answer "Yes," if you have taken or will take over the activities of another organization; you took over 25% or more of the fair market value of the net assets of another organization; or you were established upon the conversion of an organization from for-profit to non-profit status. If "Yes," complete Schedule G.	☐ Yes	☐ No
2	Are you submitting this application more than 27 months after the end of the month in which you were legally formed? If "Yes," complete Schedule E.	☐ Yes	☐ No

Part VIII   Your Specific Activities

The following "Yes" or "No" questions relate to specific activities that you may conduct. Check the appropriate box. Your answers should pertain to *past, present,* and *planned* activities. (See instructions.)

1	Do you support or oppose candidates in **political campaigns** in any way? If "Yes," explain.	☐ Yes	☐ No
2a	Do you attempt to **influence legislation**? If "Yes," explain how you attempt to influence legislation and complete line 2b. If "No," go to line 3a.	☐ Yes	☐ No
b	Have you made or are you making an **election** to have your legislative activities measured by expenditures by filing Form 5768? If "Yes," attach a copy of the Form 5768 that was already filed or attach a completed Form 5768 that you are filing with this application. If "No," describe whether your attempts to influence legislation are a substantial part of your activities. Include the time and money spent on your attempts to influence legislation as compared to your total activities.	☐ Yes	☐ No
3a	Do you or will you operate bingo or **gaming** activities? If "Yes," describe who conducts them, and list all revenue received or expected to be received and expenses paid or expected to be paid in operating these activities. **Revenue and expenses** should be provided for the time periods specified in Part IX, Financial Data.	☐ Yes	☐ No
b	Do you or will you enter into contracts or other agreements with individuals or organizations to conduct bingo or gaming for you? If "Yes," describe any written or oral arrangements that you made or intend to make, identify with whom you have or will have such arrangements, explain how the terms are or will be negotiated at arm's length, and explain how you determine or will determine you pay no more than fair market value or you will be paid at least fair market value. Attach copies of any written contracts or other agreements relating to such arrangements.	☐ Yes	☐ No
c	List the states and local jurisdictions, including Indian Reservations, in which you conduct or will conduct gaming or bingo.		

230

Part VIII　Your Specific Activities (Continued)

4a　Do you or will you undertake **fundraising**? If "Yes," check all the fundraising programs you do or will conduct. (See instructions.)　☐ **Yes**　☐ **No**

　　☐ mail solicitations　　　　　　　　　　☐ phone solicitations
　　☐ email solicitations　　　　　　　　　　☐ accept donations on your website
　　☐ personal solicitations　　　　　　　　☐ receive donations from another organization's website
　　☐ vehicle, boat, plane, or similar donations　☐ government grant solicitations
　　☐ foundation grant solicitations　　　　☐ Other

　　Attach a description of each fundraising program.

b　Do you or will you have written or oral contracts with any individuals or organizations to raise funds for you? If "Yes," describe these activities. Include all revenue and expenses from these activities and state who conducts them. Revenue and expenses should be provided for the time periods specified in Part IX, Financial Data. Also, attach a copy of any contracts or agreements.　☐ **Yes**　☐ **No**

c　Do you or will you engage in fundraising activities for other organizations? If "Yes," describe these arrangements. Include a description of the organizations for which you raise funds and attach copies of all contracts or agreements.　☐ **Yes**　☐ **No**

d　List all states and local jurisdictions in which you conduct fundraising. For each state or local jurisdiction listed, specify whether you fundraise for your own organization, you fundraise for another organization, or another organization fundraises for you.

e　Do you or will you maintain separate accounts for any contributor under which the contributor has the right to advise on the use or distribution of funds? Answer "Yes" if the donor may provide advice on the types of investments, distributions from the types of investments, or the distribution from the donor's contribution account. If "Yes," describe this program, including the type of advice that may be provided and submit copies of any written materials provided to donors.　☐ **Yes**　☐ **No**

5　Are you **affiliated** with a governmental unit? If "Yes," explain.　☐ **Yes**　☐ **No**

6a　Do you or will you engage in **economic development**? If "Yes," describe your program.　☐ **Yes**　☐ **No**
b　Describe in full who benefits from your economic development activities and how the activities promote exempt purposes.

7a　Do or will persons other than your employees or volunteers **develop** your facilities? If "Yes," describe each facility, the role of the developer, and any business or family relationship(s) between the developer and your officers, directors, or trustees.　☐ **Yes**　☐ **No**

b　Do or will persons other than your employees or volunteers **manage** your activities or facilities? If "Yes," describe each activity and facility, the role of the manager, and any business or family relationship(s) between the manager and your officers, directors, or trustees.　☐ **Yes**　☐ **No**

c　If there is a business or family relationship between any manager or developer and your officers, directors, or trustees, identify the individuals, explain the relationship, describe how contracts are negotiated at arm's length so that you pay no more than fair market value, and submit a copy of any contracts or other agreements.

8　Do you or will you enter into **joint ventures**, including partnerships or **limited liability companies** treated as partnerships, in which you share profits and losses with partners other than section 501(c)(3) organizations? If "Yes," describe the activities of these joint ventures in which you participate.　☐ **Yes**　☐ **No**

9a　Are you applying for exemption as a childcare organization under section 501(k)? If "Yes," answer lines 9b through 9d. If "No," go to line 10.　☐ **Yes**　☐ **No**

b　Do you provide child care so that parents or caretakers of children you care for can be **gainfully employed** (see instructions)? If "No," explain how you qualify as a childcare organization described in section 501(k).　☐ **Yes**　☐ **No**

c　Of the children for whom you provide child care, are 85% or more of them cared for by you to enable their parents or caretakers to be gainfully employed (see instructions)? If "No," explain how you qualify as a childcare organization described in section 501(k).　☐ **Yes**　☐ **No**

d　Are your services available to the general public? If "No," describe the specific group of people for whom your activities are available. Also, see the instructions and explain how you qualify as a childcare organization described in section 501(k).　☐ **Yes**　☐ **No**

10　Do you or will you publish, own, or have rights in music, literature, tapes, artworks, choreography, scientific discoveries, or other **intellectual property**? If "Yes," explain. Describe who owns or will own any copyrights, patents, or trademarks, whether fees are or will be charged, how the fees are determined, and how any items are or will be produced, distributed, and marketed.　☐ **Yes**　☐ **No**

Part VIII   Your Specific Activities *(Continued)*

11 Do you or will you accept contributions of: real property; conservation easements; closely held securities; intellectual property such as patents, trademarks, and copyrights; works of music or art; licenses; royalties; automobiles, boats, planes, or other vehicles; or collectibles of any type? If "Yes," describe each type of contribution, any conditions imposed by the donor on the contribution, and any agreements with the donor regarding the contribution.   ☐ **Yes**   ☐ **No**

12a Do you or will you operate in a **foreign country** or **countries?** If "Yes," answer lines 12b through 12d. If "No," go to line 13a.   ☐ **Yes**   ☐ **No**

 b Name the foreign countries and regions within the countries in which you operate.

 c Describe your operations in each country and region in which you operate.

 d Describe how your operations in each country and region further your exempt purposes.

13a Do you or will you make grants, loans, or other distributions to organization(s)? If "Yes," answer lines 13b through 13g. If "No," go to line 14a.   ☐ **Yes**   ☐ **No**

 b Describe how your grants, loans, or other distributions to organizations further your exempt purposes.

 c Do you have written contracts with each of these organizations? If "Yes," attach a copy of each contract.   ☐ **Yes**   ☐ **No**

 d Identify each recipient organization and any **relationship** between you and the recipient organization.

 e Describe the records you keep with respect to the grants, loans, or other distributions you make.

 f Describe your selection process, including whether you do any of the following:

  (i) Do you require an application form? If "Yes," attach a copy of the form.   ☐ **Yes**   ☐ **No**

  (ii) Do you require a grant proposal? If "Yes," describe whether the grant proposal specifies your responsibilities and those of the grantee, obligates the grantee to use the grant funds only for the purposes for which the grant was made, provides for periodic written reports concerning the use of grant funds, requires a final written report and an accounting of how grant funds were used, and acknowledges your authority to withhold and/or recover grant funds in case such funds are, or appear to be, misused.   ☐ **Yes**   ☐ **No**

 g Describe your procedures for oversight of distributions that assure you the resources are used to further your exempt purposes, including whether you require periodic and final reports on the use of resources.

14a Do you or will you make grants, loans, or other distributions to foreign organizations? If "Yes," answer lines 14b through 14f. If "No," go to line 15.   ☐ **Yes**   ☐ **No**

 b Provide the name of each foreign organization, the country and regions within a country in which each foreign organization operates, and describe any relationship you have with each foreign organization.

 c Does any foreign organization listed in line 14b accept contributions earmarked for a specific country or specific organization? If "Yes," list all earmarked organizations or countries.   ☐ **Yes**   ☐ **No**

 d Do your contributors know that you have ultimate authority to use contributions made to you at your discretion for purposes consistent with your exempt purposes? If "Yes," describe how you relay this information to contributors.   ☐ **Yes**   ☐ **No**

 e Do you or will you make pre-grant inquiries about the recipient organization? If "Yes," describe these inquiries, including whether you inquire about the recipient's financial status, its tax-exempt status under the Internal Revenue Code, its ability to accomplish the purpose for which the resources are provided, and other relevant information.   ☐ **Yes**   ☐ **No**

 f Do you or will you use any additional procedures to ensure that your distributions to foreign organizations are used in furtherance of your exempt purposes? If "Yes," describe these procedures, including site visits by your employees or compliance checks by impartial experts, to verify that grant funds are being used appropriately.   ☐ **Yes**   ☐ **No**

232

Part VIII	**Your Specific Activities** *(Continued)*				

15	Do you have a **close connection** with any organizations? If "Yes," explain.	☐ Yes	☐ No
16	Are you applying for exemption as a **cooperative hospital service organization** under section 501(e)? If "Yes," explain.	☐ Yes	☐ No
17	Are you applying for exemption as a **cooperative service organization of operating educational organizations** under section 501(f)? If "Yes," explain.	☐ Yes	☐ No
18	Are you applying for exemption as a **charitable risk pool** under section 501(n)? If "Yes," explain.	☐ Yes	☐ No
19	Do you or will you operate a **school**? If "Yes," complete Schedule B. Answer "Yes," whether you operate a school as your main function or as a secondary activity.	☐ Yes	☐ No
20	Is your main function to provide **hospital** or **medical care**? If "Yes," complete Schedule C.	☐ Yes	☐ No
21	Do you or will you provide **low-income housing** or housing for the **elderly** or **handicapped**? If "Yes," complete Schedule F.	☐ Yes	☐ No
22	Do you or will you provide scholarships, fellowships, educational loans, or other educational grants to individuals, including grants for travel, study, or other similar purposes? If "Yes," complete Schedule H.	☐ Yes	☐ No

Note: Private foundations may use Schedule H to request advance approval of individual grant procedures.

Form 1023 (Rev. 6-2006)   Name: EIN: −   Page **9**

Part IX   Financial Data

For purposes of this schedule, years in existence refer to completed tax years. If in existence 4 or more years, complete the schedule for the most recent 4 tax years. If in existence more than 1 year but less than 4 years, complete the statements for each year in existence and provide projections of your likely revenues and expenses based on a reasonable and good faith estimate of your future finances for a total of 3 years of financial information. If in existence less than 1 year, provide projections of your likely revenues and expenses for the current year and the 2 following years, based on a reasonable and good faith estimate of your future finances for a total of 3 years of financial information. (See instructions.)

A. Statement of Revenues and Expenses

	Type of revenue or expense	Current tax year	3 prior tax years or 2 succeeding tax years			(e) Provide Total for (a) through (d)
		(a) From.......... To	(b) From.......... To	(c) From.......... To	(d) From.......... To	
Revenues	1 Gifts, grants, and contributions received (do not include unusual grants)					
	2 Membership fees received					
	3 Gross investment income					
	4 Net unrelated business income					
	5 Taxes levied for your benefit					
	6 Value of services or facilities furnished by a governmental unit without charge (not including the value of services generally furnished to the public without charge)					
	7 Any revenue not otherwise listed above or in lines 9–12 below (attach an itemized list)					
	8 Total of lines 1 through 7					
	9 Gross receipts from admissions, merchandise sold or services performed, or furnishing of facilities in any activity that is related to your exempt purposes (attach itemized list)					
	10 Total of lines 8 and 9					
	11 Net gain or loss on sale of capital assets (attach schedule and see instructions)					
	12 **Unusual grants**					
	13 Total Revenue Add lines 10 through 12					
Expenses	14 Fundraising expenses					
	15 Contributions, gifts, grants, and similar amounts paid out (attach an itemized list)					
	16 Disbursements to or for the benefit of members (attach an itemized list)					
	17 Compensation of officers, directors, and trustees					
	18 Other salaries and wages					
	19 Interest expense					
	20 Occupancy (rent, utilities, etc.)					
	21 Depreciation and depletion					
	22 Professional fees					
	23 Any expense not otherwise classified, such as program services (attach itemized list)					
	24 Total Expenses Add lines 14 through 23					

Form **1023** (Rev. 6-2006)

234

Part IX   Financial Data *(Continued)*

	B. Balance Sheet (for your most recently completed tax year)		Year End:

Assets — (Whole dollars)

1	Cash	**1**	
2	Accounts receivable, net	**2**	
3	Inventories	**3**	
4	Bonds and notes receivable (attach an itemized list)	**4**	
5	Corporate stocks (attach an itemized list)	**5**	
6	Loans receivable (attach an itemized list)	**6**	
7	Other investments (attach an itemized list)	**7**	
8	Depreciable and depletable assets (attach an itemized list)	**8**	
9	Land	**9**	
10	Other assets (attach an itemized list)	**10**	
11	Total Assets (add lines 1 through 10)	**11**	

Liabilities

12	Accounts payable	**12**	
13	Contributions, gifts, grants, etc. payable	**13**	
14	Mortgages and notes payable (attach an itemized list)	**14**	
15	Other liabilities (attach an itemized list)	**15**	
16	Total Liabilities (add lines 12 through 15)	**16**	

Fund Balances or Net Assets

17	Total fund balances or net assets	**17**	
18	Total Liabilities and Fund Balances or Net Assets (add lines 16 and 17)	**18**	

19 Have there been any substantial changes in your assets or liabilities since the end of the period shown above? If "Yes," explain.   ☐ Yes   ☐ No

Part X   Public Charity Status

Part X is designed to classify you as an organization that is either a **private foundation** or a **public charity**. Public charity status is a more favorable tax status than private foundation status. If you are a private foundation, Part X is designed to further determine whether you are a **private operating foundation**. (See instructions.)

1a Are you a private foundation? If "Yes," go to line 1b. If "No," go to line 5 and proceed as instructed. If you are unsure, see the instructions.   ☐ Yes   ☐ No

b As a private foundation, section 508(e) requires special provisions in your organizing document in addition to those that apply to all organizations described in section 501(c)(3). Check the box to confirm that your organizing document meets this requirement, whether by express provision or by reliance on operation of state law. Attach a statement that describes specifically where your organizing document meets this requirement, such as a reference to a particular article or section in your organizing document or by operation of state law. See the instructions, including Appendix B, for information about the special provisions that need to be contained in your organizing document. Go to line 2.   ☐

2 Are you a private operating foundation? To be a private operating foundation you must engage directly in the active conduct of charitable, religious, educational, and similar activities, as opposed to indirectly carrying out these activities by providing grants to individuals or other organizations. If "Yes," go to line 3. If "No," go to the signature section of Part XI.   ☐ Yes   ☐ No

3 Have you existed for one or more years? If "Yes," attach financial information showing that you are a private operating foundation; go to the signature section of Part XI. If "No," continue to line 4.   ☐ Yes   ☐ No

4 Have you attached either (1) an affidavit or opinion of counsel, (including a written affidavit or opinion from a certified public accountant or accounting firm with expertise regarding this tax law matter), that sets forth facts concerning your operations and support to demonstrate that you are likely to satisfy the requirements to be classified as a private operating foundation; or (2) a statement describing your proposed operations as a private operating foundation?   ☐ Yes   ☐ No

5 If you answered "No" to line 1a, indicate the type of public charity status you are requesting by checking one of the choices below. You may check only one box.

The organization is not a private foundation because it is:

a 509(a)(1) and 170(b)(1)(A)(i)—a church or a convention or association of churches. Complete and attach Schedule A.   ☐

b 509(a)(1) and 170(b)(1)(A)(ii)—a **school**. Complete and attach Schedule B.   ☐

c 509(a)(1) and 170(b)(1)(A)(iii)—a **hospital**, a cooperative hospital service organization, or a medical research organization operated in conjunction with a hospital. Complete and attach Schedule C.   ☐

d 509(a)(3)—an organization supporting either one or more organizations described in line 5a through c, f, g, or h or a publicly supported section 501(c)(4), (5), or (6) organization. Complete and attach Schedule D.   ☐

Form 1023 (Rev. 6-2006)   Name: EIN: –   Page **11**

Part X   **Public Charity Status** *(Continued)*

e 509(a)(4)—an organization organized and operated exclusively for testing for public safety. ☐

f 509(a)(1) and 170(b)(1)(A)(iv)—an organization operated for the benefit of a college or university that is owned or operated by a governmental unit. ☐

g 509(a)(1) and 170(b)(1)(A)(vi)—an organization that receives a substantial part of its financial support in the form of contributions from publicly supported organizations, from a governmental unit, or from the general public. ☐

h 509(a)(2)—an organization that normally receives not more than one-third of its financial support from gross **investment income** and receives more than one-third of its financial support from contributions, membership fees, and gross receipts from activities related to its exempt functions (subject to certain exceptions). ☐

i A publicly supported organization, but unsure if it is described in 5g or 5h. The organization would like the IRS to decide the correct status. ☐

6 If you checked box g, h, or i in question 5 above, you must request either an **advance** or a **definitive ruling** by selecting one of the boxes below. Refer to the instructions to determine which type of ruling you are eligible to receive.

a **Request for Advance Ruling:** By checking this box and signing the consent, pursuant to section 6501(c)(4) of the Code you request an advance ruling and agree to extend the statute of limitations on the assessment of excise tax under section 4940 of the Code. The tax will apply only if you do not establish public support status at the end of the 5-year advance ruling period. The assessment period will be extended for the 5 advance ruling years to 8 years, 4 months, and 15 days beyond the end of the first year. You have the right to refuse or limit the extension to a mutually agreed-upon period of time or issue(s). Publication 1035, *Extending the Tax Assessment Period,* provides a more detailed explanation of your rights and the consequences of the choices you make. You may obtain Publication 1035 free of charge from the IRS web site at *www.irs.gov* or by calling toll-free 1-800-829-3676. Signing this consent will not deprive you of any appeal rights to which you would otherwise be entitled. If you decide not to extend the statute of limitations, you are not eligible for an advance ruling. ☐

Consent Fixing Period of Limitations Upon Assessment of Tax Under Section 4940 of the Internal Revenue Code

For Organization

_____   _____   _____
(Signature of Officer, Director, Trustee, or other   (Type or print name of signer)   (Date)
authorized official)

_____
(Type or print title or authority of signer)

For IRS Use Only

_____   _____   _____
IRS Director, Exempt Organizations   (Date)

b **Request for Definitive Ruling:** Check this box if you have completed one tax year of at least 8 full months and you are requesting a definitive ruling. To confirm your public support status, answer line 6b(i) if you checked box g in line 5 above. Answer line 6b(ii) if you checked box h in line 5 above. If you checked box i in line 5 above, answer both lines 6b(i) and (ii). ☐

(i) (a) Enter 2% of line 8, column (e) on Part IX-A. Statement of Revenues and Expenses. _____

(b) Attach a list showing the name and amount contributed by each person, company, or organization whose gifts totaled more than the 2% amount. If the answer is "None," check this box. ☐

(ii) (a) For each year amounts are included on lines 1, 2, and 9 of Part IX-A. Statement of Revenues and Expenses, attach a list showing the name of and amount received from each **disqualified person.** If the answer is "None," check this box. ☐

(b) For each year amounts are included on line 9 of Part IX-A. Statement of Revenues and Expenses, attach a list showing the name of and amount received from each payer, other than a disqualified person, whose payments were more than the larger of (1) 1% of line 10, Part IX-A. Statement of Revenues and Expenses, or (2) $5,000. If the answer is "None," check this box. ☐

7 Did you receive any unusual grants during any of the years shown on Part IX-A. Statement of Revenues and Expenses? If "Yes," attach a list including the name of the contributor, the date and amount of the grant, a brief description of the grant, and explain why it is unusual.   ☐ **Yes**   ☐ **No**

Form **1023** (Rev. 6-2006)

236

Part XI   User Fee Information

You must include a user fee payment with this application. It will not be processed without your paid user fee. If your average annual gross receipts have exceeded or will exceed $10,000 annually over a 4-year period, you must submit payment of $750. If your gross receipts have not exceeded or will not exceed $10,000 annually over a 4-year period, the required user fee payment is $300. See instructions for Part XI, for a definition of **gross receipts** over a 4-year period. Your check or money order must be made payable to the United States Treasury. *User fees are subject to change. Check our website at www.irs.gov and type "User Fee" in the keyword box, or call Customer Account Services at 1-877-829-5500 for current information.*

1	Have your annual gross receipts averaged or are they expected to average not more than $10,000?	☐ **Yes**	☐ **No**
	If "Yes," check the box on line 2 and enclose a user fee payment of $300 (Subject to change—see above).		
	If "No," check the box on line 3 and enclose a user fee payment of $750 (Subject to change—see above).		
2	Check the box if you have enclosed the reduced user fee payment of $300 (Subject to change).		☐
3	Check the box if you have enclosed the user fee payment of $750 (Subject to change).		☐

I declare under the penalties of perjury that I am authorized to sign this application on behalf of the above organization and that I have examined this application, including the accompanying schedules and attachments, and to the best of my knowledge it is true, correct, and complete.

**Please
Sign
Here**   ▶

--   --   ----------------------
(Signature of Officer, Director, Trustee, or other   (Type or print name of signer)   (Date)
authorized official)

(Type or print title or authority of signer)

Reminder: Send the completed Form 1023 Checklist with your filled-in-application.   Form **1023** (Rev. 6-2006)

Form 1023 (Rev. 6-2006)   Name: EIN: –   Page **13**

Schedule A. Churches

1a Do you have a written creed, statement of faith, or summary of beliefs? If "Yes," attach copies of relevant documents.   ☐ **Yes**   ☐ **No**

b Do you have a form of worship? If "Yes," describe your form of worship.   ☐ **Yes**   ☐ **No**

2a Do you have a formal code of doctrine and discipline? If "Yes," describe your code of doctrine and discipline.   ☐ **Yes**   ☐ **No**

b Do you have a distinct religious history? If "Yes," describe your religious history.   ☐ **Yes**   ☐ **No**

c Do you have a literature of your own? If "Yes," describe your literature.   ☐ **Yes**   ☐ **No**

3 Describe the organization's religious hierarchy or ecclesiastical government.

4a Do you have regularly scheduled religious services? If "Yes," describe the nature of the services and provide representative copies of relevant literature such as church bulletins.   ☐ **Yes**   ☐ **No**

b What is the average attendance at your regularly scheduled religious services?   _____

5a Do you have an established place of worship? If "Yes," refer to the instructions for the information required.   ☐ **Yes**   ☐ **No**

b Do you own the property where you have an established place of worship?   ☐ **Yes**   ☐ **No**

6 Do you have an established congregation or other regular membership group? If "No," refer to the instructions.   ☐ **Yes**   ☐ **No**

7 How many members do you have?   _____

8a Do you have a process by which an individual becomes a member? If "Yes," describe the process and complete lines 8b–8d, below.   ☐ **Yes**   ☐ **No**

b If you have members, do your members have voting rights, rights to participate in religious functions, or other rights? If "Yes," describe the rights your members have.   ☐ **Yes**   ☐ **No**

c May your members be associated with another denomination or church?   ☐ **Yes**   ☐ **No**

d Are all of your members part of the same **family**?   ☐ **Yes**   ☐ **No**

9 Do you conduct baptisms, weddings, funerals, etc.?   ☐ **Yes**   ☐ **No**

10 Do you have a school for the religious instruction of the young?   ☐ **Yes**   ☐ **No**

11a Do you have a minister or religious leader? If "Yes," describe this person's role and explain whether the minister or religious leader was ordained, commissioned, or licensed after a prescribed course of study.   ☐ **Yes**   ☐ **No**

b Do you have schools for the preparation of your ordained ministers or religious leaders?   ☐ **Yes**   ☐ **No**

12 Is your minister or religious leader also one of your officers, directors, or trustees?   ☐ **Yes**   ☐ **No**

13 Do you ordain, commission, or license ministers or religious leaders? If "Yes," describe the requirements for ordination, commission, or licensure.   ☐ **Yes**   ☐ **No**

14 Are you part of a group of churches with similar beliefs and structures? If "Yes," explain. Include the name of the group of churches.   ☐ **Yes**   ☐ **No**

15 Do you issue church charters? If "Yes," describe the requirements for issuing a charter.   ☐ **Yes**   ☐ **No**

16 Did you pay a fee for a church charter? If "Yes," attach a copy of the charter.   ☐ **Yes**   ☐ **No**

17 Do you have other information you believe should be considered regarding your status as a church? If "Yes," explain.   ☐ **Yes**   ☐ **No**

Form **1023** (Rev. 6-2006)

238

Schedule B. Schools, Colleges, and Universities

If you operate a school as an activity, complete Schedule B

Section I	**Operational Information**		
1a	Do you normally have a regularly scheduled curriculum, a regular faculty of qualified teachers, a regularly enrolled student body, and facilities where your educational activities are regularly carried on? If "No," do not complete the remainder of Schedule B.	☐ Yes	☐ No
b	Is the primary function of your school the presentation of formal instruction? If "Yes," describe your school in terms of whether it is an elementary, secondary, college, technical, or other type of school. If "No," do not complete the remainder of Schedule B.	☐ Yes	☐ No
2a	Are you a public school because you are operated by a state or subdivision of a state? If "Yes," explain how you are operated by a state or subdivision of a state. Do not complete the remainder of Schedule B.	☐ Yes	☐ No
b	Are you a public school because you are operated wholly or predominantly from government funds or property? If "Yes," explain how you are operated wholly or predominantly from government funds or property. Submit a copy of your funding agreement regarding government funding. Do not complete the remainder of Schedule B.	☐ Yes	☐ No
3	In what public school district, county, and state are you located?		
4	Were you formed or substantially expanded at the time of public school desegregation in the above school district or county?	☐ Yes	☐ No
5	Has a state or federal administrative agency or judicial body ever determined that you are racially discriminatory? If "Yes," explain.	☐ Yes	☐ No
6	Has your right to receive financial aid or assistance from a governmental agency ever been revoked or suspended? If "Yes," explain.	☐ Yes	☐ No
7	Do you or will you contract with another organization to develop, build, market, or finance your facilities? If "Yes," explain how that entity is selected, explain how the terms of any contracts or other agreements are negotiated at arm's length, and explain how you determine that you will pay no more than fair market value for services. **Note.** Make sure your answer is consistent with the information provided in Part VIII, line 7a.	☐ Yes	☐ No
8	Do you or will you manage your activities or facilities through your own employees or volunteers? If "No," attach a statement describing the activities that will be managed by others, the names of the persons or organizations that manage or will manage your activities or facilities, and how these managers were or will be selected. Also, submit copies of any contracts, proposed contracts, or other agreements regarding the provision of management services for your activities or facilities. Explain how the terms of any contracts or other agreements were or will be negotiated, and explain how you determine you will pay no more than fair market value for services. **Note.** Answer "Yes" if you manage or intend to manage your programs through your own employees or by using volunteers. Answer "No" if you engage or intend to engage a separate organization or independent contractor. Make sure your answer is consistent with the information provided in Part VIII, line 7b.	☐ Yes	☐ No

Section II	**Establishment of Racially Nondiscriminatory Policy**		
	Information required by **Revenue Procedure 75-50.**		
1	Have you adopted a racially nondiscriminatory policy as to students in your organizing document, bylaws, or by resolution of your governing body? If "Yes," state where the policy can be found or supply a copy of the policy. If "No," you must adopt a nondiscriminatory policy as to students before submitting this application. See Publication 557.	☐ Yes	☐ No
2	Do your brochures, application forms, advertisements, and catalogues dealing with student admissions, programs, and scholarships contain a statement of your racially nondiscriminatory policy?	☐ Yes	☐ No
a	If "Yes," attach a representative sample of each document.		
b	If "No," by checking the box to the right you agree that all future printed materials, including website content, will contain the required nondiscriminatory policy statement.	▶ ☐	
3	Have you published a notice of your nondiscriminatory policy in a newspaper of general circulation that serves all racial segments of the community? (See the instructions for specific requirements.) If "No," explain.	☐ Yes	☐ No
4	Does or will the organization (or any department or division within it) discriminate in any way on the basis of race with respect to admissions; use of facilities or exercise of student privileges; faculty or administrative staff; or scholarship or loan programs? If "Yes," for any of the above, explain fully.	☐ Yes	☐ No

Schedule B. Schools, Colleges, and Universities *(Continued)*

5 Complete the table below to show the racial composition for the current academic year and projected for the next academic year, of: (a) the student body, (b) the faculty, and (c) the administrative staff. Provide actual numbers rather than percentages for each racial category.

If you are not operational, submit an estimate based on the best information available (such as the racial composition of the community served).

Racial Category	(a) Student Body		(b) Faculty		(c) Administrative Staff	
	Current Year	Next Year	Current Year	Next Year	Current Year	Next Year
Total						

6 In the table below, provide the number and amount of loans and scholarships awarded to students enrolled by racial categories.

Racial Category	Number of Loans		Amount of Loans		Number of Scholarships		Amount of Scholarships	
	Current Year	Next Year	Current Year	Next Year	Current Year	Next Year	Current Year	Next Year
Total								

7a Attach a list of your incorporators, founders, board members, and donors of land or buildings, whether individuals or organizations.

   b Do any of these individuals or organizations have an objective to maintain segregated public or private school education? If "Yes," explain.   ☐ **Yes**   ☐ **No**

8 Will you maintain records according to the non-discrimination provisions contained in Revenue Procedure 75-50? If "No," explain. (See instructions.)   ☐ **Yes**   ☐ **No**

240

Schedule C. Hospitals and Medical Research Organizations

Check the box if you are a **hospital**. See the instructions for a definition of the term "hospital," which includes an organization whose principal purpose or function is providing **hospital** or **medical care**. Complete Section I below.   ☐

Check the box if you are a **medical research organization** operated in conjunction with a hospital. See the instructions for a definition of the term "medical research organization," which refers to an organization whose principal purpose or function is medical research and which is directly engaged in the continuous active conduct of medical research in conjunction with a hospital. Complete Section II.   ☐

Section I	Hospitals

1a Are all the doctors in the community eligible for staff privileges? If "No," give the reasons why and explain how the medical staff is selected.   ☐ **Yes**   ☐ **No**

2a Do you or will you provide medical services to all individuals in your community who can pay for themselves or have private health insurance? If "No," explain.   ☐ **Yes**   ☐ **No**

b Do you or will you provide medical services to all individuals in your community who participate in Medicare? If "No," explain.   ☐ **Yes**   ☐ **No**

c Do you or will you provide medical services to all individuals in your community who participate in Medicaid? If "No," explain.   ☐ **Yes**   ☐ **No**

3a Do you or will you require persons covered by Medicare or Medicaid to pay a deposit before receiving services? If "Yes," explain.   ☐ **Yes**   ☐ **No**

b Does the same deposit requirement, if any, apply to all other patients? If "No," explain.   ☐ **Yes**   ☐ **No**

4a Do you or will you maintain a full-time emergency room? If "No," explain why you do not maintain a full-time emergency room. Also, describe any emergency services that you provide.   ☐ **Yes**   ☐ **No**

b Do you have a policy on providing emergency services to persons without apparent means to pay? If "Yes," provide a copy of the policy.   ☐ **Yes**   ☐ **No**

c Do you have any arrangements with police, fire, and voluntary ambulance services for the delivery or admission of emergency cases? If "Yes," describe the arrangements, including whether they are written or oral agreements. If written, submit copies of all such agreements.   ☐ **Yes**   ☐ **No**

5a Do you provide for a portion of your services and facilities to be used for charity patients? If "Yes," answer 5b through 5e.   ☐ **Yes**   ☐ **No**

b Explain your policy regarding charity cases, including how you distinguish between charity care and bad debts. Submit a copy of your written policy.

c Provide data on your past experience in admitting charity patients, including amounts you expend for treating charity care patients and types of services you provide to charity care patients.

d Describe any arrangements you have with federal, state, or local governments or government agencies for paying for the cost of treating charity care patients. Submit copies of any written agreements.

e Do you provide services on a sliding fee schedule depending on financial ability to pay? If "Yes," submit your sliding fee schedule.   ☐ **Yes**   ☐ **No**

6a Do you or will you carry on a formal program of medical training or medical research? If "Yes," describe such programs, including the type of programs offered, the scope of such programs, and affiliations with other hospitals or medical care providers with which you carry on the medical training or research programs.   ☐ **Yes**   ☐ **No**

b Do you or will you carry on a formal program of community education? If "Yes," describe such programs, including the type of programs offered, the scope of such programs, and affiliation with other hospitals or medical care providers with which you offer community education programs.   ☐ **Yes**   ☐ **No**

7 Do you or will you provide office space to physicians carrying on their own medical practices? If "Yes," describe the criteria for who may use the space, explain the means used to determine that you are paid at least fair market value, and submit representative lease agreements.   ☐ **Yes**   ☐ **No**

8 Is your board of directors comprised of a majority of individuals who are representative of the community you serve? Include a list of each board member's name and business, financial, or professional relationship with the hospital. Also, identify each board member who is representative of the community and describe how that individual is a community representative.   ☐ **Yes**   ☐ **No**

9 Do you participate in any joint ventures? If "Yes," state your ownership percentage in each joint venture, list your investment in each joint venture, describe the tax status of other participants in each joint venture (including whether they are section 501(c)(3) organizations), describe the activities of each joint venture, describe how you exercise control over the activities of each joint venture, and describe how each joint venture furthers your exempt purposes. Also, submit copies of all agreements.   ☐ **Yes**   ☐ **No**
Note. Make sure your answer is consistent with the information provided in Part VIII, line 8.

Schedule C. Hospitals and Medical Research Organizations *(Continued)*

Section I   Hospitals *(Continued)*

10 Do you or will you manage your activities or facilities through your own employees or volunteers? If "No," attach a statement describing the activities that will be managed by others, the names of the persons or organizations that manage or will manage your activities or facilities, and how these managers were or will be selected. Also, submit copies of any contracts, proposed contracts, or other agreements regarding the provision of management services for your activities or facilities. Explain how the terms of any contracts or other agreements were or will be negotiated, and explain how you determine you will pay no more than fair market value for services. ☐ **Yes** ☐ **No**

  Note. Answer "Yes" if you do manage or intend to manage your programs through your own employees or by using volunteers. Answer "No" if you engage or intend to engage a separate organization or independent contractor. Make sure your answer is consistent with the information provided in Part VIII, line 7b.

11 Do you or will you offer recruitment incentives to physicians? If "Yes," describe your recruitment incentives and attach copies of all written recruitment incentive policies. ☐ **Yes** ☐ **No**

12 Do you or will you lease equipment, assets, or office space from physicians who have a financial or professional relationship with you? If "Yes," explain how you establish a fair market value for the lease. ☐ **Yes** ☐ **No**

13 Have you purchased medical practices, ambulatory surgery centers, or other business assets from physicians or other persons with whom you have a business relationship, aside from the purchase? If "Yes," submit a copy of each purchase and sales contract and describe how you arrived at fair market value, including copies of appraisals. ☐ **Yes** ☐ **No**

14 Have you adopted a **conflict of interest policy** consistent with the sample health care organization conflict of interest policy in Appendix A of the instructions? If "Yes," submit a copy of the policy and explain how the policy has been adopted, such as by resolution of your governing board. If "No," explain how you will avoid any conflicts of interest in your business dealings. ☐ **Yes** ☐ **No**

Section II   Medical Research Organizations

1 Name the hospitals with which you have a relationship and describe the relationship. Attach copies of written agreements with each hospital that demonstrate continuing relationships between you and the hospital(s).

2 Attach a schedule describing your present and proposed activities for the direct conduct of medical research; describe the nature of the activities, and the amount of money that has been or will be spent in carrying them out.

3 Attach a schedule of assets showing their fair market value and the portion of your assets directly devoted to medical research.

Form **1023** (Rev. 6-2006)

242

Schedule D. Section 509(a)(3) Supporting Organizations

Section I   Identifying Information About the Supported Organization(s)

1 State the names, addresses, and EINs of the supported organizations. If additional space is needed, attach a separate sheet.

Name	Address	EIN
	- -	–
	- -	–

2 Are all supported organizations listed in line 1 public charities under section 509(a)(1) or (2)? If "Yes," go to Section II. If "No," go to line 3. ☐ **Yes** ☐ **No**

3 Do the supported organizations have tax-exempt status under section 501(c)(4), 501(c)(5), or 501(c)(6)? ☐ **Yes** ☐ **No**

If "Yes," for each 501(c)(4), (5), or (6) organization supported, provide the following financial information:

- Part IX-A. Statement of Revenues and Expenses, lines 1–13 and
- Part X, lines 6b(ii)(a), 6b(ii)(b), and 7.

If "No," attach a statement describing how each organization you support is a public charity under section 509(a)(1) or (2).

Section II   Relationship with Supported Organization(s)—Three Tests

To be classified as a supporting organization, an organization must meet one of three relationship tests:

Test 1: "Operated, supervised, or controlled by" one or more publicly supported organizations, or

Test 2: "Supervised or controlled in connection with" one or more publicly supported organizations, or

Test 3: "Operated in connection with" one or more publicly supported organizations.

1 Information to establish the "operated, supervised, or controlled by" relationship (Test 1)

Is a majority of your governing board or officers elected or appointed by the supported organization(s)? If "Yes," describe the process by which your governing board is appointed and elected; go to Section III. If "No," continue to line 2. ☐ **Yes** ☐ **No**

2 Information to establish the "supervised or controlled in connection with" relationship (Test 2)

Does a majority of your governing board consist of individuals who also serve on the governing board of the supported organization(s)? If "Yes," describe the process by which your governing board is appointed and elected; go to Section III. If "No," go to line 3. ☐ **Yes** ☐ **No**

3 Information to establish the "operated in connection with" responsiveness test (Test 3)

Are you a trust from which the named supported organization(s) can enforce and compel an accounting under state law? If "Yes," explain whether you advised the supported organization(s) in writing of these rights and provide a copy of the written communication documenting this; go to Section II, line 5. If "No," go to line 4a. ☐ **Yes** ☐ **No**

4 Information to establish the alternative "operated in connection with" responsiveness test (Test 3)

a Do the officers, directors, trustees, or members of the supported organization(s) elect or appoint one or more of your officers, directors, or trustees? If "Yes," explain and provide documentation; go to line 4d, below. If "No," go to line 4b. ☐ **Yes** ☐ **No**

b Do one or more members of the governing body of the supported organization(s) also serve as your officers, directors, or trustees or hold other important offices with respect to you? If "Yes," explain and provide documentation; go to line 4d, below. If "No," go to line 4c. ☐ **Yes** ☐ **No**

c Do your officers, directors, or trustees maintain a close and continuous working relationship with the officers, directors, or trustees of the supported organization(s)? If "Yes," explain and provide documentation. ☐ **Yes** ☐ **No**

d Do the supported organization(s) have a significant voice in your investment policies, in the making and timing of grants, and in otherwise directing the use of your income or assets? If "Yes," explain and provide documentation. ☐ **Yes** ☐ **No**

e Describe and provide copies of written communications documenting how you made the supported organization(s) aware of your supporting activities.

Schedule D. Section 509(a)(3) Supporting Organizations *(Continued)*

Section II   **Relationship with Supported Organization(s)—Three Tests** *(Continued)*

5 Information to establish the "operated in connection with" integral part test (Test 3)

Do you conduct activities that would otherwise be carried out by the supported organization(s)? If "Yes," explain and go to Section III. If "No," continue to line 6a.   ☐ **Yes**   ☐ **No**

6 Information to establish the alternative "operated in connection with" integral part test (Test 3)

a Do you distribute at least 85% of your annual **net income** to the supported organization(s)? If "Yes," go to line 6b. (See instructions.)   ☐ **Yes**   ☐ **No**

If "No," state the percentage of your income that you distribute to each supported organization. Also explain how you ensure that the supported organization(s) are attentive to your operations.

b How much do you contribute annually to each supported organization? Attach a schedule.

c What is the total annual revenue of each supported organization? If you need additional space, attach a list.

d Do you or the supported organization(s) **earmark** your funds for support of a particular program or activity? If "Yes," explain.   ☐ **Yes**   ☐ **No**

7a Does your organizing document specify the supported organization(s) by name? If "Yes," state the article and paragraph number and go to Section III. If "No," answer line 7b.   ☐ **Yes**   ☐ **No**

b Attach a statement describing whether there has been an historic and continuing relationship between you and the supported organization(s).

Section III   **Organizational Test**

1a If you met relationship Test 1 or Test 2 in Section II, your organizing document must specify the supported organization(s) by name, or by naming a similar purpose or charitable class of beneficiaries. If your organizing document complies with this requirement, answer "Yes." If your organizing document does not comply with this requirement, answer "No," and see the instructions.   ☐ **Yes**   ☐ **No**

b If you met relationship Test 3 in Section II, your organizing document must generally specify the supported organization(s) by name. If your organizing document complies with this requirement, answer "Yes," and go to Section IV. If your organizing document does not comply with this requirement, answer "No," and see the instructions.   ☐ **Yes**   ☐ **No**

Section IV   **Disqualified Person Test**

You do not qualify as a supporting organization if you are **controlled** directly or indirectly by one or more **disqualified persons** (as defined in section 4946) other than **foundation managers** or one or more organizations that you support. Foundation managers who are also disqualified persons for another reason are disqualified persons with respect to you.

1a Do any persons who are disqualified persons with respect to you, (except individuals who are disqualified persons only because they are foundation managers), appoint any of your foundation managers? If "Yes," (1) describe the process by which disqualified persons appoint any of your foundation managers, (2) provide the names of these disqualified persons and the foundation managers they appoint, and (3) explain how control is vested over your operations (including assets and activities) by persons other than disqualified persons.   ☐ **Yes**   ☐ **No**

b Do any persons who have a family or business relationship with any disqualified persons with respect to you, (except individuals who are disqualified persons only because they are foundation managers), appoint any of your foundation managers? If "Yes," (1) describe the process by which individuals with a family or business relationship with disqualified persons appoint any of your foundation managers, (2) provide the names of these disqualified persons, the individuals with a family or business relationship with disqualified persons, and the foundation managers appointed, and (3) explain how control is vested over your operations (including assets and activities) in individuals other than disqualified persons.   ☐ **Yes**   ☐ **No**

c Do any persons who are disqualified persons, (except individuals who are disqualified persons only because they are foundation managers), have any influence regarding your operations, including your assets or activities? If "Yes," (1) provide the names of these disqualified persons, (2) explain how influence is exerted over your operations (including assets and activities), and (3) explain how control is vested over your operations (including assets and activities) by individuals other than disqualified persons.   ☐ **Yes**   ☐ **No**

244

Schedule E. Organizations Not Filing Form 1023 Within 27 Months of Formation

Schedule E is intended to determine whether you are eligible for tax exemption under section 501(c)(3) from the postmark date of your application or from your date of incorporation or formation, whichever is earlier. If you are not eligible for tax exemption under section 501(c)(3) from your date of incorporation or formation, Schedule E is also intended to determine whether you are eligible for tax exemption under section 501(c)(4) for the period between your date of incorporation or formation and the postmark date of your application.

1	Are you a church, association of churches, or integrated auxiliary of a church? If "Yes," complete Schedule A and stop here. Do not complete the remainder of Schedule E.	☐ Yes	☐ No
2a	Are you a public charity with annual **gross receipts** that are normally $5,000 or less? If "Yes," stop here. Answer "No" if you are a private foundation, regardless of your gross receipts.	☐ Yes	☐ No
b	If your gross receipts were normally more than $5,000, are you filing this application within 90 days from the end of the tax year in which your gross receipts were normally more than $5,000? If "Yes," stop here.	☐ Yes	☐ No
3a	Were you included as a subordinate in a group exemption application or letter? If "No," go to line 4.	☐ Yes	☐ No
b	If you were included as a subordinate in a group exemption letter, are you filing this application within 27 months from the date you were notified by the organization holding the group exemption letter or the Internal Revenue Service that you cease to be covered by the group exemption letter? If "Yes," stop here.	☐ Yes	☐ No
c	If you were included as a subordinate in a timely filed group exemption request that was denied, are you filing this application within 27 months from the postmark date of the Internal Revenue Service final adverse ruling letter? If "Yes," stop here.	☐ Yes	☐ No
4	Were you created on or before October 9, 1969? If "Yes," stop here. Do not complete the remainder of this schedule.	☐ Yes	☐ No
5	If you answered "No" to lines 1 through 4, we cannot recognize you as tax exempt from your date of formation unless you qualify for an extension of time to apply for exemption. Do you wish to request an extension of time to apply to be recognized as exempt from the date you were formed? If "Yes," attach a statement explaining why you did not file this application within the 27-month period. Do not answer lines 6, 7, or 8. If "No," go to line 6a.	☐ Yes	☐ No
6a	If you answered "No" to line 5, you can only be exempt under section 501(c)(3) from the postmark date of this application. Therefore, do you want us to treat this application as a request for tax exemption from the postmark date? If "Yes," you are eligible for an advance ruling. Complete Part X, line 6a. If "No," you will be treated as a private foundation. **Note.** Be sure your ruling eligibility agrees with your answer to Part X, line 6.	☐ Yes	☐ No
b	Do you anticipate significant changes in your sources of support in the future? If "Yes," complete line 7 below.	☐ Yes	☐ No

Form 1023 (Rev. 6-2006)　　　　Name:　　　　　　　　　　　　　　　　　　EIN:　　　–　　　　Page **21**

Schedule E. Organizations Not Filing Form 1023 Within 27 Months of Formation *(Continued)*

7 Complete this item only if you answered "Yes" to line 6b. Include projected revenue for the first two full years following the current tax year.

Type of Revenue	Projected revenue for 2 years following current tax year		
	(a) From .... To	**(b)** From .... To	**(c)** Total
1 Gifts, grants, and contributions received (do not include unusual grants)			
2 Membership fees received			
3 Gross investment income			
4 Net unrelated business income			
5 Taxes levied for your benefit			
6 Value of services or facilities furnished by a governmental unit without charge (not including the value of services generally furnished to the public without charge)			
7 Any revenue not otherwise listed above or in lines 9–12 below (attach an itemized list)			
8 Total of lines 1 through 7			
9 Gross receipts from admissions, merchandise sold, or services performed, or furnishing of facilities in any activity that is related to your exempt purposes (attach itemized list)			
10 Total of lines 8 and 9			
11 Net gain or loss on sale of capital assets (attach an itemized list)			
12 Unusual grants			
13 Total revenue. Add lines 10 through 12			

8 According to your answers, you are only eligible for tax exemption under section 501(c)(3) from the postmark date of your application. However, you may be eligible for tax exemption under section 501(c)(4) from your date of formation to the postmark date of the Form 1023. Tax exemption under section 501(c)(4) allows exemption from federal income tax, but generally not deductibility of contributions under Code section 170. Check the box at right if you want us to treat this as a request for exemption under 501(c)(4) from your date of formation to the postmark date.　　▶ ☐

Attach a completed Page 1 of Form 1024, Application for Recognition of Exemption Under Section 501(a), to this application.

Form **1023** (Rev. 6-2006)

246

Schedule F. Homes for the Elderly or Handicapped and Low-Income Housing

Section I   General Information About Your Housing

1   Describe the type of housing you provide.

2   Provide copies of any application forms you use for admission.

3   Explain how the public is made aware of your facility.

4a Provide a description of each facility.
  b   What is the total number of residents each facility can accommodate?
  c   What is your current number of residents in each facility?
  d   Describe each facility in terms of whether residents rent or purchase housing from you.

5   Attach a sample copy of your residency or homeownership contract or agreement.

6   Do you participate in any joint ventures? If "Yes," state your ownership percentage in each joint venture, list your investment in each joint venture, describe the tax status of other participants in each joint venture (including whether they are section 501(c)(3) organizations), describe the activities of each joint venture, describe how you exercise control over the activities of each joint venture, and describe how each joint venture furthers your exempt purposes. Also, submit copies of all joint venture agreements.   ☐ Yes   ☐ No

   Note. Make sure your answer is consistent with the information provided in Part VIII, line 8.

7   Do you or will you contract with another organization to develop, build, market, or finance your housing? If "Yes," explain how that entity is selected, explain how the terms of any contract(s) are negotiated at arm's length, and explain how you determine you will pay no more than fair market value for services.   ☐ Yes   ☐ No

   Note. Make sure your answer is consistent with the information provided in Part VIII, line 7a.

8   Do you or will you manage your activities or facilities through your own employees or volunteers? If "No," attach a statement describing the activities that will be managed by others, the names of the persons or organizations that manage or will manage your activities or facilities, and how these managers were or will be selected. Also, submit copies of any contracts, proposed contracts, or other agreements regarding the provision of management services for your activities or facilities. Explain how the terms of any contracts or other agreements were or will be negotiated, and explain how you determine you will pay no more than fair market value for services.   ☐ Yes   ☐ No

   Note. Answer "Yes" if you do manage or intend to manage your programs through your own employees or by using volunteers. Answer "No" if you engage or intend to engage a separate organization or independent contractor. Make sure your answer is consistent with the information provided in Part VIII, line 7b.

9   Do you participate in any government housing programs? If "Yes," describe these programs.   ☐ Yes   ☐ No

10a Do you own the facility? If "No," describe any enforceable rights you possess to purchase the facility in the future; go to line 10c. If "Yes," answer line 10b.   ☐ Yes   ☐ No

  b   How did you acquire the facility? For example, did you develop it yourself, purchase a project, etc. Attach all contracts, transfer agreements, or other documents connected with the acquisition of the facility.

  c   Do you lease the facility or the land on which it is located? If "Yes," describe the parties to the lease(s) and provide copies of all leases.   ☐ Yes   ☐ No

Form 1023 (Rev. 6-2006)   Name: EIN: −   Page **23**

Schedule F. Homes for the Elderly or Handicapped and Low-Income Housing *(Continued)*

Section II   Homes for the Elderly or Handicapped

1a Do you provide housing for the elderly? If "Yes," describe who qualifies for your housing in terms of age, infirmity, or other criteria and explain how you select persons for your housing.   ☐ **Yes**   ☐ **No**

b Do you provide housing for the handicapped? If "Yes," describe who qualifies for your housing in terms of disability, income levels, or other criteria and explain how you select persons for your housing.   ☐ **Yes**   ☐ **No**

2a Do you charge an entrance or founder's fee? If "Yes," describe what this charge covers, whether it is a one-time fee, how the fee is determined, whether it is payable in a lump sum or on an installment basis, whether it is refundable, and the circumstances, if any, under which it may be waived.   ☐ **Yes**   ☐ **No**

b Do you charge periodic fees or maintenance charges? If "Yes," describe what these charges cover and how they are determined.   ☐ **Yes**   ☐ **No**

c Is your housing affordable to a significant segment of the elderly or handicapped persons in the community? Identify your **community**. Also, if "Yes," explain how you determine your housing is affordable.   ☐ **Yes**   ☐ **No**

3a Do you have an established policy concerning residents who become unable to pay their regular charges? If "Yes," describe your established policy.   ☐ **Yes**   ☐ **No**

b Do you have any arrangements with government welfare agencies or others to absorb all or part of the cost of maintaining residents who become unable to pay their regular charges? If "Yes," describe these arrangements.   ☐ **Yes**   ☐ **No**

4 Do you have arrangements for the healthcare needs of your residents? If "Yes," describe these arrangements.   ☐ **Yes**   ☐ **No**

5 Are your facilities designed to meet the physical, emotional, recreational, social, religious, and/or other similar needs of the elderly or handicapped? If "Yes," describe these design features.   ☐ **Yes**   ☐ **No**

Section III   Low-Income Housing

1 Do you provide low-income housing? If "Yes," describe who qualifies for your housing in terms of income levels or other criteria, and describe how you select persons for your housing.   ☐ **Yes**   ☐ **No**

2 In addition to rent or mortgage payments, do residents pay periodic fees or maintenance charges? If "Yes," describe what these charges cover and how they are determined.   ☐ **Yes**   ☐ **No**

3a Is your housing affordable to low income residents? If "Yes," describe how your housing is made affordable to low-income residents.   ☐ **Yes**   ☐ **No**

Note. Revenue Procedure 96-32, 1996-1 C.B. 717, provides guidelines for providing low-income housing that will be treated as charitable. (At least 75% of the units are occupied by low-income tenants or 40% are occupied by tenants earning not more than 120% of the very low-income levels for the area.)

b Do you impose any restrictions to make sure that your housing remains affordable to low-income residents? If "Yes," describe these restrictions.   ☐ **Yes**   ☐ **No**

4 Do you provide social services to residents? If "Yes," describe these services.   ☐ **Yes**   ☐ **No**

Form **1023** (Rev. 6-2006)

Schedule G. Successors to Other Organizations

1a Are you a **successor** to a **for-profit organization**? If "Yes," explain the relationship with the **predecessor** organization that resulted in your creation and complete line 1b.   ☐ **Yes**   ☐ **No**

b Explain why you took over the activities or assets of a for-profit organization or converted from for-profit to nonprofit status.

2a Are you a successor to an organization other than a for-profit organization? Answer "Yes" if you have taken or will take over the activities of another organization; or you have taken or will take over 25% or more of the fair market value of the net assets of another organization. If "Yes," explain the relationship with the other organzation that resulted in your creation.   ☐ **Yes**   ☐ **No**

b Provide the tax status of the predecessor organization.

c Did you or did an organization to which you are a successor previously apply for tax exemption under section 501(c)(3) or any other section of the Code? If "Yes," explain how the application was resolved.   ☐ **Yes**   ☐ **No**

d Was your prior tax exemption or the tax exemption of an organization to which you are a successor revoked or suspended? If "Yes," explain. Include a description of the corrections you made to re-establish tax exemption.   ☐ **Yes**   ☐ **No**

e Explain why you took over the activities or assets of another organization.

3 Provide the name, last address, and EIN of the predecessor organization and describe its activities.
Name: _____   **EIN:** ___−_____
Address: _____

4 List the owners, partners, principal stockholders, officers, and governing board members of the predecessor organization. Attach a separate sheet if additional space is needed.

Name	Address	Share/Interest (If a for-profit)

5 Do or will any of the persons listed in line 4, maintain a working relationship with you? If "Yes," describe the relationship in detail and include copies of any agreements with any of these persons or with any for-profit organizations in which these persons own more than a 35% interest.   ☐ **Yes**   ☐ **No**

6a Were any assets transferred, whether by gift or sale, from the predecessor organization to you?   ☐ **Yes**   ☐ **No**
If "Yes," provide a list of assets, indicate the value of each asset, explain how the value was determined, and attach an appraisal, if available. For each asset listed, also explain if the transfer was by gift, sale, or combination thereof.

b Were any restrictions placed on the use or sale of the assets? If "Yes," explain the restrictions.   ☐ **Yes**   ☐ **No**

c Provide a copy of the agreement(s) of sale or transfer.

7 Were any debts or liabilities transferred from the predecessor for-profit organization to you?   ☐ **Yes**   ☐ **No**
If "Yes," provide a list of the debts or liabilities that were transferred to you, indicating the amount of each, how the amount was determined, and the name of the person to whom the debt or liability is owed.

8 Will you lease or rent any property or equipment previously owned or used by the predecessor for-profit organization, or from persons listed in line 4, or from for-profit organizations in which these persons own more than a 35% interest? If "Yes," submit a copy of the lease or rental agreement(s). Indicate how the lease or rental value of the property or equipment was determined.   ☐ **Yes**   ☐ **No**

9 Will you lease or rent property or equipment to persons listed in line 4, or to for-profit organizations in which these persons own more than a 35% interest? If "Yes," attach a list of the property or equipment, provide a copy of the lease or rental agreement(s), and indicate how the lease or rental value of the property or equipment was determined.   ☐ **Yes**   ☐ **No**

Schedule H. Organizations Providing Scholarships, Fellowships, Educational Loans, or Other Educational Grants to Individuals and Private Foundations Requesting Advance Approval of Individual Grant Procedures

| **Section I** | *Names of individual recipients are not required to be listed in Schedule H.* **Public charities and private foundations complete lines 1a through 7 of this section. See the instructions to Part X if you are not sure whether you are a public charity or a private foundation.** |

1a Describe the types of educational grants you provide to individuals, such as scholarships, fellowships, loans, etc.

b Describe the purpose and amount of your scholarships, fellowships, and other educational grants and loans that you award.

c If you award educational loans, explain the terms of the loans (interest rate, length, forgiveness, etc.).

d Specify how your program is publicized.

e Provide copies of any solicitation or announcement materials.

f Provide a sample copy of the application used.

2 Do you maintain case histories showing recipients of your scholarships, fellowships, educational loans, or other educational grants, including names, addresses, purposes of awards, amount of each grant, manner of selection, and relationship (if any) to officers, trustees, or donors of funds to you? If "No," refer to the instructions.   ☐ **Yes**   ☐ **No**

3 Describe the specific criteria you use to determine who is eligible for your program. (For example, eligibility selection criteria could consist of graduating high school students from a particular high school who will attend college, writers of scholarly works about American history, etc.)

4a Describe the specific criteria you use to select recipients. (For example, specific selection criteria could consist of prior academic performance, financial need, etc.)

b Describe how you determine the number of grants that will be made annually.

c Describe how you determine the amount of each of your grants.

d Describe any requirement or condition that you impose on recipients to obtain, maintain, or qualify for renewal of a grant. (For example, specific requirements or conditions could consist of attendance at a four-year college, maintaining a certain grade point average, teaching in public school after graduation from college, etc.)

5 Describe your procedures for supervising the scholarships, fellowships, educational loans, or other educational grants. Describe whether you obtain reports and grade transcripts from recipients, or you pay grants directly to a school under an arrangement whereby the school will apply the grant funds only for enrolled students who are in good standing. Also, describe your procedures for taking action if the terms of the award are violated.

6 Who is on the selection committee for the awards made under your program, including names of current committee members, criteria for committee membership, and the method of replacing committee members?

7 Are relatives of members of the selection committee, or of your officers, directors, or **substantial contributors** eligible for awards made under your program? If "Yes," what measures are taken to ensure unbiased selections?   ☐ **Yes**   ☐ **No**

Note. If you are a private foundation, you are not permitted to provide educational grants to **disqualified persons**. Disqualified persons include your substantial contributors and foundation managers and certain family members of disqualified persons.

| **Section II** | **Private foundations complete lines 1a through 4f of this section. Public charities do not complete this section.** |

1a If we determine that you are a private foundation, do you want this application to be considered as a request for advance approval of grant making procedures?   ☐ **Yes**   ☐ **No**   ☐ **N/A**

b For which section(s) do you wish to be considered?

- 4945(g)(1)—Scholarship or fellowship grant to an individual for study at an educational institution   ☐
- 4945(g)(3)—Other grants, including loans, to an individual for travel, study, or other similar purposes, to enhance a particular skill of the grantee or to produce a specific product   ☐

2 Do you represent that you will (1) arrange to receive and review grantee reports annually and upon completion of the purpose for which the grant was awarded, (2) investigate diversions of funds from their intended purposes, and (3) take all reasonable and appropriate steps to recover diverted funds, ensure other grant funds held by a grantee are used for their intended purposes, and withhold further payments to grantees until you obtain grantees' assurances that future diversions will not occur and that grantees will take extraordinary precautions to prevent future diversions from occurring?   ☐ **Yes**   ☐ **No**

3 Do you represent that you will maintain all records relating to individual grants, including information obtained to evaluate grantees, identify whether a grantee is a disqualified person, establish the amount and purpose of each grant, and establish that you undertook the supervision and investigation of grants described in line 2?   ☐ **Yes**   ☐ **No**

250

Schedule H. Organizations Providing Scholarships, Fellowships, Educational Loans, or Other Educational Grants to Individuals and Private Foundations Requesting Advance Approval of Individual Grant Procedures (Continued)

Section II	Private foundations complete lines 1a through 4f of this section. Public charities do not complete this section. (Continued)

4a Do you or will you award scholarships, fellowships, and educational loans to attend an educational institution based on the status of an individual being an *employee of a particular employer?* If "Yes," complete lines 4b through 4f. ☐ **Yes** ☐ **No**

b Will you comply with the seven conditions and either the percentage tests or facts and circumstances test for scholarships, fellowships, and educational loans to attend an educational institution as set forth in Revenue Procedures 76-47, 1976-2 C.B. 670, and 80-39, 1980-2 C.B. 772, which apply to inducement, selection committee, eligibility requirements, objective basis of selection, employment, course of study, and other objectives? (See lines 4c, 4d, and 4e, regarding the percentage tests.) ☐ **Yes** ☐ **No**

c Do you or will you provide scholarships, fellowships, or educational loans to attend an educational institution to employees of a particular employer? ☐ **Yes** ☐ **No** ☐ **N/A**

If "Yes," will you award grants to 10% or fewer of the eligible applicants who were actually considered by the selection committee in selecting recipients of grants in that year as provided by Revenue Procedures 76-47 and 80-39? ☐ **Yes** ☐ **No**

d Do you provide scholarships, fellowships, or educational loans to attend an educational institution to children of employees of a particular employer? ☐ **Yes** ☐ **No** ☐ **N/A**

If "Yes," will you award grants to 25% or fewer of the eligible applicants who were actually considered by the selection committee in selecting recipients of grants in that year as provided by Revenue Procedures 76-47 and 80-39? If "No," go to line 4e. ☐ **Yes** ☐ **No**

e If you provide scholarships, fellowships, or educational loans to attend an educational institution to children of employees of a particular employer, will you award grants to 10% or fewer of the number of employees' children who can be shown to be eligible for grants (whether or not they submitted an application) in that year, as provided by Revenue Procedures 76-47 and 80-39? ☐ **Yes** ☐ **No** ☐ **N/A**

If "Yes," describe how you will determine who can be shown to be eligible for grants without submitting an application, such as by obtaining written statements or other information about the expectations of employees' children to attend an educational institution. If "No," go to line 4f.

Note. Statistical or sampling techniques are not acceptable. See Revenue Procedure 85-51, 1985-2 C.B. 717, for additional information.

f If you provide scholarships, fellowships, or educational loans to attend an educational institution to *children of employees of a particular employer* without regard to either the 25% limitation described in line 4d, or the 10% limitation described in line 4e, will you award grants based on facts and circumstances that demonstrate that the grants will not be considered compensation for past, present, or future services or otherwise provide a significant benefit to the particular employer? If "Yes," describe the facts and circumstances that you believe will demonstrate that the grants are neither compensatory nor a significant benefit to the particular employer. In your explanation, describe why you cannot satisfy either the 25% test described in line 4d or the 10% test described in line 4e. ☐ **Yes** ☐ **No**

Form 1023 Checklist

(Revised June 2006)

Application for Recognition of Exemption under Section 501(c)(3) of the Internal Revenue Code

---

Note. *Retain a copy of the completed Form 1023 in your permanent records. Refer to the* General Instructions *regarding Public Inspection of approved applications.*

<u>**Check each box to finish your application (Form 1023). Send this completed Checklist with your filled-in application. If you have not answered all the items below, your application may be returned to you as incomplete.**</u>

☐ Assemble the application and materials in this order:
- Form 1023 Checklist
- Form 2848, *Power of Attorney and Declaration of Representative* (if filing)
- Form 8821, *Tax Information Authorization* (if filing)
- Expedite request (if requesting)
- Application (Form 1023 and Schedules A through H, as required)
- Articles of organization
- Amendments to articles of organization in chronological order
- Bylaws or other rules of operation and amendments
- Documentation of nondiscriminatory policy for schools, as required by Schedule B
- Form 5768, Election/Revocation of Election by an Eligible Section 501(c)(3) Organization To Make Expenditures To Influence Legislation (if filing)
- All other attachments, including explanations, financial data, and printed materials or publications. Label each page with name and EIN.

☐ User fee payment placed in envelope on top of checklist. DO NOT STAPLE or otherwise attach your check or money order to your application. Instead, just place it in the envelope.

☐ Employer Identification Number (EIN)

☐ Completed Parts I through XI of the application, including any requested information and any required Schedules A through H.
- You must provide specific details about your past, present, and planned activities.
- Generalizations or failure to answer questions in the Form 1023 application will prevent us from recognizing you as tax exempt.
- Describe your purposes and proposed activities in specific easily understood terms.
- Financial information should correspond with proposed activities.

☐ Schedules. Submit only those schedules that apply to you and check either "Yes" or "No" below.

Schedule A Yes ____ No ____		Schedule E Yes ____ No ____
Schedule B Yes ____ No ____		Schedule F Yes ____ No ____
Schedule C Yes ____ No ____		Schedule G Yes ____ No ____
Schedule D Yes ____ No ____		Schedule H Yes ____ No ____

☐ An exact copy of your complete articles of organization (creating document). Absence of the proper purpose and dissolution clauses is the number one reason for delays in the issuance of determination letters.

- Location of Purpose Clause from Part III, line 1 (Page, Article and Paragraph Number)_____
- Location of Dissolution Clause from Part III, line 2b or 2c (Page, Article and Paragraph Number) or by operation of state law _____

☐ Signature of an officer, director, trustee, or other official who is authorized to sign the application.
- Signature at Part XI of Form 1023.

☐ Your name on the application must be the same as your legal name as it appears in your articles of organization.

Send completed Form 1023, user fee payment, and all other required information, to:

Internal Revenue Service
P.O. Box 192
Covington, KY 41012-0192

If you are using express mail or a delivery service, send Form 1023, user fee payment, and attachments to:

Internal Revenue Service
201 West Rivercenter Blvd.
Attn: Extracting Stop 312
Covington, KY 41011

Index

About the Author

Mark Warda has been a Florida attorney for over twenty-five years. He received his BA with Honors in Political Science from the University of Illinois in Chicago and his JD from the University of Illinois in Champaign. He also studied law at the University of Oxford, England, and studied German in Cologne and Spanish in Barcelona.

Mark started his first business at the age of 3 when, after learning that one needs money to buy things, he started selling his drawings to visiting relatives.

While practicing law, he noticed that his clients had problems they could have avoided if they knew something about the law before they came to him. So he started Sphinx Publishing to publish self-help law books. His first book was *Landlords' Rights and Duties in Florida*, and his first printing sold out quickly—even though it had just fifty-seven pages of text typeset on a typewriter and was spiral-bound. Over the next few years he wrote several more books and eventually quit practicing law to publish the books full-time. After finding lawyers in other states interested in simplifying the law, he began publishing versions of his existing books adapted to those states.

By 1996, he found that he was spending most of his time overseeing the publishing end of the business, so he sold the company to Sourcebooks to give himself more time to write books. His works include *The Complete Limited Liability Company Kit (+CD-ROM)*, *Form Your Own Corporation, 5e (+CD-ROM)*, as well as various state-specific books he has written or coauthored.

In 1998 he started Land Trust Service Corporation to service readers of his book *Land Trusts in Florida* who were looking for dependable, affordable trustee services.

Today Mark is continuing to update his over sixty books and running Land Trust Service Corporation in Lake Wales, Florida, with his wife, Alexandra, and his new son, Mark David.